At Home in America

The Columbia History of Urban Life
Kenneth T. Jackson, General Editor

At Home in America

SECOND GENERATION NEW YORK JEWS

Deborah Dash Moore

Columbia University Press
New York 1981

The author is grateful to the following publishers for their permission to reprint certain material:

From *A Walker in the City*, copyright © 1951, 1974, by Alfred Kazin. Reprinted by permission of Harcourt Brace Jovanovich, Inc.

From "A Memoir of the Thirties," in *Steady Work*, by Irving Howe. Reprinted by permission of Harcourt Brace Jovanovich, Inc.

The author wishes to thank the American Jewish Historical Society and *The Jewish Journal of Sociology* for permission to reprint material which appeared in their publications and is grateful to *Prospects* for permission to reprint material which appeared there. She also expresses thanks to Columbia University for the following quotations from oral history memoirs in the Columbia Collection: Herbert Lehman, 1972; Theodore Kuper, 1972; Reuben Lazarus, 1975; Nathan Straus, 1975. Copyright © 1972, 1975 by the Trustees of Columbia University in the City of New York. Used with their permission.

Library of Congress Cataloging in Publication Data

Moore, Deborah Dash, 1946–
    At home in America.

    (Columbia history of urban life)
    Bibliography
    Includes index.
    1. Jews in New York (City)   2. New York (City)—
Ethnic relations.   I. Title.   II. Series.
F128.9.J5M66   974.7′1004924   80-18777
ISBN 0-231-05062-3

To Samuel Golden,

a second generation Jew
committed to the ideals
of America

Contents

List of Tables

Acknowledgments

In the course of writing a book many debts accrue, and the task of acknowledging them stirs some trepidation. Yet I am grateful for the opportunity to express publicly my indebtedness, reserving blame for errors for myself.

My greatest debt I owe to MacDonald Moore. He has nurtured this book for ten years, listening with interest as its themes were formulated, responding with valuable questions, maintaining throughout a blend of critical distance and passionate concern. The several versions of the manuscript benefited from his editorial skills, his willingness to search for just the right word, and his sense of style. I have admitted, only half-jokingly, that some of my best phrases are his.

To David Rothman, who read an earlier version of the book with a sharp eye for clarity of ideas and expression and effectiveness of organization and argument, I am most grateful. His infectious enthusiasm and vigorous criticism has sustained me through subsequent revisions. Kenneth Jackson generously read two complete versions of the book, each time making valuable suggestions which enhanced the manuscript. Walter Metzger and Herbert Gans read an earlier version of the book. Their thoughtful comments combined professional and personal perspectives and forced me to confront my underlying assumptions. I am most thankful to Arthur Goren for his insightful reading of the book. His wide knowledge of American Jewish history and his sensitivity to implications of the text uncovered layers of meaning of which I had not been fully conscious.

I appreciate the opportunity Marvin Herzog gave me to teach at the YIVO Institute's Max Weinreich Center for Advanced Jewish Studies, for I learned immeasurably from my students there. My contact with them deepened my understanding of second generation New York Jews. Specifically I want to thank Adrienne Cooper Gordon, Cary Goodman, Harriet Kraus, Gerald Sorin, Kenneth Wolpin, Howard Brown, Daphne Kis, Susan Merson, and Elinor Lerner for their interest in New York Jewish history.

While I acknowledge my specific debts in the footnotes, a number of people deserve further recognition. I appreciate the correspondence and conversations I have had with Charles Liebman, Paul Ritterband, Ismar Schorsch, and Marshall Sklare. Jack Brakarsh introduced me to the world of Jewish builders, and I am grateful particularly for the interviews granted to me by Julius Borenstein, Myron Eisenstein, Marcus Gilden, and David Tishman. The good names of Judge Elliott Golden and Robert Steingut allowed me to explore the intricacies of Brooklyn Jewish Democratic politics, and I especially appreciate the interviews granted by Judge George Abrams, Beadie Markowitz, Judge Nathan Sobel, and Stanley Steingut. Rabbi George Ende and Dr. Judah Lapson spent time with me explaining the progress of Hebrew study in the city's public high schools. Bella Golden and Zachary Baym shared their memories of teaching in the schools.

Like memories, access to documents required the concern of individuals, and I am grateful for the assistance of professionals and lay leaders in obtaining valuable records. Nathan Kaganoff at the library of the American Jewish Historical Society graciously fulfilled many of my requests by mail. Regina Reibstein literally unlocked the door of the Jewish Welfare Board library for me. Walter Socolow helped to open important files at the Board of Jewish Education. Sam Hartstein generously let me see the holdings of Yeshiva University's public relations department. I also relied on the professional expertise of the staff at the New York Public Library's Jewish Division, the library of the YIVO Institute for Jewish Research, the American Jewish Archives, and the Oral History Library of Columbia University.

I am glad to acknowledge, too, the speed and skill of Jane McAfee and Mildred S. Tubby who typed the manuscript. Bernard Gronert and Leslie Bialler at Columbia University Press have handled the book with care and dispatch. Vassar College generously gave me a grant-in-aid to cover expenses. Finally, my colleagues in the Religion Department have created a congenial atmosphere for teaching and writing; I truly value their supportive presence.

I was fortunate to have shared the rigors of graduate school with two scholars whose friendship and intellectual acuteness have given a larger significance to my work. Esther Feldblum served as an early mentor and guide both to the nature of modern Orthodoxy and to the possibilities of synthesizing an academic career with family life. Paula Hyman has brought her mastery of modern Jewish history to bear on our many discussions of the book's themes. Her commitment to the realization of the manuscript's potential, involving critical reading of successive versions, and her dedication to Jewish life and scholarship were vital to the book's fruition.

My family has helped in ways that only family can. While at times they have questioned my reconstruction of a world they knew and quarreled with my interpretations, they have never failed to encourage me. My sons have understandably shown no interest in the book, a healthy reminder of the variability of perspective. Yet Mordecai and Mikhael have lived with a working mother gracefully and have returned faithfully their parents' love and esteem.

D.D.M.

At Home in America

1

The elements that make up for most American Jews the image of
their group are to be found in the Jewish culture of New York
City; more specifically, in the culture of the Jewish lower middle
class, in the apartment houses and two-family houses of the
Bronx and Brooklyn, among those who all these years have had
to think mainly about getting along. Not all Jews actually
participate in this culture—perhaps most do not—but almost all
are ultimately connected with it. The New York pattern is the
master pattern. . . .
The crucial fact is that there are few who cannot immediately
recognize and understand its smallest forms of behavior, its
accepted attitudes, its language. If it is not "Jewish life," strictly
speaking, it is for most American Jews the area of greatest
emotional importance. It is what a Jew remembers, it is what he
has in his mind when he experiences his more private emotions
about being a Jew—affection, pity, delight, shame. Just as the
life of a small town can be said to embody the common
experience of the older Americans, so the life of New York can
be said at this particular stage in the process of acculturation to
embody the common experience of the American Jews.

Robert S. Warshow, "Poet of the Jewish Middle Class,"
Commentary (May 1946), pp. 17–18.

New York Jews

As early as 1900, Jewish observers characterized New York City as the heart of American Jewry. By 1914 there was no doubt that the pulse of New York Jewish life decisively influenced all American Jews. Even today, the heartbeat of the New York Jewish experience can be felt in Miami and Los Angeles. While New York was not America, it did represent the dominant experience of America's Jews. Since the beginning of the twentieth century, roughly half of all American Jews have lived in New York City. Indeed, they constitute the largest concentration of Jews in history.[1]

Yet because of its vast size and multiplicity of organizations, New York Jewish life has eluded sustained analysis. "There are probably a hundred people, and more, whose profession it is to discover all that can be known about the Jews in Jerusalem in the first century; there does not seem to be one who has the same duty for the Jews of New York in the twentieth century," Louis Finkelstein, the noted theologian, pointedly observed. Recently, the sociologist Marshall Sklare lamented the lack of knowledge of New York Jewish life and the resulting incomplete portrait of American Jews.[2]

The first, and perhaps most difficult, step toward an understanding of Jewish life in the United States is to analyze the creative interaction between New York Jews and their environment. In his monumental study of Jewish immigration, Irving Howe implicitly recognized the significance of the New York Jewish experience when he chose to depict the Lower East Side of New

York as the "world of our fathers." And when the Lower East
Side began its steady decline as a center of immigrant culture and
institutions, the new Jewish neighborhoods in turn presented the
best lens through which to focus on the distinctive character of
American Jewish life. On this urban frontier, second generation
New York Jews, the children of immigrants, constructed a type of
ethnicity consonant with middle-class American values. While not
all Jews shared these values, all identified the New York synthesis
as typically Jewish. Jews and New York fit together comfortably
into a recognizable pattern, what Warshow rightly calls "the master pattern."[3] New York Jews devised the grammar of American
Jewish life.

Second generation Jews developed a relationship of intimacy
with the city; many even conducted a clandestine love affair with
it. They succeeded in wedding their experiences as New Yorkers
to their existence as Jews. Through the process of becoming New
Yorkers—and by extension, also Americans—second generation
Jews redefined the meaning of Jewishness. As they built new
neighborhoods, pursued secular education in the public schools,
organized their religious and philanthropic institutions, and entered the political system, they established the limits of their assimilation into American society. Participation in the myriad
aspects of New York culture did not mark the decline of Jewish
group life—as some had feared and others had hoped. Rather, as
they became middle-class New Yorkers, second generation Jews
created the framework for their persistence as an ethnic group.
Most New York Jews persisted in associating with each other in
secular and sectarian settings. They remained Jews and brought
their children up as Jews. Only a few chose to intermarry and dis-
sociate from the group, while an articulate handful struggled to
secure recognition legitimating Jewish separateness.[4]

Out of the second generation's encounter with the city
emerged a new American Jew, one whose Jewishness was shaped
by the city's peculiar dynamic. This Jew saw himself a part of and
yet apart from New York. Irving Howe remembers the irony of
this experience: "New York did not really exist for us as a city, a
defined place we felt to be our own. Too many barriers inter-
vened, too many kinds of anxiety." And yet, Howe admits, "while
we thought of ourselves as exposed to the coldest winds of the

coldest capitalist city—and in many, many ways we were—we still lived in a somewhat sheltered world." The protection came from the comforting shadows cast by neighborhood Jewish communities in the Bronx and Brooklyn. For if Jews felt uneasy in cosmopolitan Manhattan—if they thought of New York as an alien city—they also felt at home on the streets of their own neighborhoods.[5] There they reconstructed Jewishness, shaping it to fit an American middle-class mode, adjusting it to the rigors of urban life, imbuing it with Jewish sentiments learned from their immigrant parents, and attaching it to the chain of Jewish history. The style and ethos of their ethnicity developed as the second generation acclimated itself to the fertile matrix of New York.

New York's multi-ethnic environment, its character as an immigrant entrepôt, and the changing interests of its ethnic groups, nourished this ethnicity. In New York, white Protestants struggled to uphold their American norm against succeeding waves of immigrants. A majority at the turn of the century, by 1935 they ranked third in population behind Catholics and Jews. Like Jews, New York Catholics dissented from the Protestant American norm. New York City Catholics supported parochial schools, acquiesced in the Church's ban against intermarriage, and maintained separate charitable and social organizations. Thus Irish Catholics, who persisted as an ethnic group in the city, established protective precedents for Jews who wanted to preserve Jewish group life. The New York situation supported Rabbi Mordecai M. Kaplan's observation that "a second environmental factor which indirectly yet effectively makes for the conservation of Jewish life in America is the presence in the body politic of a large and powerful group that insists upon remaining unassimilable." Referring to the Catholics, Kaplan argued that they "constitute a minority of the American people, but a minority too large, too well organized and too safely entrenched to have any apprehension about succumbing to attrition by the majority."[6]

The city's neighborhood structure also facilitated the development of diverse ethnic cultures and organizations. Ethnic groups clustered in various sections of the city, endowing these areas with a distinctive character. Groups promoted their own associations in the ethnic enclaves; and New York Jews, too, evolved their particular ethnic pattern within these multi-ethnic, parochial boundaries. The city's neighborhood structure helped ethnic groups to synthesize their cultural values and associational patterns with their social and economic group interests. "The informal and formal social groupings that make up these communities are strengthened by the fact that Jews can talk about the garment business, Irish about politics and the civil service, Italians about the state of the trucking or contracting or vegetable business," Nathan Glazer and Daniel Patrick Moynihan point out. The confluence of the immigrant heritage and American environment in New York stimulated the growth of ethnic groups. New Yorkers in turn incorporated the ethnic character of their social associations into the city's social structure: its politics, economic activities, and residential patterns. Common job experiences, neighborhood living, and reliance on similar institutions crystallized ethnicity in New York City and reinforced the diverse patterns of association at its core. Ethnicity depended no less on the strength of personal associational patterns than on the assumption of a common heritage.[7]

If the city's social structure encouraged ethnic diversity and persistence, the masses of Jews in the city sustained the vitality of a pluralist Jewish ethnicity. In New York there were many ways to be a Jew. Even within the immigrant milieu, Jews elaborated a wide range of alternatives, eschewing any consensus. As Howe astutely argues, "east European Jews brought with them considerable experience in creating 'secondary associations' that would cut through the confines, and limit the authority, of family and synagogue." Immigrant Jews "filled out the social spaces between family and state with a web of voluntary organizations." These secondary associations institutionalized a pluralist Jewish life. Immigrants had many choices among social groups which preserved a sense of peoplehood, "the essence of ethnicity." Initially an immigrant often grounded his Jewish identity through association with a *landsmanshaft*, an organization of fellow Jews from the same town or region in Europe. But increasingly immigrants discarded such parochial old-world commitments; many chose to build a Jewish life through socialism. Socialism offered them membership in an ideological community that transcended the boundaries of local concerns even though it linked Jews through such institutional ties as the Workmen's Circle (a fraternal orga-

nization) and the garment workers' unions. Even immigrants
eager to become Americans frequently discovered Jewish organizations directing the Americanization programs. These Jews often
Americanized within a Jewish milieu; they studied with fellow
Jews and were taught how to become Americans from Jewish immigrants who had preceded them. "Tacitly but shrewdly, the immigrant Jews improvised a loose pattern for their collective existence," Howe writes.

> Most wanted to maintain a distinctive Yiddish cultural life while
> penetrating individually into American society and economy; most
> wanted to insure their survival as a people while feeling free to
> break out of the ghetto; and most hoped for cultural and religious
> continuity while opting for a weak, even ramshackle community
> structure. Before the term became fashionable they made their
> way to a sort of "pluralism"—and the later decades proved them
> right.[8]

Jewish residential concentration, since it threw masses of
Jews together in close confines, encouraged ideological disputes
among groups who vied to shape the Jews' future. Immigrant Jews
brought with them across the ocean multiple Jewish value systems. What enabled Zionists to debate Socialists, Anarchists to attack Orthodox, Americanizers to compete with Survivalists, Bundists to oppose Universalists, and Yiddishists to struggle with
Hebraists was their common situation as Jewish immigrants in
New York City. They shared the same streets and parceled out
the street corners. Within these boundaries they succeeded in
transplanting through secondary social structures a common
realm of discourse.[9]

While a huge immigrant quarter like the Lower East Side was
divided into many smaller sections, the area appeared to have a
certain unity, especially from the outside. Sociologist Peter Rose
calls it "an urban equivalent of the shtetl," the small towns which
immigrant Jews left behind in Europe. The New York immigrant
quarter "came to be called a ghetto, not by those who lived and
worked and played out life's dreams there, but by the outsiders
who peered into these 'exotic' and 'oriental' enclaves." Yet the
term ghetto was a misnomer, for "a ghetto connotes forced residential permanence, entrapment." Immigrant Jews were free to

move throughout the city. Indeed, as new tenement construction created opportunities to live elsewhere, Jewish immigrants availed themselves. By 1910 many Jewish immigrants lived in Harlem, in the Bronx, and in Williamsburg and Brownsville in Brooklyn. While the Lower East Side community did not disappear, its seeming permanence belied the transiency of its residents. As older immigrants moved out, new arrivals rapidly filled their places. Estimates suggest that between 1905 and 1915, two-thirds of the Jews living on the Lower East Side left the area. Nevertheless, if residential stability eluded Jewish immigrants, residential concentration continued to characterize Jewish life.[10]

Immigrant Jews' residential concentration and mobility complemented their occupational concentration and mobility. Most Jewish immigrants earned their livelihood in the garment shops located on the Lower East Side and in the other immigrant sections. Here the confluence of work and residence transformed the public character of the streets. Jewish workers found jobs through the curbside employment markets, while pushcarts placed commerce on the sidewalks. But the immigrant areas housed both lower-class workers and the beginnings of a bourgeoisie. Thus the bitter battles between bosses and workers staged on the streets of the Lower East Side engaged the emotions of all Jewish immigrants. Class struggles ranging from garment worker walk-outs to rent strikes often became communal conflicts in the immigrant quarter. Despite their commitment to class solidarity, immigrant Jews declined to remain lower-class workers. Jewish immigrants' social mobility paralleled their residential restlessness. "Jews found the New York economy fluid and open," and they moved into white-collar positions rapidly. Yet as the earlier arrivals among the immigrants improved their economic position—and after 15 to 25 years in the United States half achieved white-collar status—more recent immigrants filled their vacated jobs. A Jewish working class endured in New York even as a Jewish middle and upper class flourished.[11]

The immigrant generation necessarily lived in two worlds, the old and the new. Immigrant Jews remembered their ties to the towns of eastern Europe and with their *landslayt* strove to plant that culture in America. The second generation appreciated these experiences, at best, as abstract ideals. In reacting to the city en-

vironment, immigrant Jews referred to both Europe and America;
their children knew only America. The immigrant generation remained a transitional generation. Nevertheless, this immigrant experience triggered a cultural explosion and released creative powers among many Jews. With these energies Jewish immigrants
shaped a moral community, which comprised "a sense of identity
and unity with one's group and a feeling of involvement" and
commitment by the individual. The second generation received
this community—sustained less by consensus or authority than by
"visions of collective fulfillment and ambitions for personal ascent"—as its Jewish inheritance. "It was the unspoken hope of
the immigrants that their visions and ambitions, the collective
dream of Jewish fulfillment and the personal wish to improve the
lot of sons and daughters, could be satisfied at the same time."
While "too radical a break in actual life patterns of generations
had made the personal and concrete experiences of the immigrant
fathers inaccessible to the sons," second generation Jews accepted
their parents' goal of linking "spiritual fulfillment with material
gratification." But the second generation turned to existing American institutions to fashion their own moral community. Indeed,
the ability of second generation Jews to recast available institutions into instruments of self-perpetuation marks their important
contribution to Jewish and to American history.[12]

The concept of a second generation inevitably suggests a first
generation, whose coherence developed around a pivotal event.
Immigration serves as the point of reference; it defines an entire
generation whose lives were reshaped by the experience. The children of immigrants, however, relate only indirectly to that point
of reference. They may turn the experience of immigration into
an object of nostalgia and idealize it, but they do not see themselves defined by it. Instead they trace for themselves a bilateral
line of descent, "selectively American on one side and selectively
ethnic on the other." The second generation shares in common
the experience of growing up American in Jewish immigrant
homes. While not a compact group in time—since mass immigration from eastern Europe extended uninterruptedly for 33 years
beginning in 1881—the second generation occupies a similar point
in space in their relationship to each other and to their immigrant
parents. Growing up in an immigrant milieu meant that "what

you believed, or said you believed, did not matter nearly as much as what you were, and what you were was not nearly so much a matter of choice as you might suppose.'' Howe recalls that ''if you found a job, it was likely to be in a 'Jewish industry' and if you went to college it was still within an essentially Jewish milieu.'' This common experience united the lives of second generation Jews. They were a cultural generation, not a chronological one.[13]

Second generation Jews found their identity defined through their relationship not only with their parents, but also with their children, the youthful third generation. Societies built on successive waves of immigration often turned to internal hierarchies based on generation, or date of arrival in the country. Nations like the United States not only ranked immigrants, but they actually developed an implicit paradigm for integrating them. This paradigm assumed that three successive generations represents ''the total time and stages necessary for an immigrant community to become assimilated and blended into a new society.'' In such a generational scheme the second generation becomes the transitional group. Giving expression to this view, the Yiddish daily *Day* lamented at the end of the High Holidays: ''Three generations rejoiced: The old—over the Torah, the middle-aged—over the business page in the newspaper, the young—over the sport page.'' Eighty years before, a French Jew had sounded the same alarm: ''The Grandfather believes, the father doubts, and the son denies.'' This paradigm of generational succession exerted tremendous appeal in its arresting vision of decline. But the paradigm distorted the course of acculturation, which was not a simple process of declension.[14]

The generational concept legitimately framed an analysis of the growth of ''a collective memory and the building of a tradition.'' As Annie Kriegel argues, it is through the relationship of generations that ''we reach an understanding of what enables an historical phenomenon to endure. Far from being its ability to command the identification of a generation, it is rather its capacity to get successive generations to accommodate to the logical nucleus which . . . ensures vitality.'' Second generation Jews, like their immigrant parents, succeeded in developing a nucleus of Jewishness, defined through secondary associations, that made being Jewish an impelling reality for their children. Thus, though second generation Jews can be seen as a transitional generation, they were not marginal. At home both in American urban culture and immigrant Jewish culture, second generation Jews could synthesize the two.[15]

Standing between the immigrants and future American generations of Jews, the second generation created a communal framework for its children. They constructed a moral community with supports borrowed from American culture, middle-class values, urban lifestyles, as well as from their immigrant Jewish heritage, fashioning an enduring structure. In fact, so successful were they in binding middle-class norms to visions of Jewish fulfillment, that their children often could not disentangle the two. In the children's eyes even the overstuffed furniture of their parents' home reflected a middle-class Jewish synthesis, as utterly bourgeois and Jewish as a decorous synagogue service. Though second generation Jews did not jettison their Jewishness, they rejected much of their immigrant background as "foreign," and adopted American styles instead. Most second generation Jews understood Yiddish, many could read the language, yet few chose to purchase a Yiddish paper. Instead they turned to the English-language press, which gradually expanded its coverage of topics of interest to Jews. Thus the development of Jewish ethnicity must be seen not as the unbroken extension of one set of Jewish values but as the reconstruction of a Jewish lifestyle consonant with the New York environment.[16]

The immense numbers of New York Jews decisively influenced the character of Jewish group life. In a city where there were many communities of 100,000 Jews (indeed, where such large aggregations of Jews were the norm) the potential existed to develop a variety of social structures which were undreamed of by Jews in smaller cities. Sheer size gave New York Jews tremendous psychological security and triggered an amazing complexity of institutions. Second generation New York Jews were free to create an ethnic community, with moral, territorial, and associational components, which was not simply a prelude to assimilation. On the contrary, they tailored their physical and institutional environment to make possible an ethnic communal alternative to assimilation. In doing so, they used acculturation to serve survivalist ends.[17]

Second generation Jews rooted their ethnic community in the neighborhood, which both fueled and limited the growth of American Jewish ethnicity. An expression of the interrelation of the city's social and spatial organization, the neighborhood was for New York Jews analogous to the American small town. The neighborhood conjured up for many Jews friendships, spatial patterns, and vaguely articulated communal values, yet it never achieved a homogeneous character. While Jews constituted a significant proportion of the residential population of their neighborhood, it was the location of their business, social, and religious institutions which appeared even more conspicuous both to those who lived nearby and those from farther away. These visible institutions labeled a neighborhood and helped to define its character. In a multi-ethnic city like New York, Jewish residential concentration in sections of the Bronx, Brooklyn, and Manhattan encouraged local associations but impeded the growth of city-wide organizations. When Jews left large immigrant neighborhoods for a host of smaller ones in the 1920s, their residential segregation increased. Thus they disproved the theories of pioneer urban sociologists like Louis Wirth. Wirth had expected residential dispersion from immigrant sections into areas of second settlement to correlate with increased assimilation into American society. Instead, second generation Jews introduced the phenomenon of greater dispersion coinciding with increased segregation.[18]

This pattern of concentrated dispersion became one of the components of Jewish ethnic persistence. Second generation Jews, like their immigrant parents before them and like their children who would follow them, combined residential segregation with mobility, and failed to develop stable neighborhoods. Rather, they chose to create and re-create new ethnic neighborhoods, constantly spreading clusters of Jewish settlements throughout the city while maintaining a high level of segregation. Although a breeding ground of provincial loyalties and parochial associations (much of one's life could be lived within the boundaries of the neighborhood), residential segregation also encouraged ideological diversity. Superficially less varied than the immigrant sections with their assortments of national and village associations, the second generation neighborhoods nurtured vitally diverse definitions of Jewishness. As with the immigrant generation, the second generation allowed that there were many ways to be a Jew. In New York City, second generation Jews kept alive secular styles of Jewish living as well as religious ones; neighborhood life, the locus of ethnic community, nourished and sustained a broad ethnic pluralism.[19]

Second generation patterns of employment in New York City strengthened Jewish ethnicity by reinforcing in the economic arena Jewish segregation from other groups. In the 1920s anti-Semitic employment practices forced Jews to rely extensively on ethnic contacts to secure work. Jews were linked by concentration in such industries as the garment trades, and by informal networks of ethnic ties in such industries as the building trades. For New York City Jews the universal business of earning a living became an exercise in ethnic group membership. Jews pursued their class concerns through their ethnic group. Second generation Jews' experience of relatively rapid, collective social mobility decisively united their ethnic group interests with those of the American urban middle class. As Jews entered a host of white-collar jobs in such fields as teaching, social work, pharmacy, and law, they formed professional associations which also enhanced their group consciousness. Growing up in an immigrant community which supported unionism, second generation Jews adapted these traditions of collective action to their new occupations. They frequently joined existing unions, as in teaching, and they occasionally created unions, as in pharmacy or social work. Through middle-class unionism and such Jewish philanthropic occupational organizations as the Jewish Teachers Association, the second generation synthesized its ethnic values and class interests. Moving into the middle class quickly reduced the class conflict which had strained the sense of community among immigrant Jews. Rapid ascent into the American middle class did not cause widespread anomie among second generation Jews. Instead they found that their new status made possible a kind of ethnic community only imagined a generation before by those who had sought to establish a legally constituted, formal Jewish community—the *Kehillah*.[20]

If middle-class status strengthened Jewish ethnicity, binding it to the neighborhood by ligaments both manifest and invisible, local institutions expressed the character of the emergent Jewish ethnic community. In the context of the neighborhood, intermediate social units contributed a public dimension to Jewish life. Instead of keeping their Jewishness within the bounds of the family (or even as the personal asset of an individual) New York Jews transformed the expression of Jewishness into a public activity. The second generation preserved a realm of public Jewish existence embodied in organizations and institutions.[21]

In New York, local institutions (schools, social groups, synagogues, and political clubs) contributed secular and religious attributes to Jewish ethnicity and supported a pluralist vision of American society. Some were formal (the schools and synagogues), others were informal (the social groups). The political clubs often fell into the category of instrumental organizations. All three types reflected Jewish associational community and fostered a sense of moral community as well. While religious organizations emerged as key agencies encouraging the persistence of Jewish ethnicity, secular alternatives existed. Taken as a whole, the institutions illustrate the varied content of Jewish ethnicity. Thus comparisons of institutional changes from immigrant to second generation neighborhoods reveal how the second generation shaped an American Jewish ethnicity.

To understand what second generation Jews achieved in New York City, one must examine at least some of their local institutions. Among the formal ones, the public school and synagogue represent outstanding examples of typical American and typical Jewish institutions respectively. As parents and teachers, second generation Jews often treated their local public school as an ethnic institution. A significant minority even sought recognition of Jewish ethnic separateness from the schools and the validation of democratic pluralism as the American creed. Other Jews tried to transform the synagogue into the core institution of Jewish life. They developed the synagogue-center, which incorporated worship, recreation, sociability, and Jewish education under one roof. The synagogue-center's program embodied the "folk religion" of American Jews, a "pattern of ritual which," Charles Liebman writes, "is supportive of Jewish communalism and ethnicity, of the Jewish home and peoplehood." Informal social clubs complemented school and synagogue, drawing into a network of Jewish association many Jews who shunned formal organizations.

Political activities gave an ideological coherence to Jewish ethnic group life. Combining support for urban welfare measures, civil rights, and civil liberties with internationalism, second generation Jews elaborated a form of liberalism as a distinctive American faith. They equated their understanding of liberalism with the national Democratic party, and beyond the party, with the American dream itself. Yet so tenaciously did Jews hold to this dogma that they adopted it as their own, as the political ideology of American Jewish ethnicity. New York Jews became "radical in thought, reformist in action, bourgeois in manner—and Jewish."[22]

While second generation Jews created a type of urban community, rooted in the neighborhood, sustained by occupational segregation, and perpetuated by local institutions, they failed to produce any city-wide counterpart. Many national and international Jewish organizations located their headquarters in the city. Their presence colored the quality of city-wide Jewish life and hindered second generation efforts to establish a cohesive New York Jewish community. The local struggles that reverberated through these Jewish organizations occasionally acquired national, or even international, significance. While second generation Jews influenced the style of the organizations, the complex interaction of these national and international Jewish organizations depended less on New York Jews than on the internal dynamics of the institutions themselves. And since New York Jewish communal life grew from the experiences of the masses of Jews, it proved to be rather intractable to the national and international organizational elites who desired to lead it.[23] Second generation Jews blurred the distinction between Uptown and Downtown Jews, between wealthy American Jews of German descent and poor eastern European Jewish immigrants, but they struggled unsuccessfully to merge the two groups into one cohesive community. Lacking a communal vision compelling enough to transcend the boundaries of neighborhood, class, and ideology, they accepted partial solutions. Second generation Jews acquiesced in the decision of some wealthy Jews to make philanthropy into a surrogate community. These Jews saw in philanthropy the possibility of using the American model of separation of church and state as a blueprint for Jewish communal organization. But advocates of philanthropy-as-community envisioned too meager a community to enlist the loyalty of most New York Jews. By contrast, one sector of the community used this strategy successfully. The fundraising drive for a Yeshiva College enabled Orthodox Jews to create a city-wide community, albeit one delimited by the ideology of modern Orthodox Judaism.

The second generation as a whole achieved a remarkable synthesis. Through secondary associations they articulated the components of Jewish ethnicity, thus encouraging multiple interpretations of Jewishness. Bounded by the flexible criteria of ethnic identity, New York Jews devised a form of urban community imbued with American middle class values, yet able to ensure the persistence of the Jewish group. The Jewish ethnic community was semi-voluntary; one did not have to take out membership, nor was one forced into the community primarily by anti-Semitism. Residence in a Jewish neighborhood and associational ties with other Jews brought one into the orbit of the community, into "a world of Jewish *un*consciousness."[24] Yet the multitude of Jewish institutions highlights the voluntary and public aspect of Jewish ethnicity—the need to affiliate explicitly, especially if one sought membership in a community extending beyond the neighborhood. The second generation ethnic community was secured by strands at once conscious and unconscious, built up through secondary and primary associations. For New York Jews this meant that their physical community was constructed by Jewish builders who attracted Jewish buyers through the invisible ties of primary bonds. It meant that work became an area of ethnic interaction fostering associational community. School and synagogue built associational and moral communal links; while in politics New York Jews treated an associational, instrumental structure as a means to moral community.

The achievements of second generation Jews first became visible in the 1920s, when new middle-class neighborhoods appeared on the map of Jewish New York. In the space of a decade cut short by the Depression, second generation Jews established enduring patterns of ethnic community. Subsequently, New York Jews continued to develop the Jewish ethnicity characteristic of the second generation. However, the emergence of a second generation in the 1920s, like the appearance of a third generation in the 1950s, should not obscure the continuing existence of immigrant life. Second generation ethnicity grew out of a dialogue with a vibrant immigrant Jewish culture. Similarly, the second generation continued as an established force long after its years of greatest innovation, the 1920s. The second generation dominated New York Jewish life through the 1950s. Indeed, among some segments of immigrant Jews, a second generation did not mature until the late 1930s. A focus on the 1920s, then, suggests an emphasis on new beginnings, on a way of life as it first blossomed.

2

But it is the apartment house that remains the emblem of the Jews' love affair with the city. Wherever Jews have formed an important segment of the urban American population, they have been the prime developers, and prime residents of apartment houses, especially of the so-called "elevator buildings," those bastions of the urban middle class. The phenomenon is best observed in New York City where this type of building has enjoyed its greatest vogue and where the Jewish preference for such housing was less influenced by non-Jewish tastes than elsewhere in the country. The elevator building was designed for people who had moved up from the working class and the walk-up building, and who, though financially able to buy a one-family home in the suburbs, chose to remain in the city. Such construction reached its apogee along the great boulevards of Brooklyn, the Bronx, and more recently, Queens—Eastern Parkway, Ocean Parkway, the Grand Concourse, and Queens Boulevard. These were essentially "Jewish" avenues, built by Jewish developers for a Jewish clientele.

Marshall Sklare, "Jews, Ethnics, and the American City,"
Commentary (April 1972), p. 72.

Jewish
Geography

A Jewish immigrant landing at the foot of the Bowery at the turn
of the century needed no English to locate the Jews of New York.
Any police officer could recognize by manner and dress the immigrant's east European origins and direct him to where the Jews
lived: the Lower East Side. The policeman knew his Jewish geography. In the peak years of the mass immigration at the beginning
of the century almost 75 percent of New York City's Jews lived in
the city's most densely crowded blocks, bounded by the East
River, the Bowery, and Monroe and 14th Streets. Over the course
of several decades Jews constructed a vibrant and visible Yiddish
working class culture in the immigrant colony. Once a Jew hit the
streets of East Broadway, the Lower East Side's most prestigious
thoroughfare (likened by Jewish intellectuals to the famed Nevsky
Prospekt in St. Petersburg), an immigrant knew she had entered a
Jewish world.[1]

By the time Congress decisively restricted substantial immigration to the United States, especially from eastern and southern Europe, a stranger searching for the Jewish quarter would
encounter difficulty. It was not that the Jews of the Lower East
Side had disappeared in 1924 (although their numbers were
shrinking daily), but New York Jews no longer concentrated in
the old immigrant section as they once had. During the decade of
the "roaring twenties," 160,000 Jews abandoned their old streets
for new neighborhoods. They left behind 100,000 Jews to fill the
spaces where previously over a quarter of a million had lived.
Halfway through the decade Jewish statisticians described New
York's Jewish demography. Surprised, they announced that the
demographic statistics revealed "the startling fact that Brooklyn

today has almost as many Jews as have the two boroughs of the Bronx and Manhattan added together and that the trend is still towards the Bronx and Brooklyn and away from Manhattan."[2]

The steady shift in the Jewish population should not have startled the Jewish statisticians. Jews had been moving to Brooklyn and the Bronx since the turn of the century. Lower East Side Jews discovered Brownsville and Williamsburg in Brooklyn with the "aid" of the Williamsburg and Manhattan bridges. The construction of their entrance ramps, completed in 1903 and 1909 respectively, dislocated thousands of Jews from their Manhattan homes and transplanted them across the river. Rapid transit facilities to Brooklyn speeded the transition. "When I was nine years old," Zalmen Yoffeh reminisced, "my mother heard of a wonderful bargain in the then sparsely-populated Brownsville—four rooms with a private bathroom. We moved there." Together with thousands of Jews the Yoffehs jouneyed to Brownsville. Other Jewish immigrants headed north to the Bronx. Many never reached the borough of parks but stopped in Harlem. There poor Jews found modern tenements east of Fifth Avenue and newly affluent immigrants settled into comfortable brownstones and apartment houses between Lenox and Seventh Avenues. Jews also brought with them to Harlem, Williamsburg, Brownsville, and the Bronx "various characteristics of the East Side." "The pushcart market on 137th Street from Brook to St. Ann's Avenues" in the Bronx replicated the original on Hester and Orchard Streets. "Overcrowding, lack of modern housing facilities brought the slums to the Bronx." Though optimists predicted "Brownsville will never have tenements," a densely populated section of 50,000 blossomed during the first decade of its discovery. In Harlem, a Jewish settlement of more than 100,000 nurtured communal institutions designed to transplant prominent features of East Side Yiddish culture. The visible signs of Jewish life in synagogues and store windows characterized these sections as spiritual and physical extensions of the Lower East Side. So successfully did these parts of Manhattan, the Bronx, and Brooklyn attract immigrant Jews that by 1916 only 25 percent of the city's Jews still lived on the Lower East Side.[3]

What warranted the note of surprise then in the statisticians' report? If Brooklyn, once "the City of Churches," now ranked, in the words of its Jewish boosters, as "the greatest Hebrew Community in the Entire World," then even astute observers of Jewish life in the city might lose their bearings. Given the trends in population since the beginning of the twentieth century, amazement came from the discovery neither of a dispersed Jewish population in the city nor of its rapid migration. Relatively late arrivals to the multi-ethnic metropolis, Jewish immigrants followed the footsteps of the Irish and Germans who preceded them and were accompanied by Italians who initially disembarked in the same period. "Between 1905 and 1925 the proportion of city residents living within four miles of City Hall tumbled from more than one half to less than one third." In 1910 Manhattan's population peaked, pointing to the physical growth of the outer city. Thirteen years later, Manhattan's Jewish population hit its acme.[4] In the future the new locale for Jewish life would be found on the streets of Brooklyn and the Bronx. A new Jewish geography was taking hold in the city and experienced observers marveled at its portents. On the city's streets appeared the first imprint of a second generation of Jews which was emerging in the 1920s.

The demographic face of New York's Jewish geography always implied an inner social reality. During the heyday of the Lower East Side, New York Jews saw themselves in geographic terms. There were the Downtown Jews—the immigrants: the poor, the Yiddish speaking, the orthodox, the radicals. Opposite them stood the Uptown Jews: the wealthy, acculturated American Jews of German-Jewish background, the Reform Jews. The schism in the Jewish community between its masses and its elite registered in the physical world. Where you lived explained what you were. But as the view from Jewish windows changed, as Jews increasingly looked out onto the tree-lined boulevards of Eastern

Table 1 Total City and Jewish Population (figures in millions)

	1920	1925	1930	1940
N.Y.C. population	5.620	5.870	6.930	7.460
Jewish population	1.640	1.750	1.830	1.950
percent Jewish	29	29	26	26

SOURCES: Horowitz and Kaplan, pp. 2–5, 15; *Jewish Population*, JCS, p. 2; Rosenwaike, p. 129.

Parkway and the Grand Concourse, the inner Jewish geography took on new contours too. The old categories of Uptown and Downtown could not characterize a community living predominantly in Brooklyn and the Bronx. Compulsively, New York Jews sought to explain to themselves the social meaning of the demographic shifts. "Once there was only one kind of Jewish neighborhood, of which the old East Side was the 'shining' example," Nathaniel Zalowitz observed in the Jewish Daily *Forward*. "But today you have a Ghetto for the Jew who owns a Rolls Royce and half a dozen other cars besides. The rich Jew no less than the poor one prefers to live among 'unsere leute' [his own kind]—and the Gentile thinks so too."[5]

Zalowitz's observation emphasized how the Jewish migration to the Bronx and Brooklyn in the 1920s destroyed the old distinctions between Uptown and Downtown Jews. The dispersal of Jews into the outer city failed to perpetuate the established pattern of densely populated immigrant neighborhoods and appeared to be producing "voluntary ghettos," no longer limited to the lower class. "What else would you call the districts in the various large American cities in which two-thirds or more of the Jews live and have their being?" Zalowitz queried. "The majority of the Jews . . . inhabit certain sections only. That, I urge, is the true earmark of Ghetto life." Another journalist writing in the *Jewish Tribune* considered the "Jewish suburban sections" in Brooklyn and the Bronx to be "object lessons in Jewish economic competence." But, he concluded, "all that is ordinarily associated with the word 'ghetto' falls away from them, except the fact that they are inhabited by Jews."[6] Both observations suggested the need for fresh definitions to explain the meaning of Jewish migration to the outer city. In the 1920s Jews were not moving into Harlem, Brownsville, Williamsburg, and the East Bronx; rather they were settling in different sections of the boroughs. They were drawing anew the map of Jewish New York.

A new middle class of Jews was emerging, fed by the profitable opportunities generated by World War I and nourished by the speculative prosperity of the 1920s. Many of the Jewish bourgeoisie belonged to the second generation of Jews in the United States. If not actually native-born of immigrant parents, these Jews acquired through their childhood experiences an

Table 2 Total and Jewish Population by Boroughs (figures in millions)

Population	1920	1925
Manhattan	2.28 (41% of city)	1.95 (33% of city)
Manhattan Jewish	.66 (40% of city)	.50 (29% of city)
	29% of boro	26% of boro
Brooklyn	2.02 (36% of city)	2.20 (38% of city)
Brooklyn Jewish	.60 (37% of city)	.80 (46% of city)
	30% of boro	36% of boro
Bronx	.73 (13% of city)	.87 (15% of city)
Bronx Jewish	.28 (17% of city)	.39 (22% of city)
	38% of boro	45% of boro
Queens	.47 (8% of city)	.72 (12% of city)
Queens Jewish	.09 (5% of city)	.06 (3% of city)
	18% of boro	8% of boro

Population	1930	1940
Manhattan	1.86 (27% of city)	1.89 (25% of city)
Manhattan Jewish	.30 (16% of city)	.27 (15% of city)
	16% of boro	14% of boro
Brooklyn	2.55 (37% of city)	2.70 (35% of city)
Brooklyn Jewish	.85 (47% of city)	.86 (48% of city)
	33% of boro	32% of boro
Bronx	1.27 (18% of city)	1.40 (19% of city)
Bronx Jewish	.59 (32% of city)	.54 (30% of city)
	45% of boro	39% of boro
Queens	1.08 (16% of city)	1.30 (17% of city)
Queens Jewish	.09 (5% of city)	.12 (6% of city)
	8% of boro	9% of boro

SOURCES: The 1920 figures from Laidlaw, p. 275. For a discussion of his estimates see Appendix. The 1925 figures from *Jewish Population*, JCS, p. 2. The 1930 and 1940 figures from Horowitz and Kaplan, p. 22.

American consciousness. They grew to maturity within the American immigrant milieu; they neither knew nor cared about the old country. Ties of *landsleyt* meant less to them than family bonds, public school friendships, and block associations. They were the Jews who picked up and moved to new neighborhoods in Brooklyn and the Bronx in the 1920s. "The young married people are going to outlying districts of the Bronx and Brooklyn," observed a settlement house worker in 1925. "Their standards of living are higher than those of their parents. They seek better homes . . . for the price they can afford to pay.''[7] In their footsteps came fabulous jumps in the number of Jewish residents in areas where previously there were few Jews.

Leaving the old immigrant sections, middle-class Jews quickly settled in a number of new neighborhoods. "Manhattan Beach is comparatively a recently occupied district by people of Jewish creed,'' observed a Brooklyn Jewish Federation fund-raiser, ever sensitive to potential sources of income. "Especially during the last two years a good many Jews have moved there as a result of the wealth they have accumulated from war activities.'' From 1920 to 1930 the middle-class Irish and white Protestant neighborhoods of Flatbush and the Grand Concourse registered increases of 250 percent and 450 percent in their Jewish popula-tions. In sparsely settled Pelham Parkway, along Bronx Park East, the number of Jewish residents jumped over 700 percent during the same decade. Similar sections in Brooklyn (including the south Flatbush, Midwood, Sheepshead Bay, and Coney Island neighborhoods), burst onto the Jewish map of New York City with 700 percent increases in Jewish population.[8] The appearance of these neighborhoods implied a revolution in values among New York Jews.

Despite differences in style, the new Jewish neighborhoods shared common characteristics underlining their inherent attrac-tion for this pioneering generation of Jews. All contrasted sharply with the immigrant sections in their suburban quality and rela-tively low population density. "In place of dingy, narrow alleys, there are clean broad streets that pay tribute to the newly arisen sense for outward beauty in the shape of trees and little gardens.'' Miles of broad tree-lined pavement set the tone for the surround-ing area. The appeal of unused land—of open fields, an oc-casional farm, or just empty lots—led many who moved out to Flatbush or the Grand Concourse to believe that they had left the city. "Crowded northward, the Jews discovered the wilds of the Bronx,'' wrote journalist Konrad Bercovici in 1923. "The doctors advised them to go and live there when they had a 'touch of con-sumption.' It was the 'country.' '' The long subway ride into Man-hattan confirmed the impression of living in the suburbs. As the editors of the New York Regional Survey noted, "the word 'su-

burb' must not be interpreted too narrowly. The contrast is between neighborhoods in which the land is heavily covered with
buildings and others where a good deal of it is open in the form of
parks, gardens or ground surrounding detached houses,'' they
explained. "Compared to Manhattan and the old wards of Brooklyn, large portions of the outer boroughs are definitely suburban
in character although their aspect may not be rural."[9]

The presence of small farms and undeveloped parcels of land
helped to retain the suburban feeling of many sections of Brooklyn and the Bronx during the 1920s. When Harry Golden moved
with his family to Vyse Avenue in the Bronx in 1918 he "could
still see the goat farms.'' In 1921 almost half of the land in the
Bensonhurst, Midwood, and Sheepshead Bay sections of Brooklyn
remained unimproved. Six years later Bronx builder Myron Eisenstein still had to chase goats off his apartment house lot near
Montefiore Hospital on Wayne Avenue before beginning construction. In the Bronx "there was at first no competition with the
slums, and construction went on more systematically and at a
quiet pace. The Bronx, therefore, became a residential area, like
a suburban area where people wish to raise their children in a
quieter atmosphere.'' In 1936 an anonymous historian of the Jewish Communal Center of Flatbush admitted in retrospect that "we
who have immigrated to the Flatbush Community within the past
few years, find it difficult to think of this suburb of the metropolitan district in terms of an unpopulated and countrified settlement. This was the case during 1914–1915." Second generation
Jew Anna Bortz remembered that even as late as 1929 when she
moved to "Evergreen Estates'' on Westchester Avenue in the Crotona section of the Bronx, it "was a beautiful new building out in
the country.'' Yet Evergreen Estates was a large, six-story apartment complex, hardly the housing reflective of a suburban setting.
In the same spirit, ten years later the builders of "a suburb in the
Heart of the Bronx'' advertised their apartment house at 2175
Cedar Avenue as located in "Rustic surroundings—A beautiful,
tree-lined street—Overlooking the Hall of Fame Park, New York
University and the Harlem River."[10]

Obviously the type of house did not need to be suburban in
style to attract Jewish residents. The predominance of apartment
houses in the new neighborhoods suggested that Jews wanted

New apartment houses under construction in the "suburban" Bronx in 1928 along Pelham Parkway, east of White Plains Road. *Courtesy of the Bronx County Historical Society, New York City.*

modern homes, sporting the latest conveniences. The same advertisement promising "rustic surroundings" also boasted: "adjacent to the best shopping center in the Bronx—Fordham Road." Similarly, Myron Eisenstein advertised the courtyard garden, which was "filled with foliage and traced by flagstone walks," of his six-story apartment house on Wayne Avenue as providing "all the fresh-air atmosphere of the suburban home close to the city's convenience." Such homes cost substantial sums to rent or buy; to live in one implied the achievement of middle-class status. The new houses contrasted with those in the older immigrant sections of the city. "In place of the dismal tenements, there are residences for one or two families ranging in rank from the modest red brick house to the stuccoed and sometimes over ornamental 'mansion.' " In fact, some Jews who moved out of congested city neighborhoods had acquired sufficient income to spend around $100 a month for rent. In 1921 Municipal Court Judge Harry Robitzek noted in regard to recent housing that "figures, reduced to an irreducible minimum, show that it is impossible to build a modern apartment house now that can rent its rooms for less than $25 a month each." Yet rents for new apart-

ments on side streets cost less than on a major boulevard like the
Grand Concourse. Tenants at 2175 Cedar Avenue spent as little
as $70 a month for a four room apartment. Clearly, none of this
housing competed with old-law tenement apartments built before
the minimum standards set by the housing law of 1901. These
rented for an average of $500 a year in 1921. Advertisers sensed
the acute desire for new middle-class homes after the tight housing market of World War I had eased. Praising their Brooklyn
product, the advertisements promised: "Modern throughout.
Steam heat, electric light, gas, hardwood floors, bathroom and
kitchen Spanish tile. Own your own fireproof stucco house."[11]

As the rapid rate of housing construction continued, some
Jews sought out the newest homes. Recently completed apartment
buildings not only attracted Jews from immigrant sections who
were ready to move up, but appealed as well to Jews from older
buildings in the neighborhood. Others who preferred not to pay
any more for rent discovered that by shifting location (from Harlem to the Grand Concourse for example) they could avoid rent
increases. A contemporary observer recognized the critical role of
new housing in 1925, pointing out that "the decreasing number of
Jews in Williamsburg, South Brooklyn, Bay Ridge and Green-
point indicate their removal to other sections where increases are
evident. New sections of Brooklyn, Flatbush particularly, are
being developed with modern homes and apartment houses," he
continued. These areas were "attracting people from the older
and more congested districts, not only of Brooklyn, but of Manhattan as well. This migration of Jews from one district of Brooklyn to another," he predicted, "will take place as long as the
present building development continues in Brooklyn, opening up
better residential areas for those who improve their economic status." Indeed, the newness of the houses often carried more weight
with potential residents than their style. By the late twenties, two-
year-old apartments could not command the same rents as recently completed ones and landlords often offered adjustments to
keep their tenants from moving. "The West Bronx, almost as a
whole, consists of large, spacious, and modern apartment
houses," noted one writer in the 1930s. "Most of the buildings are
very new; but even the oldest in this part of the Bronx are constantly kept in repair, are always having modern improvements

installed, and therefore never fall into the state where they might appear incongruous next to their newer neighbors."[12]

Jews saw middle-class housing not only as a sign of their economic status but as a symbol of their acculturation as well. "Immigrants who settle on the East Side of New York do not remain there any longer than they can help," Harry Schneiderman, assistant secretary of the American Jewish Committee, remarked in 1941. "Those who settle there do so because of the low rents, which, in turn, are made possible by the smallness of the apartments, the lack of air and light." Schneiderman pointed to the correlation of housing standards and American values in the eyes of New York City Jews. But moving to the suburban outer city involved more than acquiring a taste for nature and enough capital to afford middle class housing. Second generation Jews also migrated to the Bronx and Brooklyn in the 1920s to trade the foreignness of immigrant sections for an American neighborhood. In doing so, they fulfilled the ambitions of their immigrant parents. "The immigrant ghetto from the beginning was entered into only to be abandoned," observes historian Ben Halpern. "The generation that entered the immigrant ghetto was confronted by one overwhelming task: to get out, or to enable the next generation to get out. This task they accomplished." Second generation Jews' suburban residence implied a willingness to live among Gentiles. "I think it is also true that as immigrant Jews become more Americanized, they become less and less inclined to live in neighborhoods which are compactly inhabited by co-religionists," Schneiderman mused. "Progress in assimilation leads to a desire to live in neighborhoods which are 'American.' This trend is responsible for the fact that Jews pioneered in the settlement of many of the outlying sections of the city as soon as transportation facilities were provided."[13]

Schneiderman's easy equation of American with non-Jewish overlooked the distinctively American Jewish tone the new Brooklyn and Bronx neighborhoods rapidly acquired. As Zalowitz astutely observed,

> People used to imagine years ago that as soon as the Jews will shed their 'greenness' they will mix with the Gentiles, be accepted in Gentile society, move into Gentile neighborhoods, and be absorbed in a decade or less. Nothing of the sort has happened. The Jews in

their northward march from the dingy and sordid East Side did move into Gentile sections—and the Gentiles immediately began to get out. This is the story of the Bronx, of Flatbush, . . . even of Riverside Drive and West End Avenue.

Indeed, it took Jews a while to realize that the suburban and middle-class values which they identified as American and which guided their search for housing also implied a less densely populated Jewish neighborhood. Writing in the late 1920s, novelist Michael Gold described his mother's frightened response to the prospect of living isolated in a single family house in pre-war Borough Park:

> My mother would not go in. She remained on the porch like a beggar. With troubled eyes she stared around at the suburb, at the lots covered with slush and weeds, at the eight banal houses. On our way home, my father asked my mother: "Well, what do you think of it now, Katie?"
> "I don't like it," said my mother.
> "And why not?" my father said indignantly. "Are you so much in love with that sewer of an East Side?"
> "No," said my mother. "But I will miss the neighbors on Christie Street."

So, too, in 1929 Yoffeh chronicled his family's first abortive attempt to move to Brownsville:

> What a horrible experience. Our nearest neighbor was over fifty yards away. At night the street was deserted and quiet. Gentiles lived across the way; one had to walk two and three blocks to reach a store. What self-respecting Jew could live in such a neighborhood?

The Yoffehs gave up and "moved back to the East Side in mid-August."

> The street we moved to was filled with pushcarts. A continual roar arose from the occupants and it was with difficulty that one made his way through the crowds. Here and there were heaps of rotting fruit. The stench and the heat, as I look back on it, were unendurable. Yet we were all happy to be back. Back on the East Side, back in a Jew's world.

But Brownsville educated the Yoffeh family. "To live, a family of eight, in three rooms, seemed to us quite normal, as was being

Cultivating a love of nature in Brownsville, Brooklyn.
Farm gardens at the corner of Pitkin Avenue and Chester Street, circa 1910.

without a bathroom and sharing the toilet with three neighbors,''
Zalmen Yoffeh recalled. "In winter all the windows were kept
shut day and night, and in summer we slept on the roofs and on
the fire-escapes. Nothing was wrong with that,'' until they learned
of other possibilities.[14]

Second generation Jews moving from Brownsville and Williamsburg, from the Lower East Side and Harlem, needed no such
education. They knew that they were acquiring a middle-class
American environment and leaving behind an immigrant, foreign
world. Secure in their Jewishness they did not flee from who they
were. Rather they redefined the meaning of Jewishness as they
rewrote New York's Jewish geography. Their migration produced
the seeming paradox of concentrated dispersal.[15]

For all their mobility throughout the city, by 1930 most Jews
lived in sections significantly segregated from the Gentile population. The 1920s' trend toward greater dispersal in Brooklyn and
the Bronx and the corresponding abandonment of Manhattan did
not reduce the segregated aspect of Jewish residential life. In fact,
as the migration picked up speed, Jewish residential concentration increased. In 1920 only 54 percent of New York's Jews lived
in neighborhoods at least 40 percent Jewish in population. By
1925 the percentage jumped to 64 percent, and at the end of the
decade 72 percent of Jewish New Yorkers resided in sections with
a critical mass of Jews. An index of dissimilarity computing the

extent of Jewish residential concentration in neighborhoods throughout the city measures on a scale of 0 to 1 a steady increase in segregation from .4 in 1920 to .5 in 1925 to .6 in 1930.

As Jews concentrated in a larger number of neighborhoods, a new norm emerged. In the 1920s the neighborhoods where Jews made up close to 50 percent of the population took the place of the previous Uptown–Downtown pattern. Instead of a handful of crowded, poor Downtown sections complementing a diffuse, rich, elite Uptown, many ethnically mixed Jewish neighborhoods appeared. Here Jews could rub shoulders with some Gentiles even as the neighborhoods isolated Jews from most non-Jewish New Yorkers. These new areas also reflected greater differentiation in wealth among New York Jews. Less densely populated, with modern housing, offering an opportunity to live with Gentiles as well as Jews, the new neighborhoods attracted Jews of all incomes. By 1930 even many upper-class Jews lived in Jewish neighborhoods. "The common notion," concluded statistician Julius Maller in 1934, "that Jewish areas are located only on the Lower East Side or in other poor districts is unfounded." Second generation Jews, too, chose to live together, as long as they lived in a new, middle-class American neighborhood. As a result, with an increasing number of Jewish neighborhoods scattered in the outer city came a rise in Jewish ethnic segregation in New York as measured by an index of dissimilarity. The index of dissimilarity shows the extent to which the second generation clustered together in sections of the city rather than residing, evenly distributed, among Gentiles. Indeed, the process of migration intensified Jewish residential segregation. During the Depression, when Jewish mobility declined, the extent of Jewish concentration leveled off at a new plateau.[16] The new Jewish geography resembled a patchwork quilt securely blanketing three boroughs.

Table 3 Index of Dissimilarity for Jews in New York City

1920	.38
1925	.52
1930	.58
1940	.56

Index computed from figures for 1920 from Laidlaw, pp. 292; for 1925 from Laidlaw, pp. 73–81 and *Jewish Population*, JCS, pp. 4, 6–7; for 1930 and 1940 from Horowitz and Kaplan, pp. 98, 100, 102, 104.

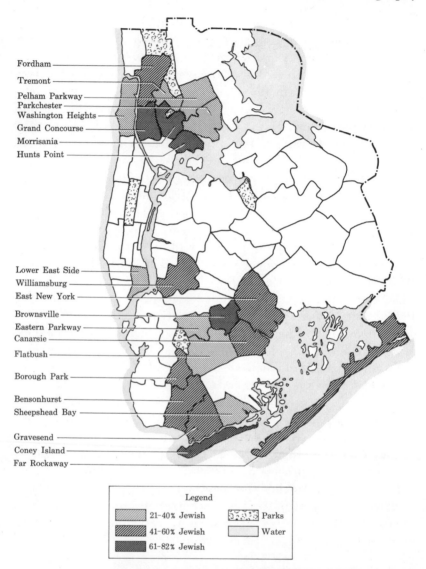

Figure 1. Map of Jewish Neighborhoods in New York City in 1930
SOURCE: C. Morris Horowitz and Lawrence J. Kaplan, *The Estimated Jewish Population of the New York Area 1900–1975* (New York: Federation of Jewish Philanthropies of New York, 1959).

Yet why did the Jews' conscious search to implement their desire for a comfortable suburban middle-class life—values they shared with other New Yorkers—draw them toward some neighborhoods and not others? From 1920 to 1930 Brooklyn and the

Bronx each gained close to half a million residents, but their Jewish population increased at a greater pace. Brooklyn had more than 800,000 Jews in 1930 (a third of its population) while the Bronx had almost 600,000 Jews (close to half of the borough's residents). Yet while 75 percent of New York City's Jews chose to live in either the Bronx or Brooklyn, only 46 percent of the city's Gentile population agreed with their choice. From 1920 to 1940 Queens tripled its population, but most Jews ignored the borough except for the stretch of beach in the Rockaways. Even within the Bronx and Brooklyn, Jews gravitated toward some sections and avoided others. Wherein lay the attraction of Flatbush compared to Fort Hamilton in Brooklyn, of the Grand Concourse to Gun Hill Road in the Bronx? All were middle-class neighborhoods; but Jews chose to live in some and not in others.

Jewish intracity migration in the 1920s recorded an ethnic variation on the general theme of urban growth. As New York City rapidly expanded into its outlying, low-density areas, Jews and non-Jews alike followed the transit lines to new homes in less congested neighborhoods. Drawn by a vision of American suburban bourgeois living, they sought out substantial houses with the most modern amenities.[17] But though they started off down the tracks together, Jews and Gentiles arrived at different stations. Underneath the process of urban growth lay a network of ethnic ties which subtly directed the city's migrations, producing at one stroke similar but ethnically distinct middle-class city neighborhoods.

In searching for new homes Jews, like other New Yorkers, found their choices limited initially by transportation facilities. A person needed to be able to reach his job, and investing in a modern home did not necessarily include laying out more than a dime a day in subway or elevated fares. Transportation unlocked the door to urban expansion. Construction of 260 miles of rapid transit facilities in New York between 1914 and 1921 preceded the city's residential building boom. The new track brought large areas of Brooklyn and the Bronx within reach of Manhattan and its jobs. Indeed "not only has the multiplication of rapid transit routes serving the inner zone facilitated the dispersal of the residential population to outer sections, but it has also aided the trend toward concentration of business uses, which have virtually driven out residences over large areas."[18]

Building the White Plains Road extension in the Bronx.
View from Gun Hill Road looking east toward White Plains Road and the Third
Avenue El. *Courtesy of the Bronx County Historical Society, New York City.*

The reciprocal relationship between rapid transit and residential expansion appears vividly in a comparison of the 1920 and
1930 distribution of the Bronx population. In 1920 the most
crowded neighborhoods clustered within a quarter mile of the two
major transit lines running through the central Bronx: the Third
Avenue Elevated and the Interborough Rapid Transit (IRT). But
the almost simultaneous completion of three new lines promoted
the growth of a host of middle-class neighborhoods near their
routes. The White Plains Road extension in 1917, the western
Jerome Avenue line, and the eastern Pelham Bay line spurred
massive population shifts. During the Depression, when most
housing construction came to a standstill, the construction of the
Independent (IND) subway under the Grand Concourse encouraged continued building of apartment houses along the Concourse and on neighboring streets. Sections of the Bronx lacking
inexpensive transportation remained sparsely populated throughout both decades.[19]

But Jews and other New Yorkers needed more than transportation to reach their new homes. The availability of public services shaped the city's emerging housing patterns. Zoning laws
sketched out a broad outline of potential urban growth. Construction of residences in undeveloped sections of New York depended

on City Hall's willingness to grade and pave streets, run water lines and sewage mains, and provide gas and electricity. The existence of such essential services enticed builders, as one advertisement for 297 lots in Manhattan Beach suggested. "Over a Million Dollars Spent in city improvements, such as water, sewers, gas, electricity, sidewalks, curbs, boulevards, avenues, etc. without regard to expense," it proclaimed.[20]

Yet it availed Jews little if builders took advantage of the transit facilities and public services to build only small apartments. As second generation Jews came of age, they desired homes appropriate for their growing families. New York Jews presented an age profile slightly younger than the general city population. They were relatively recent immigrants to New York and most Jewish immigrants were teenagers or in their twenties. With the maturation of a second generation, many more Jews began to raise families. The new buildings constructed in Brooklyn and the Bronx fulfilled their expectations. The houses catered to growing families and offered spacious apartments of three, four, and five rooms. These apartments often contained large living rooms of 22

Transportation unlocked the door to urban expansion.
The 138th Street crosstown line between Alexander and Willis Avenues in the Bronx with the Third Avenue El, which ran between blocks up to 144th Street, in the background. *Courtesy of the Bronx County Historical Society, New York City.*

feet by 14 feet and those with more than one bedroom included a second bathroom as well. Advertisements extolled the virtues of the new construction in the Pelham Parkway area, urging New Yorkers to "Buy where kiddies grow husky in the open air." Newspaperman Leon Wexelstein boosted Brooklyn, which "has been proffering all these years not merely flats in crowded apartment houses, but one- and two-family houses, with ample space around for genuine home life, for a care-free and natural rearing of children." By 1924 Rabbi Alexander Basel could observe in regard to the Grand Concourse that "thousands of young married couples have selected this section as a most ideal place where to settle and raise the young generation."[21]

Eager as they were to reach the Grand Concourse or Flatbush, Jews discovered when they arrived that other ethnic groups had preceded them. Ethnic Irish and German New Yorkers, who constituted a majority of the city's population in 1900, were enjoying the beauties of the Bronx and Brooklyn as early as the turn of the century. By the time the Jews were rushing out to Brownsville or the East Bronx, the Irish had moved into the Concourse and parts of Flatbush. And they continued to move. The Germans left Yorkville for Queens during the same decade that the Jews went to the Concourse. Ethnic succession characterized New York's residential neighborhoods, with earlier immigrants preceding later arrivals. Starting on the bottom rung of the residential ladder, each immigrant group climbed its way up, never quite reaching the ones who came earlier.[22]

But ethnic succession alone cannot explain the distinctive Jewish patchwork-quilt geography in the city. Jews rarely enjoyed a completely free choice of available housing. In certain sections of the city they encountered persistent discrimination and anti-Semitism. One of the most significant housing developments in Queens, the large innovative group of garden apartments built by the Queensboro Corporation in the 1920s, restricted Jewish tenants and cooperators. "Riding on a Fifth Avenue bus in New York, one may notice advertisements of the desirable residential development in Jackson Heights: 'Restrictions, Convenience, Service,' " observed newspaper columnists Heywood Broun and George Britt. Some sections of Flatbush also resisted Jewish residents as did Sea Gate in Coney Island. One apartment building on

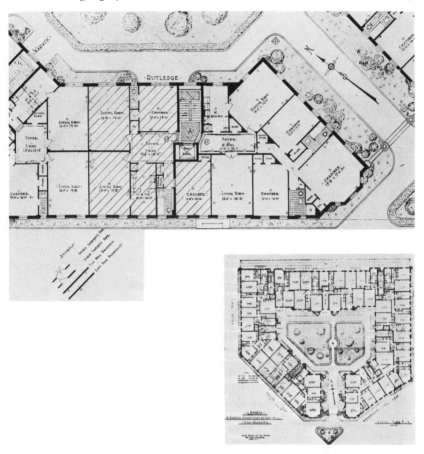

Floor plan of several large apartments in the Lenru on Wayne Avenue and East 210th Street, built by Myron Eisenstein in 1927 and designed by Charles Kreymborg. The layout of the building, with multiple entrances, allowed each apartment to have cross-ventilation and every room to have a window.

Caton Avenue and Westminster Road advertised: "Sensibly priced, sensibly built, sensibly restricted." More exclusive buildings in expensive sections of Brooklyn and Manhattan relied on word of mouth. Wealthy Brooklyn Jews settled along Eastern Parkway near Prospect Park, avoiding Park Slope and Brooklyn Heights, which had been known since the nineteenth century as Yankee neighborhoods, and which continued to bar Jews throughout the 1920s and 1930s. So, too, the Fieldston section of Riverdale in the Bronx restricted Jewish residents.[23]

Such prejudice distressed Jews, and they fought unsuccessfully to break down the barriers of discrimination in housing. But a lawsuit filed against the Jackson Heights development failed to open any doors to Jews. In 1927 Judge Burt Humphrey ruled that the renting agent had the right to refuse to accept Jews irrespective of their character and ability to pay the rent. The American Jewish Committee, the most prominent American Jewish defense organization in New York in the 1920s, found no way to prevent private building owners from discriminating against Jews. Although the Committee's head, Louis Marshall, succeeded in getting in 1913 an amendment to the New York Civil Rights Act that prohibited discriminatory hotel advertising, the law proved to be unenforceable. Chastened by this experience in the legal arena, the Committee concentrated its efforts on educational campaigns and public appeals.[24]

But anti-Semitism shaped Jewish housing patterns less decisively than did Jewish associational networks. Jews decided where to live based on information they received from friends and relatives. Seldom did Jews choose a new home solely in response to discrimination. Kinship built Jewish neighborhoods more effectively than anti-Semitism. Jews learned from their associates whom to trust as a builder of quality homes, where to go to get mortgages, what were the most attractive features of a new section. And because most Jews wanted to be "at home" in their neighborhood, they were happiest living near other Jews.[25]

Jewish builders recognized these informally acknowledged desires and subtly guided Jews to their new homes. In the 1920s Jewish builders eagerly set out to satisfy their fellow Jews' demand for modern housing. They relied on the ethnic associational network to get them residents. Thus Jewish builders helped to create new Jewish neighborhoods. Choosing to build in Flatbush or along the Concourse, Jewish builders drew Jews to these sections of the city. The demands of a Jewish housing market and of Jewish builders' profit margins mandated the construction of new housing—both single and multi-family dwellings—which produced remarkably similar middle-class neighborhoods in Brooklyn and the Bronx. In New York City the general process of suburban development in the growth of the outer city received a special twist: the bonds of ethnicity supported ethnically separate construction industries catering to an ethnically distinct housing market.[26]

By establishing a foothold in the industry, immigrant Jews laid the foundation for the widespread Jewish activity in all aspects of real estate and building characteristic of the 1920s. As early as the 1890s, immigrant Jews eyed the lucrative real estate market on the Lower East Side where the masses, crowded into tenements, pushed up land and building values. Investing first in Lower East Side real estate and then in properties in other sections where Jews settled—like Harlem and Brownsville—secured the future of those few who had succeeded in accumulating capital. Some, like Harris Mandelbaum, even made a fortune out of buying and selling tenements. The passion for quick profits fed curbside real estate markets. "The scene was the corner of Fifth Avenue and One Hundred and Sixteenth Street . . . a spot that usually swarmed with Yiddish-speaking real-estate speculators," Abraham Cahan wrote in his novel of Jewish success in America. "It was a gesticulating, jabbering, whispering, excited throng, resembling the crowd of curb-brokers on Broad Street." So many Jews took a chance to invest in real estate after the turn of the century that by World War I Cahan, the perceptive editor of the Yiddish Daily *Forward,* could ridicule the "realestatenik:"

> Small tradesmen of the slums, and even working-men, were investing their savings in houses and lots. Jewish carpenters, housepainters, bricklayers, or installment peddlers became builders of tenements or frame dwellings, real-estate speculators. Deals were being closed, and poor men were making thousands of dollars in

less time than it took them to drink the glass of tea or the plate of
sorrel soup over which the transaction took place. Women, too,
were ardently dabbling in real estate.

The rush of Jews to Brownsville lifted land values there, and
prices on $50 lots soared to $3,000 in just two years. "The
hangout of the real estate speculators was a cafe on Pitkin Avenue," the former *Freiheit* editor Melech Epstein remembered.
"Houses were bought and sold over a cup of coffee." The boom in
Brownsville also enticed Jews into the construction industry.[27]

Harry Fischel, a Russian immigrant with architectural training, pioneered in building tenements on the Lower East Side on
irregularly shaped lots. His expertise allowed him to depart
"from the stereotyped ideas of tenement construction, from stock
plans." In his footsteps came other Jewish builders and a demand
also developed "for Jewish mechanics and artisans in every
branch of the building industry." Indeed, "the entrance of Jewish workers in the building trades ran parallel with the entrance
of Jewish builders in that field." Yet despite the success of such
builders as Fischel on the Lower East Side or the Goell brothers
(Jacob and Charles) in Brownsville, relatively few Jews possessed
sufficient capital to pursue opportunities in the construction industry. Large numbers of immigrant Jewish workers also found it
difficult to enter the building field. Skilled Jewish immigrants discovered after the depression of the 1890s that they could not join
the building trades unions. Entrenched union workers, many of
Irish descent, "opposed the admittance of Jews." Excessive initia-
tion fees, as high as $100, closed the unions' doors to most Jewish
workers. Their exclusion from the building trades' Brotherhoods
effectively restricted their work to "alteration" jobs, remodeling
old tenements. In response, Jews founded Alteration Building
Trades Unions in the various trades beginning in 1904. But the
established craft unions refused to recognize them. "The organized crafts succeeded in pushing the Jews out of new buildings."
Thus, the experience of immigrant Jews in the construction industry before World War I barely hinted at the scope of Jewish
post-war activities.[28]

The restrictive environment in construction collapsed after
the war. The acute housing shortage produced by a virtual stand-

still in construction during the war sparked public outrage in 1919. "Construction of new homes ceased during the war, the absence of rent control encouraged a speculative fever of buying and selling apartment houses," Epstein recalled. "By raising the rent, the new owner automatically raised the value of the house for resale." But the attempts at "rent gouging . . . provoked a wave of spontaneous strikes in the Jewish section of the city," Epstein continued. "Some blocks were actually littered with the furniture of evicted families." The tenants' grievances reached Albany and the state legislature authorized the Lockwood Committee to investigate housing conditions in the city. With Samuel Untermyer serving as counsel, the Lockwood investigations recommended emergency rent legislation to stabilize rents and regulate increases. To spur construction the Committee proposed ten-year tax abatements on new housing as an incentive. New York City hastily accepted both recommendations; City Hall was especially eager to encourage new residential construction in 1921. The Lockwood Committee also looked into the kickback racket in the Building Trades Council and undermined the corrupt authority of its head, Robert Brindell. The exposure of Brindell strengthened the hands of Jewish leaders in the Brotherhood of Painters. They had won union acceptance of Jews in 1914 when Jewish workers gained a wage increase putting them on a par with Brotherhood workers. With Brindell under fire, the painters garnered support for their demands for a five-day week.[29]

By 1921 promising conditions tempted both Jewish builders and workers to take advantage of opportunities in new residential construction. In those years a modern five-story apartment house cost $40,000 to $50,000 and took only eight months to build. A building begun in February could be finished by October in time to rent. Bank loans, secured at each stage of construction, made it relatively easy to enter the building field. The extensive use of amortizing mortgages, advocated by Fischel and adopted widely by banks and loan associations during the war, eased the money market for new construction. Builders purchased Brooklyn and Bronx real estate at reasonable prices in the early 1920s. The standard apartment house, 100′ by 100′, required four lots, and 25′ by 100′ lots on the Grand Concourse, for example, sold for $3,700. (By 1930 feverish land speculation had driven prices up to $10,000 and even $20,000 a lot.) At $2,000 per apartment, a building with four apartments to a floor, each with three or four rooms and a bathroom, rented at prices middle-class New Yorkers could afford to pay. The substantial $10,000 profit the builder collected enticed many Jews who had accumulated some capital during the war into this burgeoning field.[30]

The tax abatements, strong demands for new housing, amortizing mortgages, available real estate, reasonable construction costs and timetables ignited a tremendous building boom in New York City. In 1919 Stanley Isaacs, a future borough president of Manhattan, entered the real estate business to make his fortune. "It was a period of the grossest exploitation," he recalled, "a period of wild excitement in real estate." Over the course of the decade builders constructed 156,772 new apartments in the Bronx and 144,905 in Brooklyn. These figures represented respectively a 228 and 208 percent increase in apartment construction compared to the previous decade. Such rapid residential expansion provided previously unheard-of opportunities for Jews to enter the building trades as entrepreneurs. Wexelstein exuberantly dubbed it "the awakening."[31]

The "notorious housing shortage" stimulated the "irrepressible ambition" of Brooklyn Jews who, in Wexelstein's words, "ran lustily when they heard the bell of opportunity tolling its promise." These "new builders were springing up all over," taking advantage of the post-war situation to remake the face of the borough. "Aflame with schemes, plans and ambitions for bigger things," Wexelstein boosted Brooklyn's new breed of builder. "Here they are, grown rich, prosperous, financially independent," he wrote exultantly; "here they are, strutting in front of their skyscrapers, and breathing freely with their chests out." Michael Gold viewed the embourgeoisement of the Jewish builders through less celebratory spectacles. Writing of his painter father, who was bitten by the building bug, Gold described the Sunday when "we traveled to Borough Park to see the house and lot Zechariah was persuading my father to buy. It was a dreary day of fall," he wrote.

> The suburb was a place of half-finished skeleton houses and piles of lumber and brick. Paved streets ran in rows between empty fields where only the weeds rattled. Real estate signs were stuck

everywhere. In the midst of some rusty cans and muck would be a
sign shouting "This Wonderful Apartment House Site for Sale!" In
a muddy pool where ducks paddled, another sign read: "Why Pay
Rent? Build Your House in God's Country."[32]

Others objected to the widespread entrance of Jews into the
real estate and construction business. H. S. Black, chairman of
the board of the United States Realty and Improvement Company, referring to Jews, publicly protested in 1929 that "the
foreign element" was a "disturbing feature in real estate today."
By comparison, "when I came to New York thirty-five years ago,
this was conspicuous by its absence and under no circumstances
would a foreigner own or operate property; he always rented," he
remarked. "During the past few years, however, conditions have
changed and there are probably more foreigners in the real estate
field now than native-born." Black's resentment led him to exag-
gerate the extent of Jewish activity. Of approximately 10,000 New
York builders in the 1930s, Jews accounted for 4,000 (40 percent). The number of Jewish construction workers came to 48,000
(or 15 percent of the total workforce in the industry). Yet, as
Broun and Britt observed, Jews made up "eighty percent of the
speculative and operating group" in real estate. Jews trained as
architects also became prominent; twelve of fifteen well-known de-
signers of apartment houses in the Grand Concourse during the
interwar decades were Jewish. They maintained a similar, highly
visible profile in construction. Indeed, Jewish builder success
stories cluttered the desks of metropolitan newspaper editors.
"All manner of Jewish 'success' blurbs comes to the newspapers,"
Stanley Walker complained in the *American Mercury* in 1927.
"There is a Jewish real estate dealer who, every time he buys a
new building, announces that he once sold newspapers on that
very corner. If his press agent is to be believed," Walker continued, "he has sold papers on every street corner from Grand
Street to Columbus Circle."[33]

The transformation from newsboy to builder appeared marvelous in the eyes of many who gravitated to construction in the
1920s. As with any new area, most Jews entered the building industry with little or no previous experience. Reviewing the history
of Brooklyn builders, Wexelstein recorded a wide variety of prior
occupations: peddler, druggist, carpenter, tailor, contractor,

and, of course, newsboy. The new opportunities tempted those
who disliked their current work. Bored with knit goods, Julius
Borenstein left to build apartments in the Bronx. Jacob Berg
abandoned embroidery for construction in Brooklyn. Others
joined their fathers in the field, as did David Tishman and Abraham Halperin. The early pioneers brought their friends into the
business. With no specific career plans when he graduated from
college, Myron Eisenstein joined a friend in the building industry
who needed help. Jacob Berg introduced his friends into the business; Julius Borenstein got his start from a friend. As the construction industry expanded, those who worked in allied fields as
carpenters, plumbers, or electricians often switched into building
houses themselves. Samuel Minskoff parleyed a successful plumb-
ing business into a substantial building career in the Bronx. So,
too, Abraham Weissman switched from paperhanging to building.[34]

    Because much of the builder's job involved the coordination
and supervision of the work of various subcontractors, very few
of the Jewish builders—even those who joined their fathers in
construction—received any prior training as builders, architects,
or engineers. Of the 70 Brooklyn Jewish builders Wexelstein described, only five had studied architecture or engineering. Most
entered a short apprenticeship on the job where they learned how
to oversee the entire construction process. After building one
house, they set out on their own. But their lack of prior training
did not bother most Jewish builders. Eisenstein admitted that he
knew nothing about construction when he started working for his
friend. Nevertheless, he would walk out boldly on the scaffolding
and try to tell the bricklayers what to do. Builders usually left the
design of the house to the architects. The architects prepared the
blueprints and filed the plans with the city. Yet, despite their
meager training, Jewish builders generally felt that after they had
built one house, acquiring the entrepreneurial skills, they knew
the industry.[35]

    The industry they knew soon acquired an ethnic Jewish fla-
vor. The informal ethnic contacts which drew Jews into the construction business prevailed within the industry itself. In the
1920s most Jewish builders specialized in residential construction,
especially apartment house building. This field offered the largest

opportunities for individuals with limited capital. In Brooklyn and the Bronx, Jews rapidly became predominant in apartment house construction. Indeed, by the middle of the decade large segments of the building trades constituted areas of self-contained Jewish economic activity. Working out of a home office, usually the dining table, many Jewish builders relied on a favorite Jewish architect to design their buildings. A handshake between a Jewish builder and his Jewish contractors often sealed their agreement. The contractors in turn usually employed Jewish workers, especially in the "Jewish" trades.[36]

Contemporary folklore distributed the building trades according to an ethnic calculus. Italians specialized in concrete pouring, Swedes held the reputation for fine carpentry, the Irish ruled in steam fitting. Jews predominated as painters, rough carpenters, and sheet metal workers. Such folklore flourished on a foundation of fact. In 1936 estimates suggested that there were 18,000 Jewish carpenters and 8,000 Jewish painters in the city. In fact, the construction industry was second only to the needle trades as an employer to Jews. The fields allied to construction also attracted Jews; they worked as plumbers, glaziers, and electricians. Although the building trades employed only 5 percent of all Jews who worked (compared with 10 percent of all gainful workers in New York City), roughly a quarter of the union members were Jewish. In fact, the approximately 18,000 Jewish building trade union members in 1929 ranked second after the estimated 71,000 Jews in the needle trades unions. While they were not admitted to the Gentile skilled craft Brotherhoods until 1914, by the 1920s Jews predominated in at least half a dozen locals in Brooklyn, the Bronx, and Manhattan.[37]

Contractors came to the old immigrant sections of the city to hire their Jewish workers. On Sunday mornings painters congregated at the "East Side Painters Exchange" in front of the Romanian Synagogue at Rivington and Allen Streets. With their "turkey" in hand (their painter's overalls) they waited for the contractor, derisively called a "cockroach" boss, to pick his men. In Brownsville, the corner of Stone and Pitkin Avenues (in front of the Jewish-owned Municipal Bank) served as the meeting place where "carpenters, painters, electricians and masons assemble to talk shop and find employment. Boss painters and contractors

walk from group to group, picking their men," observed writer
Irving Ripps. "I liked listening to the painters talk about their
famous union boss, Jake the Bum, and to the unending disputes
between left wing and right wing, which had been in friction with
each other for so long, so automatically bristled and flared as
soon as a word was said, that the embattled daily life of the union
came alive for me," critic Alfred Kazin recalled. "The men would
stand around for hours—smoking, gossiping, boasting of their
children, until it was time to go home for the great Sabbath mid-
day meal."[38]

As Jewish workers gathered together on the street corners
and in union local meetings, so Jewish builders gravitated toward
a few blocks in each borough. At the Real Estate Center on 149th
Street in the Bronx an ethnic style shaped the contours of business associations. Its Brooklyn counterpart, a stretch of Court
Street, drew Jewish bankers, lawyers, real-estate brokers, insurance men, and builders. Jewish ethnic associations often brought
builder and banker together to finance new construction. A handful of small commercial banks whose principal directors were
Jews loaned money to many Jewish apartment house builders.
These bankers often lived in the neighborhood where they worked
and participated actively in the business ventures of their clients.
The reciprocal relationship between builder and banker occasionally led successful Jewish builders into banking. The Municipal Bank in Brooklyn included several builders on its board
of directors. Both Max Alpert, a well-to-do "trimmings" man and
builder in Brooklyn, and Morris Dlugasch, who built 500 two-
family houses in Flatbush during the early 1920s, joined the Municipal Bank board.[39]

A formal associational network complemented the informal
ethnic contacts among Jews in the construction industry. Within
each borough Jewish builders created organizations which paral-
lelled the union locals. Since Jews predominated in the field of
apartment house construction in Brooklyn and the Bronx, they
endowed the two organizations of apartment house builders in
those boroughs with ethnic attributes. As in Local 1011 of the
Brotherhood of Painters in Brownsville or the East Bronx, Jews
made up the majority of members of the Bronx Building Industry
League and the Associated Builders of Kings County. Founded in

1914 to combat "irresponsible" combinations of houses that supplied construction material and of local labor unions, the Associated Builders of Kings County in ten years grew rapidly from a handful of men to a group of 200 substantial builders. At the headquarters of the Bronx Building Industry League and the Associated Builders, sociality mixed with business. Though its members no longer spoke the Jewish workers' Yiddish at the League's weekly evening meetings, a Jewish ambience pervaded the associations. Cards and stories supplied the ethnic context in which information was passed and deals were made. Brokers, contractors, and lawyers looking for business with builders frequented the organizations, which provided their members with a network of contacts in a congenial atmosphere.[40]

Yet the close ties among Jewish builders remained local ones; localism fostered ethnic associations. Rarely did Jewish builders cross borough lines in the 1920s. From the perspective of Bronx builders Brooklyn could have been as remote as San Francisco. It was not until the Depression that Brooklyn Jewish builders ventured into Queens while Bronx builders crossed the Harlem river into upper Manhattan to construct apartments in Washington Heights. Then the organizational localism began to diminish. Reflecting these new trends, the Associated Builders changed its name to include Queens County. But the strength of the organizations lay in their localism, in their ability to provide the ethnic business and social contacts for Jewish entrepreneurs in the local construction industry.[41]

The common ethnicity uniting Jewish builders formally and informally with Jews in other aspects of the construction industry ultimately extended to the tenants of the buildings. Most Jewish builders in Brooklyn and the Bronx owned and managed the houses they built. Not surprisingly, they sought out tenants among Jews. At the least, they refused to restrict their buildings. As Broun and Britt observed, "the breaking of restrictions in rented apartments . . . came through the refusal of Jewish operators and builders to recognize such community agreements. Buying property which had been considered sacrosanct to Gentiles, they proceeded to fill vacancies with applicants who appeared personally acceptable, regardless of whether they were Jews or Gentiles." Word of mouth functioned as advertising among Jews.

On Sunday, renting day, "builder on premises" characterized Jewish builders' renting style. Like other Bronx builders, Eisenstein stood in front of his newly finished apartment house each fall trying to induce prospective tenants to put down a $10 deposit. Sunday was also the day for snooping around to see what competitors were doing. Once Eisenstein showed off all the details of his fifth-floor model apartment to a very interested man—a sure buy he thought. Later he found out that his prospective tenant was the builder of an apartment house down the block.[42]

The pattern of residential construction of Jewish builders correlated with the trend of Jewish migration. "The Brooklyn movement has all been into the one-family, two-family, and apartment house sections," Jewish statisticians observed in 1928. Furthermore Brooklyn, they felt, "indicated sharply the method of Jewish population trends. Original settlements are made into regions with one-family houses. . . . The next wave moves into two-family houses. The final wave is an apartment house population because the rise in land values forbids the erection of smaller dwellings." Wealthy Jews pioneered in purchasing homes in new neighborhoods, but most Jews moved up the residential ladder step by step. Typically, Jews left Brownsville for East Flatbush and from there went to Flatbush or Eastern Parkway. Gradually the pull of friends and relatives who had moved to a new neighborhood registered its impact on those left behind. In an echo of the days of mass immigration, Jew followed Jew to seek new homes in Brooklyn and the Bronx. Riding the IRT from Manhattan to his home in Brownsville, Kazin understood the ethnic contiguity of subway stops. "Franklin Avenue was where the Jews began—but all middle-class Jews, alrightniks, making out 'all right' in the New World," he wrote. From the "wide and tree-lined Eastern Parkway" the train traveled through successive Jewish neighborhoods "past the rickety 'two-family' private houses built in the fever of Brownsville's last real-estate boom; and then into Brownsville itself." A similar situation prevailed in the Bronx, where "perhaps every West Bronxite was formerly a resident of the other side of this borough." Occasionally Jewish builders tried to hasten this process of collective ethnic mobility. In 1921 Realty Associates advertised the attraction of living near friends and featured a "club" offer on houses in Crown Heights:

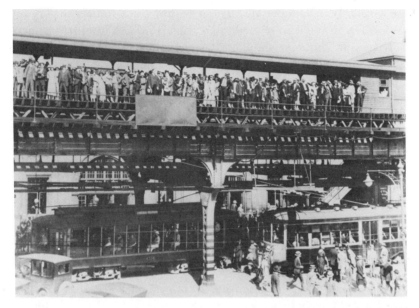

Waiting for the train on the Fifth Avenue El line in Brooklyn around 1920. Beneath the tracks are the Flatbush and Seventh Avenue streetcars. *Courtesy of the Museum of the City of New York.*

buy two houses and save $250 each, buy three houses and save $500 each. "An opportunity both to select your neighbor and make money" the ad insisted. But given the local orientation of Jewish builders, they rarely searched for tenants outside of the borough. If they advertised at all, Jewish builders usually relied on local papers known to be read by many second generation Jews, such as the *Bronx Home News.* Generally the ethnic associational network tenanted their buildings. Most Jewish-built housing adjoined older Jewish sections and these areas gradually became new Jewish neighborhoods. As the number of vacancies in the housing market increased, people moved more easily. Thus the sorting process which drew Jews to certain areas accelerated throughout the 1920s.[43]

Jewish builders transformed extensive parts of the Bronx and Brooklyn with their rapid construction of apartment houses. "Vast areas of meadowland and rock were turned by them, as by a magic wand, into densely populated avenues and streets of brick and mortar," Cahan wrote. "Under the spell of their activity cit-

ies larger than Odessa sprang up within the confines of Greater
New York in the course of three or four years.'' Joseph Schwartz,
a Brooklyn builder, thought the changes "marvelous.'' "There
was a time when one could look out from where I live (Crown
Street) in the direction of Flatbush and Brownsville and see substantial plots of vacant land intervening between the two points,''
he remarked in 1924. "Now the sections merge into one another
almost imperceptibly. . . . And dense rows of well-built and modern homes stretch to Flatbush and obscure the open view which
only a brief few years ago we had.'' Rabbi Basel concurred with
Schwartz's assessment and described the Jews' impact on the
Grand Concourse in similar terms. "A section, which only a few
years ago consisted of barren hills, has been turned by their
efforts into one of the most modern and prosperous sections of
New York City,'' he wrote in 1925.[44]

Indeed, Jewish builders molded the character of the future
Jewish neighborhoods. Choosing architects who worked in the Art
Deco style, Jewish builders helped to make that style the hallmark
of ostentatious middle-class apartment living in New York City.

Moses Ginsberg's four-story modern apartment building, 421 Crown Street, near
the northeast corner of Brooklyn Avenue, designed by Emery Roth (1929).
Courtesy of the Museum of the City of New York.

Façades with lively geometric patterns, recessed entranceways, metal ornaments, and curved corner windows predominated along the Grand Concourse. But most decoration appeared on the interior. "Whether it be mosaic ceilings, tiled floors, incised elevator doors or metal reflecting radiator covers, the mixture of wood, metal, glass, brick, and concrete" created an "elegant environment" of clean lines and exuberant display. In the lobbies indirect lighting, ornamentation of chrome and glass, and occasionally a mural celebrated the new art moderne of the period, "a sleek style that spoke of modern technology and progress." "In the poor man's dream he visualizes himself in a Grand Concourse apartment, with a sunken living room and a pink tile bathroom, with a canopy outside the building, a lobby with mirrors and golden cupids on the ceilings and a noiseless lift which you can operate by merely pressing a button." On the Concourse the ideal of middle-class luxury correlated with apartment house living. The design of many Art Deco buildings reflected fantasy. The architect often created through dramatic effects "a sense of the Broadway stage." In the hallways "there are black-and-white tiled floors, laid out to resemble marble; there are gilded, pilastered walls, heavy mirrors, tables and chairs . . . and rococo flambeaux on the walls, unfortunately requiring the prosaic aid of electricity," wrote Ruth Glazer with a touch of sarcasm. Through the Art Deco style, which reflected the mass culture of the period and its love for the theatrical, Jewish builders brought the American dream of housing as a status symbol within the reach of those who could afford only to rent.[45]

These apartments attracted second generation Jews who often chose to invest their money in business rather than in houses. By 1937 estimates suggested that Jews owned close to two-thirds of the 34,000 factories in New York City and a similar percentage of the 104,000 wholesale and retail establishments, and the 11,000 restaurants and lunchrooms. Having put their money into businesses, many Jews either could not afford or did not care to invest in a private house. And when they did purchase real estate, they tended to regard it "as a commodity to be traded rather than as an economic good to be consumed." Marshall Sklare considers this attitude a true reflection of the Jews' "urban perspective."[46]

The apartment houses so popular among Jewish builders allowed them to synthesize Jewish ethnic and American values. Recognizing the importance placed on housing as a measure of achievement in American society, Jewish builders introduced the most modern conveniences into their apartment buildings. As soon as automatic elevators became economically feasible in the early 1920s, the builders installed them. In 1927 Eisenstein featured the "newest type, self-operating Otis elevators" in his Bronx apartment house. "Absolutely foolproof" a brochure assured prospective tenants. Similarly, Jewish builders eagerly replaced ice boxes with refrigerators later in the decade. In Flatbush the apartments offered "spacious rooms, stained glass windows, parquet floors and beamed ceilings." Grand Concourse apartments included step-down living rooms, large entrance foyers, tiled sun decks on the roof or recreation rooms in the basement. By placing these symbols of the middle class in apartments, Jewish builders compensated for the lower status American society accorded to apartment houses. Concurrently, Jewish builders helped second generation Jews to purchase an ethnic version of the American dream.[47]

Though the apartment house ranked below a private home in the scale of American housing values, it encouraged greater ethnic density in a neighborhood. Jewish understanding of American society demanded that Jews not live in "ghettos," i.e. that they live down the block from some non-Jewish Americans. The apartment house offered them this opportunity as well as the chance to move up collectively.[48]

A glimpse at the physical structure of the new Brooklyn and Bronx neighborhoods also reveals the synthesis of Jewish ethnic and American values developed by Jewish builders. Through their choice and placement of houses, Jewish builders created a neighborhood of residences. They restricted retail stores and commercial space to special shopping streets. Although many stores contained living quarters above them, the majority of apartment houses functioned exclusively as residences. The neighborhood which emerged, defined by the confluence of stores, homes, and transit facilities, extended the feeling of the park it often bordered. Americans, especially the Progressives whom Jews had encountered in the settlement houses, emphasized the importance of light and space for a proper home environment and railed against the indiscriminate mixing of residential, commercial, and manufacturing activities characteristic of immigrant neighborhoods. They also attacked the congestion of immigrant quarters, which they felt destroyed a sense of community, advocating instead greenery to provide a rootedness in land. Jewish builders acknowledged these values and placed their large apartment buildings along tree-lined boulevards or on side-street corners. But such locations satisfied Jewish ethnic values as well, allowing Jews to share the streets with Gentiles even while living among Jews. Jewish builders searched for lots in an "unspoiled" neighborhood. There they might be the first to erect an apartment house which would be unique among the private homes. In 1920 the Grand Concourse epitomized such an unspoiled neighborhood; it was an area dominated by Gentile-owned single-family brick houses, many only ten years old. A decade later the Grand Concourse was an integrated American Jewish neighborhood where Jews lived mostly in the apartment houses and their non-Jewish neighbors resided in the private homes on the side streets.[49]

Not all Jewish builders pursued an ethnic version of the middle-class American ideal. In the 1920s, a handful of dedicated socialists, such men as Baruch Brodski and Abraham Kazan, sought to wed the virtues of middle-class housing to the requirements of the cooperative commonwealth. Under their initiative housing cooperatives for Jewish workers arose in the Bronx. The Amalgamated Clothing Workers of America underwrote extensive construction of apartments to be sold to Jewish workers, ultimately sponsoring the largest cooperative housing project near Van Cortlandt Park. The apartments of three to five rooms cost an average of $300 to $500 per room to buy, with monthly maintenance fees of $12 to $15 per room—within the budget of many workers. But, as Joseph Schlossberg, general secretary of the Amalgamated, indicated "the cause for congratulations is not in the lower rental co-operators will be required to pay." Rather these apartments brought the "blessings of beautiful homes, with sufficient sunlight and fresh air, and in delightful surroundings . . . to the families of wage workers." Indeed, the emphasis on a suburban environment and on the values of greenery, light, and

The interior courtyard gardens of the Amalgamated Clothing Workers coopera-
tive apartments, designed by Springsteen and Goldhammer, at Sedgewick
Avenue and Gun Hill Road, in 1929 shortly after they were completed.
Courtesy of the Museum of the City of New York.

air, circumscribed Jewish workers' search for ideal housing.
"One of the appeals of the land they found for the Coops was that
it was in a relatively undeveloped area right across the street from
Bronx Park," Calvin Trillin recorded in regard to the Workers
Cooperative Colony. "The workers' committee that met with the
architect emphasized sunlight and cross-ventilation and the sort
of inner courtyards that could be turned into gardens." In fact,
the workers stipulated "that every room would have at least one
window." But the *New York City Guide* faulted the development,
which occupied two city blocks and comprised four red brick and
stone apartment buildings, for failing "to make a strong architectural impression because of an ill-advised attempt to put 'cute
cottage' feelings into so large a housing group."[50]

However, the cooperatives offered Jewish workers the American amenities in an ideological setting. As Trillin observed, "in
the late twenties, a Jewish garment worker who wanted to move

his family from the squalor of the Lower East Side to the relatively sylvan north Bronx could select an apartment on the basis of ideology." The cooperative concept appealed to many segments of the Jewish working class which united to build housing. In addition to the Amalgamated and the Workers Cooperative Colony, the Sholem Aleichem movement, the Labor Zionist Farband, the Typographical Union, and the Jewish Butchers Union all sponsored cooperative housing projects. "Someone who happened to be an active supporter of the Social Democratic wing of the Jewish labor movement—the wing whose views were reflected by Abraham Cahan in the *Jewish Daily Forward*, the wing that had, after a ferocious struggle with the radicals, retained control of the largest clothing unions—would probably try to obtain an apartment in the Bronx cooperative project sponsored by the Amalgamated Clothing Workers," Trillin wrote.

> An adherent of the Labor Zionist movement could go to the Farband Houses. A follower of Hayim Zhitlovsky, the leader of a movement absorbed with the preservation of secular Jewish culture, could live in a cooperative called the Sholem Aleichem Houses. A radical—someone who continued to defend the Soviet revolution after other Socialists had turned against it, someone who subscribed to the *Morgen Freiheit*, a Yiddish daily that was then faithfully pro-Soviet, and read the *Forward* only to see what the enemy was up to—could move to the Workers Cooperative Colony.[51]

The cooperatives represented an ideological variation within the ethnic Jewish building industry, an example of Jewish builders uniting with Jewish workers to construct housing tailored to their socialist specifications. Sponsored by Jewish organizations, erected by Jewish builders, the apartments were bought by Jewish workers. But the cooperatives' influence extended beyond their immediate boundaries. In several cases the cooperatives created Jewish neighborhoods virtually overnight. Through the cooperatives, Jewish workers developed an alternative ethnic community to the immigrant quarter. The product of conscious design, the cooperatives also provided a variation on the major American Jewish theme of middle-class ethnic community. But most second generation Jews chose a middle-class secular ethnicity, unencumbered with a radical ideology.

Light and airy kitchen in the Amalgamated cooperative houses,
with gas stove and icebox, 1929. *Courtesy of the Museum
of the City of New York.*

Hastening to impose an image on the city's vacant lots, Jewish builders erected a monument to themselves in the shape of the
neighborhoods they developed. "Where else in the city did the
apartment dweller have an attractive environment that was built
to human scale?" queried two architecture critics. Jewish builders
translated a "belief in optimum housing for the working citizen"
into "streets graced by Art Deco buildings with fine gardens,
shopping streets and a most incredible array of building styles."
The names carved into apartment house lintels reflected the aspirations of many Jewish builders. On the streets of the Bronx and

Modern livingroom in the Amalgamated cooperative houses,
with overstuffed furniture and rococo electric flambeaux on the wall, 1929.
Courtesy of the Museum of the City of New York.

Brooklyn, Jewish builders engraved their pride and their success.
"Dora Court," the "Louise Apartments," or perhaps an acro-
nym, the "Lenru," named in honor of a wife or daughter, testified
to the sense of achievement Jewish builders felt.[52]

The Chanin brothers, Henry and Irwin, symbolized the aspirations of most Jewish builders. Starting their careers in 1919
with a $7,000 frame house in Bensonhurst, they completed a $15
million exemplar of Art Deco architecture only a decade later.
The 56-story Chanin building on 42nd Street and Lexington Avenue in midtown Manhattan proclaimed on its heavily ornamented
façade and in its lobby: "New York: City of Opportunity." The
Jews who flocked to rent the apartments in Brookyn and the
Bronx concurred. To live in Flatbush or on the Grand Concourse, to walk its streets lined with stately maples, spelled success.[53]

The collective mobility of second generation Jews fueled the
migrations creating new neighborhoods in Brooklyn and the

Bronx. Helping to maintain Jewish ethnic identity, a large but
compact neighborhood emerged where enough Jews lived to support special school facilities, synagogues, recreation centers, social clubs, and gathering places. Sanitary living quarters, greenery to provide esthetic pleasure and a rootedness in land, and
modern apartments large enough to contain one nuclear family
composed the components of an improved urban environment.
The high value of land so close to Manhattan restricted the
acreage allowed to private homes. Until widespread use of the automobile as a substitute for walking and rapid transit, neighborhood boundaries remained compact, defined by the confluence
of residences, stores, and transit facilities. In the 1920s and 1930s
apartment dwellers shared the sidewalks with residents of private
houses. In the sheltered new neighborhood the heady optimism of
success would nourish the distinctive characteristics of New York
Jewish life, producing unconsciously a model of urban community.

3

The social legitimization of class position motivated a mass flight from the ghetto only to result in a reconcentration of Jews in the higher income areas of the city. This formed the physical basis for a new kind of ghetto, a closed community of middle class Jews whose social life was carried on exclusively with Jews of appropriate status. These were "gilded" ghettoes in which the institutions paralleled those of the American middle class, but whose participants were all Jews. Of course, not all Jews were equally successful economically and class and status differences began to develop among them. . . . Paradoxically achievement of majority values generated and actually reinforced the social foundations of the second generation Jewish community.

Seymour Leventman, "From Shtetl to Suburb,"
The Ghetto and Beyond, ed. Peter I. Rose
(New York: Random House, 1969), pp. 43–44.

A World
of Its Own

The chemistry of migration synthesized a new Jewish community in New York City. The new address of Jews indicated the nature of the developing ethnic community, one bounded by the neighborhood. Jews used the neighborhood, with its interrelation of social and spatial organization, as the warp on which they wove the fabric of community. Such a community grew, in writer Vivian Gornick's words, from "a concretely shared experience powered by commonly held ideals and rooted in the rhythms of daily life."[1] The Jewish neighborhood provided the physical framework in which Jews constructed a moral and associational community.

The neighborhood served Jews as individuals and as members of a group. It offered individual Jews an environment which mediated the stresses of acculturation. Just by going about his mundane activities in the neighborhood, a New York City Jew could feel equally American and Jewish—and unthreatened. "In an odd way and for a brief period, Brownsville fulfilled the age-old Jewish need for a sanctuary, an escape from the consciousness (if not the fact) of being a minority in exile," William Poster recalled. "To a child, at any rate, Brownsville was a kind of grimy Eretz Yisrael without Arabs—living in a world all Jewish, where no alien group imposed its standards, he was secure in his own nature." Neighborhood living provided the context for ethnic Jewish identification. This context was natural, informal, almost invisible, its American and Jewish components inextricably woven into a matrix of local activity. Such neighborhood life encouraged many Jews to develop a sense of Jewish identity independent of any formal Jewish organizational association. "On *Pesach* and

Yom Kippur we did not have to be 'observing' Jews to know that
we were Jews," Gornick remembered. "The whole world shut
down, everyone dressed immaculately, and a sense of awe thick-
ened the very air we breathed." The local friendships and contacts Jews made within their neighborhood transformed its physical environment into a moral community. Jews identified with
their Jewish neighbors and gained a sense of wholeness from the
texture of local life. Within the sheltering neighborhood, Jews
pursued everyday activities which, through the primary ties of
family and friends, became ethnically cohesive.[2]

But the new Jewish neighborhoods served as more than the
catalyst for a sense of community built on primary associations;
they also housed many Jewish institutions. New York City Jews
pursued their cultural and political interests within the neighborhood, creating more formal associations and organizations to
further these specific group ends. Institutions in turn channeled
the developing reconstruction of Jewishness in the neighborhood.
Alternative styles of Jewish ethnic group life emerged in the network of Jewish settlements scattered throughout the Bronx and
Brooklyn. Each neighborhood gradually acquired a collective
persona and each tended to be exclusive, a world of its own. In
the 1920s Jews wedded the "close proximity, co-operation, intimate social contact, and strong feeling of social consciousness"
characteristic of an urban neighborhood to a host of ethnic activities.[3] This somewhat unorthodox marriage produced an unlikely
brood of children: provincial loyalties, parochial associations,
and ideological diversity. At their new addresses New York Jews
found both individual freedom and ethnic continuity.

"The Fourth American City" the *Forward* called Jewish New
York in 1927. Yet in looking for these New York Jews the *Forward* discovered that "each Jewish community is in most of its
requirements a self-contained and practically self-sustaining
unit." The rapid migration of Jews and their new residential
segregation dissolved New York Jews into a congery of provincial
Jews: Flatbush Jews, Brighton Jews, Williamsburg Jews, Grand
Concourse Jews, Crotona Jews, East Bronx Jews. Individual Jews
often knew who they were because of where they lived. "We were
Brownsville—*Brunzvil*, as the old folks said—the dust of the
earth to all Jews with money," Kazin remembered. While up in

Bella Lasker and Samuel Golden
at home in their first Brownsville apartment
of the top floor of 134 Chester Street,
between Pitkin and Sutter Avenues.
Bella's brother Morris and Sam's brother
Israel also lived there, sharing
one of the bedrooms of the five-room
apartment (circa 1920).

the East Bronx, recalled Gornick, "the organic quality of the atmosphere told us who we were, gave us boundary and idiomatic
reference, shaped the face of the culture in which each of us assumed a vital, albeit primitive, sense of identity." And in a memoir of the same East Bronx neighborhood, Irving Howe wrote:
"The Jewish community enclosed one, not through choice as
much as through experience and instinct, and often not very
gently or with the most refined manners."[4]
    Despite the social mobility which created these areas of sec-
ond and third settlement, the neighborhoods were at once parochial, individualized, and tolerant. Ideological battles became
Jewish family quarrels. "The dominating characteristic of the
streets on which I grew was Jewishness in all its rich variety,"
Gornick recalled. "Down the street were Orthodox Jews, up the
street were Zionists, in the middle of the street were shtetl Jews,
get-rich-quick Jews, European humanist Jews." Neighborhoods
developed as specialized arenas for intraethnic debating, the sort
of constant conflict that defines the common Jewishness of all concerned. Howe recalled that "the Jewish neighborhood was prepared to listen to almost anyone, with its characteristic mixture of
skepticism, interest and amusement." Parochial associational patterns and a certain provincialism spawned ideological diversity.
Individual Jews also possessed the freedom to trade one neigh-

borhood for another, and thus to attain a new status and a new
Jewish identity. Jewish social mobility confirmed that "changes of
economic and social status . . . tend to be registered in changes
of location." Kazin characterized Brownsville as "notoriously a
place that measured all success by our skill in getting away from
it." In the Bronx it was "the ambition of almost every East
'Bronxer' to some time reach the point in life where he can afford
to become a resident of the West Bronx."[5]

While class differences separated Jewish neighborhoods into
self-contained worlds, other Jewish criteria differentiated one
neighborhood from another. For example, by the 1930s, to talk of
Williamsburg Jews usually meant speaking of Orthodox Jews. The
East Bronx, especially the Pelham Parkway area, held a reputation for radicalism while Borough Park often brought to mind
Zionist fervor. Often new neighborhoods first obtained their Jewish ideological slant from the builders who pioneered in their development. And since Jews gravitated to neighborhoods based on
information offered by friends and relatives, migration accelerated the process of ideological specialization. As Jews expressed
their cultural and political interests they erected visible signposts
of the area's emerging character on its streets. The types of Jewish organizations thriving in each section often reflected the particular persona of the neighborhood, serving as a guide to its
unique world.[6] Thus a survey of representative middle-class Jewish neighborhoods reveals the matrix of Jewish ethnicity, which
grew out of these urban communities.

Having arrived in new neighborhoods with different attitudes
from their immigrant parents, second generation Jews found that
neighborhood living encouraged them to alter their politics and to
restructure their organizations even as it reinforced in-group social patterns. As New York City Jews acculturated, they embedded their values in a modern form of urban community. This
emergent ethnicity merged American middle-class values with
Jewish collective experience. Yet perceived against the backdrop
of immigrant Jewish life, the synthesis appeared bland and homogenized. Some observers found it "difficult to discern which is
a distinctly Jewish Community" since there was "often an absence of the distinguishing characteristics of the popular conception of a Jewish neighborhood." Writing on "How the Jewish

Suburb Became a Jewish Community" in 1928, S. Mutterperl was at a loss to locate the roots of ethnic cohesion in the new Jewish neighborhoods. He saw "no strong social bond" because of the newness of these neighborhoods, and for similar reasons he discovered "no intellectual bond. It has, of course, a racial bond, but it fails to operate, is a pale and passive thing." Most seriously, "it has no religious bond. It is almost a contradiction in terms to say that a Jewish community has no religious bond, but there are dozens of Jewish sections of which this can be said."[7]

Mutterperl saw only the external sense of security, the visible middle-class attributes of the new neighborhoods. He could not even find what set the Jews apart from their Gentile neighbors. Others recognized that the mere clustering of Jews in new neighborhoods would "serve as one of our greatest bulwarks in our struggle against absorption in the maelstrom of Anglo-Saxon civilization, but that at the same time it will be one of the potent causes of anti-Semitic feeling." Zalowitz perceived not only the feature of self-segregation but the diversity of Jewish neighborhood life as well. "There are Ghettos for foreign born Jews and Ghettos for native born Jews," he wrote; "Ghettos for poor Jews and Ghettos for middle class and for rich Jews, for Russian Jews and for German Jews. The East Side is one kind of a Ghetto, Washington Heights another kind, West Bronx a third, Riverside Drive a fourth . . . and Brooklyn has a dozen different kinds and styles of Ghettos of its own."[8] Between Mutterperl and Zalowitz lay the old image of the Lower East Side and its claim to represent a normative tradition of Jewish life for American Jews.

Despite a declining population, the Lower East Side endured as a viable and visible immigrant community from 1920 to 1940. It united even those immigrants who moved away, drawing them back to its streets through the claims of *landsmanshaftn*. *Landslayt* who had lived near each other on the Lower East Side, in the Romanian, Galician, or Russian areas, usually left their old-country bonds behind when they moved to new neighborhoods. But they returned periodically to Clinton Hall or the *Forward* building on East Broadway to renew these ties at meetings of their *landsmanshaftn*. These fraternal and mutual benefit societies clung to the East Side's streets; they belonged in the immigrant milieu and most found it difficult to adjust to the demands of

Table 4 Jewish Neighborhoods in 1930 (figures in thousands)

Neighborhood	Family Median Income	Density per sq. mile	Population	% Jewish
IMMIGRANT NEIGHBORHOODS				
Lower East Side	$1,360	163,000	261,000	39
Williamsburg	$2,000	80,000	192,000	41
Brownsville	$2,490	92,000	208,000	82
East Bronx	$2,770	130,000	253,000	67
SECOND GENERATION NEIGHBOR-HOODS				
Upper West Side	$8,700	123,000	203,000	23
Flatbush	$4,320	44,000	172,000	33
Borough Park	$4,040	50,000	111,000	55
Washington Hghts.	$4,030	86,000	169,000	39
Eastern Parkway	$3,980	70,000	148,000	36
Brighton Beach	$3,780	15,000	60,000	77
Grand Concourse	$3,750	83,000	177,000	71
Pelham Parkway	$3,490	29,000	85,000	40

SOURCES: The estimated population and percent Jewish from Horowitz and Kaplan, pp. 98, 100, 102. The estimated median annual family income (based on rentals or cost of housing) and density (persons per square mile) from New York City Market Analysis (1933). A fixed ratio of one to five—rentals to income—was used as the basis for computation (i.e. annual rent multiplied by five). For owned homes, the Census reported value was assumed to be 100 times the monthly rental.

middle-class neighborhood life. The Lower East Side also survived as "the focal point of Jewish culture . . . the cradle of the Jewish press and Jewish literature . . . centering about Rutgers Square." Those who stayed on the East Side "were loath to leave the old scenes, the old synagogues, the old shops and the old schools, the old streets so slightly changed, the old theaters and . . . the famous restaurants."[9]

The Lower East Side provided an emotional point of reference for both first and second generation Jews. It spawned, above all, the myth of the immigrant neighborhood as an organic community. It summoned up memories of childhood for many Jews who had left its streets. "The East Side of my boyhood was a completely Jewish world. The language of our home was Yiddish. The newspapers that came into our home were Yiddish. The store signs were all in Yiddish," Yoffeh recalled. "The only holidays we observed were Jewish holidays. . . . As Friday night approached, the pushcarts left the street, the stores began to close. . . . Early

Saturday morning found the streets deserted; everybody was in *schul.*" [10] Such recollections belied the diversity of East Side life and contributed to a vision of a holistic immigrant Jewish culture which could only put to shame the current Jewish life on the streets of the Bronx and Brooklyn. The nostalgic eye viewed the road from the East Side to Flatbush or the Concourse as a downhill path along which Jewishness was discarded for American affluence.

Among those who escaped its poverty, the Lower East Side also generated nostalgia for the moral fiber that had inured Jews to their impoverished circumstances and had girded them to the task of leaving the immigrant neighborhood. This vision emphasized the constricting poverty and spiritual breadth of immigrant Jewish life. Its theme announced the triumph of Jewish spirit over matter, a victory measured in terms of dollars and sense. Like the memory of a holistic community, the American Jewish success story gained credibility from aspects of the reality of the Lower East Side. Throughout the 1920s and 1930s the old immigrant quarter remained one of the poorest, with rents among the lowest in the city (apartments could be rented for five to six dollars per room). The Lower East Side also continued to thrive as a neighborhood of small businesses, 75 percent of them owned by Jews. In 1930 the area still housed 12,000 shops, among them over 500 butcher shops and candy stores, and over 400 barber shops, restaurants, and cleaning and dyeing stores. Yet more than the East Side realities sustained the image of Jewish rags-to-riches. Of all the organizations which derived from the Lower East Side, the Grand Street Boys Association fostered most insistently the Lower East Side's moral meaning as the source of the American Jewish self-made man. Jonah Goldstein, judge, Democratic politician, and third president of the Association, defined a Grand Street Boy as "one who once lived on East Broadway or Madison Street, -went to school on Norfolk or Henry,-learned the facts of life on Allen Street, -was in business on 7th Avenue, -and lived on Central Park West." Founded in 1920 as a social group meeting at the Odd Fellows Hall on Forsythe Street, the Grand Street Boys Association quickly attracted a large and affluent membership, previous residence on the Lower East Side being its only membership requirement. In 1924 the Association erected its own

clubhouse on 55th Street containing entertainment and sports facilities. The Association saw the road from the Lower East Side as
an uphill path along which Jews acquired American amenities as
rewards for diligence and hard work.[11]

The vision of an organic, uniquely spiritual Lower East Side
gave New York Jews a yardstick with which to measure the extent
of their transformation. For Jews, the "gilded ghetto" of the
Upper West Side was the opposite of the Lower East Side. It appeared as the upper class apotheosis of Jewish acculturation. Its
world contrasted vividly with immigrant Jewish life on the East
Side. "The epic of the Jewish immigrant from Ellis Island to Riverside Drive" captured the full distance Jews traveled in becoming Americans. On the Upper West Side "they think of the Jews
of the Bronx and Brooklyn as not having 'arrived,' " admitted
one resident, "and the East Side is more distant in their past than
the Second Temple." Home of the "alrightnik," one "who has
not only become relatively wealthy, but also smug and compla-
cent," a Central Park West address symbolized for many Jews
the ultimate sign of success. "Eighty-Sixth Street is the Main
Street of the most compact and prosperous Jewish community in
the city of New York," wrote Aaron Frankel about his neighborhood. "It may well be the most Jewish Street in New York. In
any case, it is reputedly that street where Jews feel most comfortably at home." Frankel described the Upper West Side as
"packed with movie theaters, with dress and haberdashery shops
and 'beauty bars,' and an amazing number of lingerie shops. . . .
Grocery, butcher, and dairy stores abound," he continued, "as do
the bakery shops dispensing in little blue boxes lush pastries that
are almost the sacramental bread of the neighborhood." "In this
neighborhood one sees evidences of ostentatious consumption,"
Jewish writer H. K. Blatt acidly noted, "fashionable and expensive clothes, flashy and genuine jewelry, highly powered motor
cars often driven by chauffeurs." Less bitterly Frankel described
"the heavy brown buildings, in which apartments heaped fifteen
stories or more . . . rise on both sides of Eighty Sixth Street and
cut a narrow path in the sooty sky." Yet he concurred that "up
and down the wide street the curbs are always crowded with shiny
cars." The reality of the Upper West Side's affluence—its estimated median annual income of $8,700 in 1930 placed its resi-

dents in the upper class—confirmed the vision of the neighborhood as the "gilded ghetto" alternative to the genuine
immigrant "ghetto." And the Upper West Side suffered in comparison. "The ghetto of old had been the preserver of Judaism,"
fulminated Louis Marshall in 1927. "The gilded ghetto of today
has no spiritual values." Yet "spread through an area thirty
blocks long and four blocks wide are also some twenty synagogues," Frankel observed. "By actual count, one need never go
more than ten blocks, and most of the time only five or six, to find
the synagogue of one's inclination."[12]

The sharp contrast drawn between Jewish life on the Lower
East Side and Upper West Side obscured the reality of an emerging new Jewish world. Life in Brownsville evoked no mythic memories in the 1920s and 1930s. Its reality of working-class poverty
and white-collar marginality defied transcendence. An "egali-
tarianism of tone and manners" reigned in Brownsville. Lacking
the Lower East Side's centrality for Jewish immigrant life and its
cultural dynamism which embraced both right and left wings,

Brooklyn home of immigrant painter,
Ike Davidson (on left),
with his second generation nephew,
Barney Golden and Barney's father,
Mordecai Golden (circa 1915).

Brownsville could aspire only to be known as the "East Side of
Brooklyn." The home of immigrant parents and their native-born
children, Brownsville encompassed on a small scale the range of
Jewish working-class life. Its physical milieu reflected the variety
found among its residents. "Built up nearly overnight on run-
down farmland, Brownsville, in the 20's, had come to occupy an
area of about two square miles set apart," recalled Poster, "by
such natural boundaries as the IRT El on Livonia Avenue, the

BMT El on Junius Street, the junction of Pitkin Avenue's macadam with the greensward of Eastern Parkway at Howard Avenue, and the Liberty Avenue trolley." Brooklyn's most densely populated section, Brownsville's monthly rents ranged from a low of six dollars per room in old buildings to a high of seventeen dollars per room in some of the newest houses constructed after World War I, Brownsville's last building boom. Brownsville also supported its own light industries (mainly garment manufacturing), business streets, and pushcart markets. "The open air market on Belmont Avenue," writer Irving Ripps characterized in 1941 as "the cynosure for local housewives. . . . Here Yiddish is the shopkeepers' talk, and all the varieties of kosher foods, as well as delicacies particularly favored by Jews, are the leading articles of sale. In winter the hucksters bundle up in sweaters and stand around wood fires." Poster described a walk down the "seven blocks of furniture stores on Rockaway Avenue" as "a girl's domestic daydream of plushy sofas and gleaming mahogany bedroom suites." In 1942, Pitkin Avenue, the main thoroughfare, boasted 372 stores lining the fourteen blocks stretching from Stone to Ralph Avenues. "Pitkin Avenue is what Brownsville is most proud of," Kazin wrote, where

> the neon glare suddenly lights up all the self-conscious confusion of Brownsville's show street. Banks, Woolworth's, classy shops, loan companies, Loew's Pitkin, the Yiddish theater, the Little Oriental restaurant—except for Brownsville's ancestral stress in the food, the Yiddish theater, the left wing–right wing arguments around the tables in Hoffman's Cafeteria, the Zionist appeals along the route, it might be Main Street in any moderately large town.[13]

As a miniature East Side, Brownsville defied the trend to collective specialization among new Jewish neighborhoods. "The most prosperous merchant of Pitkin Avenue and the poorest potato peddler," Poster observed, "were likely to live in the same house or adjacent ones, and to buy most of their food, clothing, and furniture at the same stores—if only out of a lack of desire or time to do otherwise." Brownsville's organizational activities embraced the entire spectrum of Jewish political and cultural associations. Jews of various persuasions competed with each other for Brownsville's streets. Each organization staked a claim to su-

premacy by supporting a visible building as a physical symbol of
its collective presence in the world of the neighborhood. The
Labor Lyceum at Sackman Street and Liberty Avenue testified to
Brownsville's vigorous radical community. A "shrine of the neighborhood," the Labor Lyceum housed the meetings of union locals,
the lectures and debates of socialists, as well as numerous Yiddish
cultural and social activities. The Hebrew Free School on Stone
Avenue, the largest and most famous of Brownsville's communally
supported modern Talmud Torahs, stood for Jewish religious
conservatism. Brownsville's more orthodox elements erected a parochial elementary school, the Yeshiva Rabbi Chaim Berlin; and
by 1930 they added a high school. The proponents of Americanization, usually those who were making money in the new world,
supported the Hebrew Educational Society (H.E.S.) on Hopkinson and Sutter Avenues. Brooklyn's first Jewish community center, H.E.S. provided the neighborhood with a host of educational,
recreational, and social services. The Adath Israel of Brownsville
served as the central address for various and vociferous Zionist
groups. Only the multitude of fraternal organizations popular
among Brownsville's Jews lacked an outstanding physical presence. The elaborate clubhouses of the Jewish Huron and Non-
Pareil clubs on Brownsville's outskirts pointed to the aspirations
of the neighborhood's hundreds of social and athletic clubs.[14]

Neither Williamsburg nor the East Bronx sustained the vigorous multiplicity of Brownsville. By the 1930s certain Jewish
groups dominated each neighborhood, set the tone, and overshadowed the other existing organizations. Williamsburg, particularly, went through an extensive transformation. Once the neighborhood of Brooklyn's middle-class German Jews, Williamsburg
in the 1890s "was a very ritzy section and only the very rich
resided here. Walking down Hewes Street from Bedford Avenue
was like walking into a park, with trees and well-cared-for gardens on both sides of the street." In the early decades of the twentieth century immigrant Jews crowded into Williamsburg, producing another microcosm of the East Side. Yet affluent residents
clung to the area around Bedford Avenue with its comfortable
brownstones. "Here the wide street, the speeding automobiles,
and the scattering of fine houses produced an air of gentility,"
novelist Daniel Fuchs wrote. "The sidewalks were lined with

young trees presented to the community by the American Legion in loving memory of the war dead." Fuchs thought "they looked pathetic and city-worn, but occasionally, at some street corner, a great oak or maple lifted its muscular trunk to the sky. They were planted in pavement and looked unreal," he concluded.[15]

The 1920s building boom enticed away many of Williamsburg's well-to-do residents. As they left, the neighborhood contracted; eventually the heart of Jewish Williamsburg centered along Bedford, Lee, Marcy, and Division Streets, where the better housing existed. The neighborhood's physical contraction paralleled an economic, social, and cultural consolidation. Williamsburg became increasingly homogeneous. As middle-class Jews left the neighborhood, Williamsburg's occupational distribution narrowed. In 1923 a survey pointed to substantial numbers of middle-class Jews in the area. Thirteen years later Williamsburg housed a disproportionate number of Brooklyn families on home relief. Estimates of the Jewish occupational distribution indicated that close to one-third of Williamsburg Jews worked in the clothing factories near the area while another third engaged in retail trade on the local streets. One-tenth earned a livelihood as neighborhood professionals and another one-tenth held clerical positions. The extensive coincidence of work and residence in the same neighborhood fostered an ethnic intimacy in Williamsburg.[16]

By the 1930s Williamsburg was known as an Orthodox neighborhood. Despite the steady drain of almost half of Williamsburg's Jews to such affluent neighborhoods as Flatbush and Borough Park, pupil enrollment in the local Hebrew schools remained constant. Orthodox Jewish activities overshadowed those of socialist and Zionist Jews. As one Orthodox resident saw it, "Williamsburg became really Jewish after the war, when the richer Jews moved to Flatbush and Crown Heights, and the plain people moved here from the East Side and other neighborhoods of *Greene*." Williamsburg's local leadership increasingly centered around such Orthodox organizations as Young Israel, Agudath Israel, and the parochial school, Yeshiva Torah Vodaath. These organizations eclipsed such older established agencies as the Williamsburg and Brooklyn YM-YWHA's. While the Y's board members moved to new neighborhoods, the Yeshiva attracted new supporters during the 1930s. Soon "the stores in the streets changed owners and carried Jewish merchandise, foods, and re- ligious articles." By the end of the decade observers noted that "every second man wears a beard and the children on Lee Ave- nue are Jewish and most of them have a *yarmulke* and go to a Yeshivah."[17]

The East Bronx moved in a different direction. It was the most economically heterogeneous of the immigrant Jewish neigh- borhoods, and a vigorous secular Jewish life flourished on its streets. "Jewishness was the great leveler" in the East Bronx, where close to half of the borough's Jews lived. This area, also called Morrisania, included many subsections: Hunts Point in the Southeast, South Bronx in the blocks below 149th Street, the Tremont or Crotona section around Crotona Park. The principal Bronx immigrant Jewish neighborhood, the East Bronx also wel- comed middle-class Jews, who lived on its better residential streets near Crotona Park or Southern Boulevard. Such blocks boasted "fine brick apartment houses, some with elevators, with embossed tin and carved granite cornices, wrought-iron stair rails, polished-brass mailboxes and marble lobbies." They at- tracted Jews from Manhattan throughout the 1920s, especially "the working person who had made it, or who could afford bet- ter." Some residents even saw Crotona Park East as "the Central Park West of the Bronx." In the middle of the park was a large lake where one "could rent rowboats or fish for carp or sunfish." The park also offered tennis and handball courts, a bocci rink, and a big field "usually filled with picnickers." Yet the relative luxury of Charlotte Street which ended at Crotona Park stood cheek-by-jowl to the more modest tenements of Wilkins Avenue. The eastern section of the East Bronx, along Simpson and Fox Streets, averaged monthly rents as low as six dollars a room, "a duplication of the ghetto." This district combined factories, ware- houses, and garages on its western edges with pushcart markets, and shopping streets on East 163rd Street and Prospect Avenue. In the 1920s the once residential Bathgate Avenue became "a street emporium stretching from 174th Street to Claremont Park- way. The gutter was lined with pushcarts selling clothes, food, furniture," Morris Freedman recalled. "The stores had open doorways and overflowed onto the sidewalks."[18]

Simpson Street in the East Bronx, corner of East 163rd Street, looking toward Westchester Avenue in 1920. *Courtesy of the Museum of the City of New York.*

The East Bronx acquired a reputation for radicalism. On Washington Avenue the activities of the Yiddish schools, Workmen's Circle clubs, union locals, and socialist meeting halls overshadowed those of the *landsmanshaft chevras* and the Yeshiva Rabbi Israel Salanter, the Bronx's only Jewish day school in the 1920s. The few synagogues and talmud torahs hugged the middle-class blocks or clustered near Hunts Point. Jewish radical organizations exerted more influence in the neighborhood than religious groups. Sensitive to such trends, the program of the local settlement house, Bronx House, reflected this emphasis. Bronx House encouraged efforts to establish retail cooperatives, taught consumer education, and featured many left-wing Yiddish speakers in its lecture series. At its Institute of Jewish Culture it even offered classes in the Yiddish language, promising a "non-ideological" approach. The public schools, too, responded to the dominant trend, opening their doors to night classes in Yiddish and to union meetings. The ILGWU's Unity Centers also sponsored many activities in the neighborhood, often using public school facilities.[19]

In these predominantly lower-class neighborhoods, Brownsville, Williamsburg, and the East Bronx, the Jews made the streets their own. Relatively few non-Jews lived in such densely populated immigrant Jewish sections. Indeed, the neighborhood gave a Jewish tone to otherwise neutral activity. "You might be shouting at the top of your lungs against reformism or Stalin's betrayals, but for the middle-aged garment worker strolling along Southern Boulevard you were just a bright and cocky Jewish boy, a talkative little *pisher*," Howe recalls ironically. The ethnic Jewish characteristics of the immigrant, working-class neighborhood provided a model of Jewish living which overshadowed a second-generation, middle-class alternative. The substantial contrast in class between immigrant and second generation neighborhoods obscured the continuities in structure, for middle-class Jews continued to endow the urban environment with ethnic attributes. However, the ethnic content of middle-class neighborhoods acquired a new surface sheen and restrained private quality. Looking at the main arteries of the West Bronx, one resident asked rhetorically, "What streets anywhere can match them in their sheer number of food stores, ice-cream parlors, delicatessens, restaurants, specialty shops for women and children, haber-

Along the shopping hub of the East Bronx, Third Avenue and 149th Street, looking north under the el in 1918. *Courtesy of The Bronx County Historical Society, New York City.*

dasheries, and that special institution of the area, the 'hardware' store." The profusion and style of stores in part marked the middle-class neighborhood as a Jewish environment. Hindsight revealed that "living on Ocean Parkway in Brooklyn or Mosholu Parkway in the Bronx meant yielding all one's senses to a Jewish ambience." Eventually even middle-class neighborhoods would transmit a Jewish tinge to secular activities pursued within their boundaries.[20]

Middle-class comfort characterized the emerging Jewish neighborhoods. Their relative affluence modified the Jewishness of local institutions. On the Grand Concourse, in Flatbush, Borough Park, or even Pelham Parkway, a middle-class way of Jewish living appeared.

In the Bronx, "the height of prosperity" was manifested on the Grand Concourse. Socialist and writer Paul Jacobs remembered the neighborhood of his childhood: "We lived in an apartment house on a quiet tree-lined street in the upper Bronx, just off the Grand Concourse. Most of the houses on the block were one-family homes, two or three stories high with stoops in front and yards in back." Located west of Webster Avenue and stretching to the Harlem River, the Grand Concourse neighborhood started at Franz Siegel Park, "complete with bandstand and Sunday afternoon concerts," and spread northward until it reached 181st Street. At the far end of the Concourse was the big shopping area which Ruth Glazer called "the lodestar of Bronx life." The Grand Concourse became known for its "fancy" apartment houses where "ritzy" Jews lived. Howe remembered them as "forbidding apartment houses" to a poor, East Bronx youth in the 1930s. Indeed, the WPA *New York City Guide* described the Grand Concourse in 1939 as "the Park Avenue of middle class Bronx residents," adding that "a lease to an apartment in one of its many large buildings is considered evidence of at least moderate business success." The Concourse attracted "manufacturers and tradesmen, doctors, dentists, lawyers, engineers, school teachers, salesmen and minor executives . . . the envy of the Jewish poor," wrote one WPA writer. Yet most of its professionals and businessmen earned enough only to place them securely in the middle class. Glazer, who lived in the neighborhood, located the Grand Concourse "in time midway between the Lower

East Side (or the East Bronx) and West Side of Manhattan." She characterized it as "a community whose residents seem occupied full time in discovering the wonderful things produced by the world that can be had for even the moderate amount of money at their disposal." Nonetheless, the Concourse aspired to be the Upper West Side of the Bronx. The Jewish doctors' offices on the Concourse copied the "elaborately equipped . . . waiting rooms of physicians on Park Avenue." "The Bronx Jewish socialites aspire to live on this wide boulevard and enjoy the social prestige it bestows on its inhabitants," noted a WPA writer.[21]

The Concourse did not forget its Jewishness in the pursuit of middle-class security. "Jewish traditions and mores are observed, but with a certain degree of restraint. Jewish holidays are observed and gefilte fish are relished by these Jews. But, there is a conscious attempt to merge with the general mode of life of the American population." As Glazer remembered, "although the

Pushing baby carriages along the tree-lined Grand Concourse at 168th Street. Photo taken in 1952. *Courtesy of The Bronx County Historical Society, New York City.*

Sabbath may not be observed in other respects, for Friday night
and Saturday one buys *chaleh*." Grand Concourse Jews participated in an intense synagogue-building spree in the 1920s, a conscious attempt to fit in with the American style of life. Jacobs
recalled that "one block away there was a church and down the
street an Orthodox synagogue, which we didn't attend; for my
parents were Reform Jews who belonged to a brick temple on the
Concourse." In the Bronx such organizational activity highlighted
the Concourse as the epitome of second generation Jewish affluence. But in many ways the Grand Concourse resembled several
middle-class neighborhoods in Brooklyn.[22]

A more suburban type of middle-class Jewish neighborhood
developed in Brooklyn. Like the Grand Concourse, Flatbush
emerged abruptly in the early 1920s as a typical New York Jewish
neighborhood. The early Jewish settlers in Flatbush were pioneers. "It was with a great deal of speculation that Jewish families had decided to reside in this part of Brooklyn. Instead of
using the usual streets and asphalted highways of today, these
settlers would walk through fields in order to reach each other's
home or the Brighton line station." In the space of ten years
rapid migration transformed Flatbush and subdivisions gobbled
up its fields. By 1925 Flatbush's possibilities as a new Jewish
neighborhood appeared secure. "Residents of Flatbush are
looked upon with envious eyes by those living elsewhere—not only
because Flatbush is a picturesque, open and delightful place in
which to make one's home," Wexelstein wrote enthusiastically,
"but because, also, it now has its own shopping centers which can
cope adequately with the demands of its population." Flatbush attracted Jewish businessmen and professionals; it became an
"upper-middle-class enclave." In 1926 Flatbush ranked only
slightly behind its northern neighbor, Eastern Parkway, in contributions to the United Jewish Campaign. As on the Grand Concourse, Jewish organizational activity in Flatbush centered in the
substantial neighborhood synagogues.[23]

The Borough Park section of Brooklyn contrasted with the
upstart newness of Flatbush. A relatively old district, Borough
Park appeared in 1920 "to be about the wealthiest Jewish section
in Brooklyn. I was told that they are considered to be the '400' of
Brooklyn," commented a field worker for the Brooklyn Federa-

Growing up in south Flatbush.
Helen and Martin Dash on the steps of their one-family house at 1758 East
9th Street, looking toward the apartment building on the corner of Kings
Highway (circa 1928).

tion of Jewish Charities. "The rich section extends from about
46th Street to 60th Street. Between 37th Street and 46th Street is
the 'east side' of Borough Park, with its small orthodox congregations." From the neighborhood of the Jewish elite in 1920,
Borough Park increasingly developed into a middle-class area as
the wealthy Jews left for the newer districts of Flatbush and Eastern Parkway. By 1930 the more expensive section of Borough
Park had narrowed to the blocks between 46th Street and 53rd
Street. During the Depression Borough Park evolved further into
a neighborhood of small businessmen and wage earners, many of
whom owned their own homes.[24]

   The Jewish organizations in Borough Park reflected the
changing population of the neighborhood. As Borough Park contained two Jewish subcommunities, so it included two sets of Jewish institutions. In the less affluent part of the neighborhood a
group of six heavily used Yiddish schools flourished. Borough
Park also housed a number of Jewish philanthropic organizations, most of them established before 1920. Upper-class Jews

usually turned first to philanthropy as a mode of Jewish group activity. As the wealthy left, however, the Orthodox and Conservative synagogue leaders assumed positions of prominence in the community, changing its Jewish character in the process. These men created a Jewish Community Council in 1929 and promoted widespread support for Zionist causes and the idea of Jewish peoplehood in America. Middle-class Borough Park Jews preferred to give their funds to the United Palestine Appeal rather than support the non-Zionist Joint Distribution Committee through the United Jewish Campaign. They also helped to develop a form of cultural Zionism which embraced middle-class modernism as a form of Jewish expression and secured Zionism's future as a Jewish group activity.[25]

Alternative middle-class Jewish neighborhoods also existed. Not quite as affluent, they combined comfortable housing, often in sparsely settled sections of the city, with a radical, secular Jewish lifestyle. Located predominantly in the Bronx, they drew their tone from the housing cooperatives in their midst. Yiddish writer B. B. Weinrebe characterized the cooperatives as "cultural centers. They organize discussions, lectures, concerts; they have founded and are supporting their own workers' schools and kindergartens; youth clubs, libraries and have even engaged in publishing activities. They have become important centers of Jewish culture, in the Yiddish language," he concluded, "and are spreading their influence among the entire Jewish working population of New York City." In the Workers Cooperative Colony "the most important day of the year was neither Yom Kippur nor Christmas but May Day." Tanya Rosenberg remembered that day "as the only holiday when you really felt a holiday spirit, all through the halls and courts." In the Pelham Parkway section, east of Bronx Park, "a good proportion of the Jewish people residing in this neighborhood is of the Yiddish speaking group. A large number of them are Socialists and Communists," Jack Horden, the Jewish Education Association statistician, observed in 1935.[26]

A few of the new neighborhoods replicated the immigrant model. A middle-class area, the Brighton Beach neighborhood of Coney Island was "considered a miniature East Side." "A densely populated year-round residential area, with closely

Boarding the Amalgamated's cooperative bus, used to reach the subway and elevated lines, in 1929. *Courtesy of the Museum of the City of New York.*

packed apartment houses," Brighton Beach was located between the lower-class neighborhood of Coney Island and affluent Manhattan Beach. "Brighton itself was the middle-class axis of this seesaw, sometimes tipping its families up and sometimes down." During the Depression Milton Klonsky remembered that he "could sense the anxiety of everyone to keep his place on the balance." As in the East Side, "the Brighton Jews range from strict orthodoxy to radicalism, each with his religious and political centers, welfare and youth clubs," observed Yiddish writer B. Weinstein. "The main street, Brighton Beach Avenue, with its rumbling elevated overhead, is comparable to an East Side market on Hester or Rivington Street. Thronging the streets are peddlers selling different wares, Bagels, hot peas, knishes, and on Fridays, candles for the Sabbath." The influx of temporary residents which transformed Coney Island each summer did not disrupt the Jewish life of those permanently living in Brighton Beach.[27]

Other new middle-class Jewish neighborhoods in New York

City fit the patterns suggested by Brighton Beach or Pelham Parkway, Flatbush or the Grand Concourse. Only the Upper West Side ranked as an upper-class Jewish neighborhood in the 1920s and 1930s. Yet in important respects Brooklyn's Eastern Parkway replicated the Upper West Side. Like Harlem before the first World War, these neighborhoods attracted Jews with both German and east European backgrounds. On Eastern Parkway the neighborhood synagogues included the prestigious Union Temple, old Brooklyn Jewry's religious address, as well as the Brooklyn Jewish Center, the new monument of second generation east European Jews. The massive apartment houses lining Eastern Parkway produced an impression of solid respectability associated with West End Avenue. In addition, many of the elite Brooklyn Jewish social and fraternal clubs attracted members from the section. Jews on both Eastern Parkway and the Upper West Side contributed substantial sums to Zionist fund-raising campaigns. Washington Heights, a middle-class Manhattan Jewish neighborhood, resembled Borough Park. Originally the home of wealthy Jews, Washington Heights gradually lost them to Central Park West. In the 1920s Washington Heights attracted Jews from Harlem, and in the 1930s the neighborhood drew thousands of German Jewish refugees who came to live near distant American relatives who had helped them. The establishment of Yeshiva College in the late 1920s served as a magnet pulling Orthodox Jews to the neighborhood. As in Borough Park, Washington Heights' Jewish leaders organized a Jewish Community Council to coordinate local organizational activities.[28]

The diversity of Jewish neighborhoods compensated for their individual provincialism. Rental costs made New York's newer Jewish neighborhoods relatively homogeneous; the poor rarely shared the streets with the middle class.[29] Yet the second-generation neighborhoods also retained aspects of the immigrant milieu and housed a variety of Jewish organizations which reflected the ideological tendencies of area residents. In the idiosyncratic soils of different neighborhoods there developed alternative styles of ethnic group life. Orthodoxy was either modern and middle class, as in Borough Park, or immigrant and lower class, as in Williamsburg. So, too, second generation Jewish radicals living in the Mosholu and Pelham Parkway sections created a stylistic and substantive alternative to immigrant lower-class radicalism.

Substantial apartment houses lined Eastern Parkway by 1925. The Martha
Washington apartment pictured here was located between Washington
and Underhill Streets, and faced the northern boundary of Prospect Park.
Courtesy of the Museum of the City of New York.

The new neighborhoods shared common characteristics in
their physical and social structure. Jews brought to the streets a
pattern of association and they transformed public places into
arenas of Jewish interaction. The parks and boulevards Jews
prized so highly served as the setting for ethnic expression. "Saturday afternoon on the Grand Concourse is the perfect time to
watch a Jewish crowd pass in endless procession," observed one
writer. In the East Bronx, Wilkins Avenue was "the Sabbath
promenade, the Rosh Hashanah gathering place, for the neighborhood." In Brooklyn, Jews walked down Eastern Parkway or
Ocean Parkway; in Coney Island it was the Boardwalk; while in
Manhattan, Jews strolled along Riverside Drive or Central Park
West. Young Jews took to the streets not only for Sabbath prome-

nades. Boys played ball on the streets while girls jumped rope or played hopscotch. Adolescents also turned to the streets for their socializing. "There never seemed any place to go. The thought of bringing my friends home was inconceivable," Howe wrote. "So we walked the streets, never needing to tell one another why we chose this neutral setting for our escape at evening. . . . In the summer, after meetings, we would parade across the middle bulge of the Bronx."[30]

When winter came the candy stores and cafeterias replaced parks as forums to debate politics and art. People gathered at candy stores "to discuss politics and unionism." Local kids "made pocket change by hanging out at Leboff's candy store [one of five on Charlotte Street], and calling neighborhood people to the phone." Hoffman's Cafeterias on Pitkin, Flatbush, and Brighton Beach Avenues also catered to the radical element. Howe recalled that "in the winter, when the Bronx is gray and icy, there were cafeterias in which the older comrades, those who had jobs or were on WPA, bought coffee while the rest of us filled the chairs." Other cafeterias, like Dubrow's or Garfield's in Brooklyn, aspired to opulent elegance. Garfield's dubbed itself "the cafeteria of refinement." Located on the corner of Church and Flatbush Avenues, diagonally across from the Reformed Protestant Dutch Church, Garfield's boasted an interior decorated with mosaics done in the Art Moderne style. Dubrow's, a dairy cafeteria, also served as a neighborhood meeting spot with its attractive location by the elevated station, on a shopping street like Kings Highway.[31]

For married women, children provided the excuse to stroll along the sidewalks. The first Jews moving into Flatbush found no baby carriages on the street, but by 1930 Jewish mothers pushing prams had appeared. Klonsky remembered that "parks were crowded with mothers wheeling baby carriages" in Brighton Beach during the 1930s. In lower-class Jewish neighborhoods the women sat on the stoops. Kazin recalled that "as soon as I could see . . . the old women in their housedresses sitting in front of the tenements like priestesses of an ancient cult," he knew he was home in Brownsville. After dinner along the Boston Post Road in the Bronx "people would come down with their chairs and sit around on the sidewalk while the children played. It was like a picnic, a neighborhood picnic." Older people also sat on the benches placed along the center greensward of the large boulevards like Eastern Parkway and the Grand Concourse. The chess tables in particular attracted a steady clientele of Jewish men. The Jewish neighborhood lent an ethnic dimension to these aspects of urban life.[32]

The association patterns inherent in neighborhood living encouraged Jewish ethnic persistence, allowing New York's Jewish

Mothers and children in baby carriages enjoy the greensward and benches along Crotona Parkway in the Bronx, circa 1917. *Courtesy of the Museum of the City of New York.*

neighborhoods to support strong communal boundaries. Because of Jewish self-segregation in New York City neighborhoods, "four-fifths of all the Jews . . . practically have no social contact with the Gentiles. . . . It means that for the overwhelming majority of the Jews in America assimilation in any true sense of the term is absolutely out of the question," Zalowitz concluded. "It means that despite the fact that we have attended American public schools and universities, read American papers and books, pa-

tronize the same theatres and subways and buses, we are kept
and keep ourselves at arm's length from the bulk of the American
population."[33] Having reached neighborhoods which appeared to
be "American" when they lived in immigrant areas, some New
York Jews now turned around and saw only the Jewish aspects of
their neighborhoods. The American city still eluded them.

Ultimately Jews succeeded so well in making American urban
neighborhoods into ethnic Jewish communities that many saw
New York City as something separate and distant. These Jews
juxtaposed "the city" to their neighborhood, perceiving the
former as foreign territory. "We were of the city, but somehow
not in it," Kazin wrote.

> I saw New York as a foreign city. . . . That the two were joined in
> me I never knew then. . . . We were the end of the line. We were
> the children of the immigrants who had camped at the city's back
> door. . . . "New York" was what we put last on our address, but
> first in thinking of the others around us. *They* were New York, the
> Gentiles, America.

Gornick wrote that "we of the second generation were frightened
of America also—but we hungered for it more than we feared it.
Manhattan for us was Araby." Howe, too, admitted that

> New York did not really exist for us as a city, a defined place we
> felt to be our own. Too many barriers intervened, too many kinds
> of anxiety. In the thirties New York was not merely the vital me-
> tropolis, brimming with politics and contention, that has since
> become a sentimental legend; it was also brutal, ugly, frightening,
> the foul-smelling jungle. . . . New York was the embodiment of
> that alien world which every boy raised in a Jewish immigrant
> home had been taught, whether he realized it or not, to look upon
> with suspicion. It was "their" city in ways that one's parents could
> hardly have explained, and hardly needed to; and later, once I
> had absorbed the values of the Movement, it became "their" city
> in a new and, as it seemed to me, deeper sense.[34]

But if Jews knew who they were in relation to each other in
the neighborhood, they also tried to replicate aspects of *their*
world in the alien city itself. "In our very distance from the
city—caused, I suspect, less by a considered 'alienation' than by
a difficulty of access, a puritanical refusal of possibilities, and an

unacknowledged shyness beneath our pose of bravado—'' Howe remembered, "we made for ourselves a kind of underground city consisting of a series of stopping places where we could ease the strain of restlessness and feel indifferent to our lack of money." Looking at New York from another perspective Yoffeh remarked on the impact of Jewish neighborhood life on the city. "The Ghetto is spreading out, is taking in more territory, and becoming, in the process, diluted," he argued. "But it has left its imprint upon New York. I do not only mean that Jews may now be found in every part of the town," he went on, for the "process of Ghettoizing New York has been much more subtle. . . . It has given the very Gentiles a Jewish tinge." The Yiddish playwright Peretz Hirschbein went further, arguing that "it can hardly be said that New York is in America, it would be more true to say that it is at the rim of it. It often seems to me," he mused, "that if you could give New York one big push it would roll all the way across the ocean over into Europe."[35]

Did the neighborhood enclose Jews? Did it spread Jewish influence throughout the city? Indeed, the Jewish neighborhood managed to do both. It tied Jews to ethnic apron strings as it reshaped the quality of New York City life. Nourishing an unconsciously Jewish world, it freed Jews to perceive other horizons.

The security, accommodation, and community of informal primary ties found within the neighborhood's cosy parameters sufficed for many New York City Jews. But others also wished to associate through explicitly Jewish American institutions. The marginality lurking at the borders of the neighborhood impelled them to develop secondary institutions to ensure the survival of their Jewish ethnicity and American middle-class status. For such Jews, generally a minority, it was not enough to patronize Jewish food shops, to walk past synagogues, to see Jewish faces on the tree-lined streets. Many of these joined civic or Jewish organizations to promote within the neighborhood an institutional synthesis of American and Jewish values. Second generation Jews wrought structural and programmatic changes in their local civic and Jewish institutions, fashioning out of middle-class affluence the sinews of a new kind of Jewish life. These institutional innovations articulated the nature of American Jewish ethnicity, in important ways defining the second generation New York Jew.

4

Their children . . . lived their early lives scurrying between two worlds. For most, the centripetal attraction of the wider society often transmitted by public school teachers was too compelling to resist. They were to learn . . . to adjust their style of life to fit more readily into that toward which they aspired.

Peter I. Rose, "The Ghetto and Beyond,"
in *The Ghetto and Beyond: Essays on Jewish Life in America*,
ed. Rose (New York: Random House, 1969), p. 9.

Ethnic Identity and the Neighborhood School

Among local American institutions centered in the neighborhood, the public school influenced second generation Jews with singular authority. School was for immigrant Jews, and especially for their children, the preeminent American institution—the local representative of American society, the repository of its ideal values, and the symbol of its aspirations. Immigrants juxtaposed the public school to the Russian state schools and the traditional Jewish religious schools they had known. American public schools offered Jews access to American society and contact with non-Jewish Americans. A secondary institution of socialization, the public school promoted primary associations among its pupils. Children learned not only from their teachers, but from each other as well. "In Brownsville when I knew it, school was a major occupation, not only of the children alone but of the whole neighborhood," Samuel Tenenbaum remembered. "Every teacher was discussed with the minute detail a jeweler devotes to a watch; the principal of the local public school had the same authority and prestige as the most learned dean of our most respected university."[1] The public school's influence extended beyond its classrooms. It pervaded the lives of the pupils and their parents.

As the neighborhood's representative American institution, the public school stood apart from immigrant Jews and their children. Controlled and staffed predominantly by non-Jews, public schools in immigrant neighborhoods wrenched Jewish students away from the culture of their parents through Americanization programs. "Americanization is a spiritual thing," declared New York City's Superintendent of Schools in 1918. "Broadly speaking, we mean by it an appreciation of the institutions of this coun-

The main reading room of the children's branch of the public library in
Brownsville, an important adjunct to the public school. August 1930.
Courtesy of the Museum of the City of New York.

try, absolute forgetfulness of all obligations or connections with
other countries because of descent or birth.'' The public schools
accepted the burden of Americanization, the task of weaning their
pupils away from their ethnic heritage. In their zeal to transform
the immigrant "little savages" into "little citizens," the public
schools became potential arenas of conflict between Gentile
teachers and Jewish students.[2]

Americanization in the public schools emphasized the culturally symbolic importance of language. Teachers denigrated
Yiddish, associating it with the lower class, "unAmerican" culture of their pupils' parents. An extremely zealous Americanizer
like the German Jewish Julia Richman, district superintendent of
the Lower East Side schools during the first decade of the twentieth century, even forbade children to speak Yiddish among
themselves during recess or in the halls and bathrooms. Richman
encouraged teachers to monitor their pupils and wash out with
soap the mouth's of those who relapsed. Mastery of English sig-

nified the formal cultural baptism—the acceptance into American life—of these new Americans. "Thus the public school graduate grows up to know that he must despise his parents with their poor knowledge of English, that he must be thoroughly conversant with the batting averages, and that he must possess a large quantity of Americanism—100 percent at least!" Jewish educator Isaac Berkson wrote scornfully.[3]

The public school's Americanization process involved more than that of secular socialization—the inculcation of an Anglo-Saxon normative culture associated with the English language. The public school also carried a religious burden. "The school's goal might be called religious," argues religious historian Robert Michaelsen, not only in terms of "achieving moral character but also in the development of a sense of community, of a common identity as Americans." The public schools became "the chief instrument for eliciting and inculcating public piety." Educators assumed that they could exclude "the particularities and peculiarities of religion," usually dubbed sectarianism, while they fostered "the general elements, those assumed to be held in common by all or most of the people. The former divide; the latter unite. And because the latter unite," notes Michaelsen, they help to produce the common assumptions and commitments which serve as the basis of American public piety. "The public school has been, then, a favorite vehicle for engaging in 'common religionizing,' " he concludes.[4] Jews, however, found such common religionizing heavily Christian in tone, even if educators perceived it as non-sectarian.

But the public schools offered immigrant Jews a carrot as well as a stick: they promised social mobility as a reward for school success. "To Brownsville," Tenenbaum recalled, "school represented a glorious future that would rescue it from want, deprivation and ugliness." Indeed by 1914, sociologist Colin Greer argues, "the triumph of the public school as the chief mechanism of social democracy was both an article of popular faith and a canon of historical scholarship." What Greer calls "the Great School Legend" took hold during the years of mass immigration. Schools "were believed to provide common experience for diverse children they were to equip with the wherewithal for responsible citizenship and economic prosperity."[5] The public schools equalized their pupils. The linking of Americanization with social mobility in the public schools assumed the open character of American society. It tied to a capitalist economy both a definition of American nationality based on Anglo-Saxon culture and a public piety based on a common nonsectarian, but Christian, faith.

Immigrant Jews experienced the public schools' challenge as an incentive and as a dismissal. In their response to the public schools they expressed attitudes derived from traditional Jewish values toward education. In eastern Europe Jews saw religious education as fulfilling three intertwined goals: transmitting Jewish religious culture, providing for the child's ethnic identity, and fitting him into the social structure. Jewish attitudes combined an identificational with an instrumental view of education. Jews based their educational decisions on the principle of *takhlis*, "the maxim that all of one's final activities must be goal-directed and lead to some positive final result." As Moses Kligsberg notes, "one did not hesitate choosing long years of deprivation, hunger, and loneliness, far from home, in a yeshiva or apprenticeship, were one convinced that it led to *takhlis*." And in eastern Europe, for many years learning was the best trade, providing status and financial security. Goal-oriented Jewish immigrants kept the principle of *takhlis*, but discarded the old values of eastern Europe and adopted such new ones as wealth-without-learning or secular-status-without-Jewish-knowledge. This entailed splitting apart their view of education and creating two parallel educational systems. In America the Jewish immigrants' instrumental attitude toward education found its fulfillment in the public schools. Jewish immigrants accepted the public school's promised reward of secular status, the chance to become a doctor or lawyer, or more modestly, a pharmacist or teacher. But Jewish immigrants resisted identifying with the public school completely. Instead they established several Jewish educational systems to inculcate Jewish identity in their children. The existence of the traditional religious *heders* as well as the innovative socialist and nationalist radical schools indicated a partial rejection of the public school. Supplementary Jewish education implied a desire on the part of immigrant parents to immunize their children against the nonsectarian Christian character of the public school so that they could reap its benefits without becoming infected.[6]

Cooperative kindergarten in the Amalgamated houses in the Bronx, 1929,
synthesized Jewish socialist and American values. *Courtesy of the
Museum of the City of New York.*

Jewish immigrants also brought with them a vision of
America that did not square with the public school's image. Some
saw America as an open society, its culture not yet fixed, its
greatness still in the future. The melting pot ideal, as the English
writer Israel Zangwill articulated it, captured the imagination of
immigrant Jews. "America is God's Crucible, the great Melting-
Pot where all the races of Europe are melting and re-forming!"
Zangwill's Jewish hero proclaims: "God is making the American.
. . . the real American has not yet arrived." For immigrants
committed to radical socialism, their vision of America assumed a
class dimension. Eager "to establish some harmony between his
dreams and his experience," the Jewish radical intellectual explicitly recognized "the ideological role of art in involving man in the
process of creation of cultural forms." As Michael Gold argued in
1927, Jewish needle trades workers "have built up a richer and
intenser mass culture than that of bank presidents or Greenwich
Villagers or even Theater Guild audiences." Jewish socialists distinguished between American elite and popular cultures and
sought to develop an American workers' culture. On such grounds

they too challenged the Americanization promoted by the public schools.[7]

But immigrant Jews rarely tried to change the public schools' program. "The older generation of Jews accepted as inevitable the partition of the child's personality between the public school and the Jewish school, between the home and the street," observed a second generation parent, Fannie Neumann, in the 1920s. "They relied upon the Hebrew school to undo the 'mischief' of the unJewish environment by supplying strong doses of Judaism as an antidote to the virus of assimilation." These methods produced tension in the child, a dualism not easily overcome. "The traditional Jewish passion for higher education, as well as many another 'Jewish trait' simply fell apart under the violent impact of street life," William Poster recalled of his Brownsville youth in the 1930s. "The lure of punchball, movies, and 'working,' proved stronger than parental authority or desire."[8]

Second generation Jews who moved into the new middle-class neighborhoods mitigated the conflict engendered by the public schools in part by changing the schools themselves. No longer outsiders to the routine of public education and having achieved a higher status (reflected in their change of residence), second generation Jews persistently pressured the public schools to accommodate Jewish ethnicity. If the public schools' definition of Americanism and its expressions of public piety could be modified, conceivably Jews could identify with the schools. As they worked to overcome the conflicts produced by the public education of immigrant children, middle-class Jews developed yet another alternative vision of American culture. The new ideal of democratic pluralism they championed incorporated aspects of Jewishness and Americanism in a secular synthesis, which was grounded in the reality of their middle-class status.

The public school's transition from the dominant institution of Americanization in the immigrant neighborhood to one accepting American Jewish identity accompanied a steady shift in the ethnic character of the teaching staff. The preponderant majority of Christian teachers in the public schools in immigrant sections fundamentally had shaped the Jewish child's encounter with the school. Americanization, taught by Christian teachers, heightened the distance between the school and its pupils. Jewish students on the Lower East Side saw teachers as "strange, awesome beings. . . . We knew they were not Jewish, most of them, but neither did they fit into our conception of Christians," Yoffeh recalled. Christians, the young Yoffeh knew, "were an ignorant lot. Yet these teachers were so clever, seemed to know everything." Statistics confirm the foreignness of the public school teachers to their immigrant pupils. In 1910 immigrants and their children made up over 70 percent of the school population. Conversely, the majority of the teachers in New York City were native-born, although almost half of these had foreign-born parents. The largest second generation contingent was Irish, who made up almost 20 percent of the total, while a mere 6 percent were Jewish.[9]

An overwhelming majority of immigrant Jews sent their children to the public schools. Well into the 1930s Jewish parochial schools attracted only 2 percent of the city's Jewish children. Given the residential concentration of immigrant Jews and the local character of the public schools, Jewish children often discovered that they constituted 90 percent of a school's enrollment—a situation that limited the interethnic contact within the school to teacher-pupil contact. This relationship often was filled with tension. "Paternalistically, the public schools responded to its new foreign and lower-class clientele by catering to their 'sanitary' and 'behavioral' difficulties, rather than by attempting to do much about academic performance," Greer writes. The influence of Jewish pupils or their immigrant parents on the public school paled before the power of the teachers and administrators. Irate Lower East Side Jews failed to rebuff Julia Richman's slander of them. Richman led marches of teachers and pupils through Lower East Side streets in an anti-pushcart campaign and attacked "desperately ignorant" Russian Jewish parents for starving their children during the depression of 1907–1908.[10] While Richman's crusade reflected attitudes held by many German Jews toward east European Jewish immigrants, the social structure within the school also would have to change if Jews were to modify any aspect of the school's program.

Beginning in the years around World War I and accelerating in the 1920s and 1930s, Jews joined the city's public school teaching staff. The percentage of new teachers who were Jewish increased steadily from 1920 to 1940. In 1920, 26 percent of the

Young teachers at P.S. 165 on their way home in Brownsville in 1920.
From left to right (lower row): Frances Feeman, —?—, Bella Golden;
(upper row) Sadie Reibstein, Ida Wirth, (?).

teachers entering the New York City public school system were
Jews; by 1930 Jews made up 44 percent of the new teachers, and
by 1940, they composed 56 percent of the new teachers. Immigrants and their children learned a version of American life
under the tutelage of teachers named Jones, O'Reilly, Smith, and
Kennedy; the second generation and their children would also
know teachers named Golden, Kaplan, and Kaminsky.[11]

The changing nature of the schools' personnel was particularly evident in Jewish neighborhoods. The Board of Education
tried to match the background of the teachers with their pupils.
Therefore, increasingly larger numbers of Jewish teachers and
principals began to instruct Jewish pupils. Even as early as 1914,
the 68 teachers at P.S. 120 on Rivington Street (25 of whom were
Jewish) were supervised by a Jewish principal and assistant principal. The Board facilitated this ethnic correspondence of teaching staff and students not out of any interest in the immigrants'
culture, but rather as a means of promoting the native-born
teachers to "better" schools in middle-class neighborhoods. Yet
the shift occasionally enabled immigrant Jews and their children
to influence public school policy decisions. In Brownsville, where
by 1927 over 30 percent of the teachers were Jewish, a radical
Jewish principal tacitly could encourage his students to protest
the Gary Plan, an ill-conceived program to revamp public educa-

Bella Golden with her fourth-grade class, at P.S. 165, during a play period
outside in the fields bordering the school (circa 1920).

tion. During a hotly contested four-way mayoralty election in
1917, Alexander Fichandler, principal of the newly constructed
P.S. 165 on Lot and Hopkinson Streets at the outskirts of
Brownsville, quietly exulted when his pupils struck the school in
protest against the proposed Gary Plan. A socialist, Fichandler
posted anti-war cartoons on the school bulletin boards and modified the rigid structure characteristic of New York City public
schools, permitting his pupils to walk in the halls rather than
march stiffly two-by-two.[12]

But the entrance of second generation Jews into teaching did
not affect only the old immigrant neighborhoods. In such new sections as the Grand Concourse and Flatbush the increase in the
Jewish student population paralleled the increase of Jewish
teachers in the public schools. In the space of a decade a 70 percent increase in Jewish students accompanied an 87 percent increase in the percentage of Jewish teachers in Grand Concourse
schools. Despite the cutbacks in licensing and staffing during the
Depression, the proportion of Jewish teachers in Flatbush schools
leaped 108 percent in ten years, although the number of Jewish
students grew less rapidly.[13]

The changing composition of the public schools' teacher and
student populations in Jewish neighborhoods influenced the social
relationships within the school and facilitated outside Jewish ef-

Table 5 Jewish Pupils and Teachers in Public Schools (in percent)

	Grand Concourse	*Flatbush*
Jewish pupils		
1924	40	48
1934	68	57
Jewish teachers		
1927	16	12
1937	30	25

SOURCES: Jewish pupils from Jewish Education Association, Jewish Child Population Study; Jewish teachers from New York City Department of Education, *List of Members*.
(Note: Determination of Jewish teachers based on onomastic criteria.)

forts to transform the local public school's values. Bridging the chasm between home and school rested on the resolution of the conflict between American teachers and foreign pupils. As second generation Jewish teachers just out of college took jobs in such newly established high schools as Abraham Lincoln and Thomas Jefferson, both located in Brooklyn and serving substantial numbers of Jewish students, the teacher–pupil relationship within the schools underwent a subtle transformation. Bright Jewish adolescents warmed to their teachers and shared many extracurricular interests with them. At Lincoln, the journalism teacher supervising the school's newspaper, *The Lincoln Log*, also found time to play ping-pong with the student editor in chief. Irving

The library squad on the roof of the Annex to Abraham Lincoln High School in 1935 where camaraderie flourished between teachers and students.

Hudson, a student at Lincoln, remembers shooting golf balls on Coney Island with his English teacher, Charlie Steingardt. Unmarried teachers received, and often accepted, invitations to student parties. This milieu dissipated the ethnic antagonisms that second generation teachers often had experienced as children and changed the schools' social structure. The large number of Jewish teachers entering the city's public school system laid the basis for a rapprochement with Jewish parents.[14]

The changes in school personnel also reflected the Board of Education's desire to extend the school's Americanization functions. Sociologist Sherry Gorelick argues that immigrant Jewish workers "created the problems of worker control and political strife which inspired the business class to solve those training and social control problems by expanding the schools, and hiring the sons and daughters of immigrants to socialize the sons and daughters of immigrants." In the early 1920s the Board commenced a vast expansion program designed to reach the large numbers of children denied admission to school or attending half-time sessions. The Board "built, completed, and opened one new school house every twelve days for nearly ten years," recalled Theodore Kuper, advisor to the president of the Board of Education. From May 1924 to September 1929 the Board of Education oversaw the construction of 130 new school buildings in its efforts to keep pace with the growing and shifting city school population.[15] These new projects gave second generation Jews the chance to enter recently created positions in new public schools in the rapidly growing middle-class Jewish neighborhoods.

The increase in the number of Jewish teachers occurred within the context of an expanding educational system in the city. Like the school construction program, the number of teachers employed mushroomed during the 1920s. In 1903 a mere 13,000 teachers taught over 600,000 pupils in the city's public schools; by 1925 more than 22,000 teachers instructed approximately 850,000 students. In one school year, 1921–1922, the Board of Education sought to fill almost 1,000 vacancies in the city's public schools. The expansion of instructional opportunities also allowed some Jews to move up into administrative positions. In 1924 Dr. Elias Lieberman left his job teaching English in Bushwick High

School to become the first principal of the newly constructed Thomas Jefferson High School, which served Brownsville pupils.[16]

Not only did the field of education grow, but the recruitment, training, and control of teachers also changed. The Board of Education removed teacher certification from local school boards and gave the task to a city-wide Board of Examiners. New regulations for teachers stipulated at least a high school diploma. While teacher training programs made teaching a profession, the parallel expansion of administration bureaucratized it. These changes accompanied the transformation of New York City's schools "into a hierarchical system—an educational career ladder." As higher education became more democratic with the development of public high schools and the growth of City College, the school system stimulated "both greater individual freedom, and greater centralized control."[17]

A channel of mobility, education increasingly attracted second generation Jews, enticed by the profession's intellectual outlook, job security, and modest but comfortable salaries. Before World War I, grade school teachers started working for $15 a week, which compared unfavorably with the weekly earnings of skilled garment workers. But salary raises after the war rescued teachers' wages from the inroads of inflation. The new schedule of teachers' pay adopted in 1920 gave annual salaries of $1,500 to $2,900 to elementary teachers, while junior and senior high school teachers earned from $1,900 to $3,700. These salaries promised teachers a chance at middle-class status. A subsequent raise in 1928 boosted elementary school salaries to the $1,600 to $3,500 range, and secondary school salaries to $2,040 to $4,200, securing the middle-class position of the latter. Jews also appreciated the teachers' work schedule, which permitted them to observe the Sabbath and holidays without fear of losing their jobs. The free training and the bureaucratized appointment system allowed many Jews to leap the hurdles of prejudice which restricted their employment in other white-collar jobs. Although the Board of Examiners regularly penalized Jewish applicants for certification if their speech was Yiddish-accented—treating their *t*'s and *d*'s and sibilant *s*'s as unacceptable "accents"—the installation of a standardized civil service approach to teacher appointments permitted many Jews to find jobs in the field.[18]

The absorption of second generation Jewish teachers, and to a lesser extent Jewish principals, into the city's educational system introduced a Jewish component into the public schools. In the 1920s the Board of Education inadvertently encouraged Jewish teachers to work in Jewish neighborhood public schools through its policy of transferring teachers to schools located close to their homes. A response to the changing residential patterns of the city's school age population, the transfers increased ethnic homogeneity within the local schools. From 1924 to 1929 the Board of Education effected over 12,000 teacher transfers, involving over half the teaching force. The Board justified the transfers on the grounds of health and convenience to the teachers, who would not be forced to travel extensively to reach their jobs.[19]

The growing presence of Jewish teachers within the school system encouraged the creation of Jewish associational networks. Often the increased Jewish-Gentile contact among teachers spurred separatism, not friendship. In many public schools where Jews made up a significant minority of the staff, teacher rooms became effectively segregated: teachers walking into the "wrong" room for lunch were made to feel unwelcome. These ethnic strains chilled even the liberal atmosphere of P.S. 165. But Jewish teachers did not restrict their associations to the informal teacher room groups. As soon as their numbers warranted, Jewish teachers organized to amplify their collective voice. In 1916 Jews helped form the first teachers union in the city, which became Local 5 of the American Federation of Teachers. Celia Zitron, active for many years in the union, characterizes this early group of 600 teachers as socialists, pacifists, and supporters of women's rights. During the quiet years following the Lusk Committee's investigation of radicalism in the AFT in 1919–1920, many Jewish teachers joined the union. In the 1930s, Jewish teachers participated in the union's internal factional struggles. As the Depression wore on, the union held forums and presented lesson plans to combat anti-Semitism, picketed the Nazi-German consulate, and collected funds for refugees from Hitler.[20]

Jews also established and joined specifically Jewish teacher associations. In 1924 the Jewish Education Association, devoted primarily to promoting supplementary Jewish education in New York City, founded an Advisory Council to bring together Jewish public school teachers and principals. Composed of 30 principals, 275 delegates representing an equal number of public schools, and 165 associate members, the Council worked to advance supplementary Jewish religious education in the city. At the same time, Jewish philanthropic organizations recognized Jewish teachers as a new constituency and appealed to them for support. In 1926 the Brooklyn Federation of Jewish Charities created the Brooklyn Jewish Teachers Association to facilitate its fund-raising. A successful social venture, the Jewish Teachers Association soon became independent from the Federation. In 1927 the Association enrolled 1,000 members and sponsored such social events as dances and dinners. In the Bronx the local Federation created the Bronx Jewish Teachers Committee, headed by Jacob Shuffro, principal of the recently opened P.S. 64 on Walton Avenue, near the Concourse.[21]

The simultaneous integration of Jewish teachers and principals into the public schools and the Jewish institutional community brought the city's education system within the reach of second generation Jewish parents. Fortified by their achievement of economic security, some of these parents turned to the public schools in their neighborhoods and demanded that they produce their promised educational reward of social mobility. These parents hardly worried about whether or not the schools enforced such rules as bringing a clean handkerchief to school each day. Instead they turned their attention to how well the school encouraged the accumulation of knowledge. These second generation Jews perceived the public school system as a ladder and pushed their children to climb to the highest rungs.[22]

During the 1920s and 1930s a popular myth emerged—that of Jewish love of learning, translated into social mobility via secular education. As Gorelick points out, "for the Jewish passion for education to result in upward mobility, there had to be an educational system which was so organized as to provide an avenue of mobility, and educational achievements had to be relevant to occupational success. Before the end of the nineteenth century," she concludes, "neither of those two conditions obtained." In 1910, 60 percent of the New York City children who graduated from elementary school went on to high school, but only 16 percent of those students completed high school in four years. In this select group, were 16 percent of east European Jews, a higher percentage than that of Germans or native whites. Yet this elite of Jewish youth constituted a bare 2 percent of their age group. The vast majority of Jewish teenagers could not afford even a public high school education. Furthermore, this education bore little real relationship to the jobs available, even the white-collar ones.[23]

By the mid-1920s the situation had changed dramatically. The 1920s first provided the "hard core of reality behind the story which depicts the entry of the eastern European Jewish immigrant into the small business enterprise and then of his son into the university and the professions." Secure within the ethnic boundaries of their middle-class neighborhoods, second generation Jews went on to scale the walls of a larger American society. In 1922 the city's white Protestant Americans achieved the distinction of being least behind in school grade level. By 1931 Julius Maller reported that a survey of public schools in 270 neighborhoods found the least amount of "slow progress" among Jews. As the Depression drew to a close, the new Jewish neighborhoods of Flatbush and the Grand Concourse ranked among the city's best. Their schools boasted the highest number of successfully achieving pupils. Jews also flocked to the high schools in disproportionate numbers during these years. Although city high school enrollments skyrocketed thanks to the extension of age levels in the compulsory education law and the limited employment opportunities during the Depression, by 1934 Jews made up over 70 percent of the student body in all of the local high schools serving such neighborhoods as Flatbush, Brownsville, and the Grand Concourse. As Greer observes, "economic stability for the group preceded its entry into the broader middle-class stage via education." Since the public school reinforced economic status rather than transformed it, as middle-class Americans, Jews could take advantage of the school system by the 1920s. Additionally, given the public school's tendency to reflect the cultural background of its students, second generation Jews could hold a new mirror before the school system, demanding that it acknowledge American Jewish ethnicity.[24]

Most second generation Jews remembered the schools' Americanization activities as the most threatening to their sense of identity. The thrust of those efforts in immigrant Jewish neigh-

borhoods were on mastering the English language. The public
school authorities defined proper English as the key to American
life. Through the English language the schools transmitted American values and customs, promising students a share in American
society and its opportunities. By comparison, the schools down-
graded Yiddish language and culture. Knowing Yiddish better
than English at the age of five, Irving Howe recalled his "first day
of kindergarten as if it were a visit to a new country. The teacher
asked the children to identify various common objects," he continued.

> When my turn came she held up a fork and without hesitation I
> called out its Yiddish name, a *goopel*. The whole class burst out
> laughing at me with that special cruelty children can have. That af-
> ternoon I told my parents I had made up my mind never to speak
> Yiddish to them again, though I would not give any reasons.

Though in retrospect Howe sees that "the pained embarrassment
that seeps through this recollection was due less to anyone's mal-
ice or ill-will than to inherent difficulties in making the transition
from immigrant home to American school," the memory un-
derlines the estrangement between home and school produced by
Americanization programs.[25]

Others felt that the attack on Yiddish by the public school
went further than Howe acknowledged. Even a Yiddish accent
could be an embarrassing barrier, as Norman Podhoretz learned.
The idea of his favorite teacher (who he later discovered was Jewish) meeting his mother, he remembered, "was more than I could
bear: my mother, who spoke with a Yiddish accent and of whom,
until that sickening moment, I had never known I was so ashamed
and so ready to betray." Another Brownsville public school pupil
and later a teacher himself, Zachary Baym, admitted that he
always felt somewhat ashamed whenever his parents visited the
school.[26]

Teacher Bella Golden's memories of her Brownsville childhood confirmed the importance of speaking proper English. "One
morning when I came in late I was sent into the boys' classroom
next door. What a disgrace and how I wept," Golden recalled.
"When I returned to my classroom I may have said something
'fresh' to my teacher and she slapped me. At home I told my

mother. She was incensed and wrote a letter to the principal. I was most proud to carry this letter," Golden continued, explaining that "unlike any of the other children's mothers, my mother could write English and we were going 'to show the teacher' I couldn't be treated in this fashion." In Golden's eyes her mother's British accent and ignorance of Yiddish gave her a special status and allowed her to approach a Brownsville public school principal as an equal. As sociologist Peter Rose observed, second generation Jews discovered "often through bitter experience, that the accent, dress and manners learned in their neighborhoods precluded easy access into the American mainstream."[27]

Alfred Kazin's description of his and his immigrant parents' relationship to the public school as an American institution portrays the tensions that engulfed many second generation Jews in the 1920s:

> Our families and teachers seemed tacitly agreed that we were somehow to be a little ashamed of what we were. Yet it was always hard to say why this should be so. It was certainly not—in Brownsville—because we were Jews, or simply because we spoke another language at home, or were absent on our holy days. It was rather that a "refined," "correct," "nice" English was required of us at school that we did not naturally speak, and that our teachers could never be quite sure we would keep. This English was peculiarly the ladder of advancement. Every future young lawyer was known by it. Even the Communists and Socialists on Pitkin Avenue spoke it. It was bright and clean and polished. We were expected to show it off like a new pair of shoes. When the teacher sharply called a question out, then your name, you were expected to leap up, face the class, and eject those new words fluently off the tongue.

Not all Jewish youths acquiesced in the public school's program. Some expressed their hatred of the system by dropping out or stayed in school but failed to pass on to the higher grades. Others deliberately flouted school rules, becoming troublemakers.[28]

Since the struggle over the symbolic importance of language epitomized the conflict over Americanization in the public schools, a few concerned second generation Jews turned to Hebrew as a means of gaining legitimacy for Jewish culture within the public school. These middle-class Jews recognized the symbolic value of Hebrew. By championing it they sought to redefine the Jews' relationship to a Jewish language within the framework of the public schools. They also hoped to overcome the sense of embarrassment produced by the degradation of Yiddish language and Jewish culture. But instead of fostering a positive appreciation of Yiddish language and culture, linked in the minds of many middle-class second generation Jews with immigrant radicalism or orthodoxy or just plain foreign-ness, they turned to Hebrew. Speaking English at home to their children, these second generation Jews saw in Hebrew a symbol of a secular Jewish ethnicity compatible with Progressive Americanism. Their successful efforts to include Hebrew in the high school curriculum revealed the willingness of a public school system no longer bent on Americanization to accept Jewish culture.

The promotion of Hebrew depended on a definition of Americanism as an expression of democratic pluralism. In contrast to the melting pot image or the socialists' cosmopolitan vision of America, democratic pluralism derived from Progressive notions of nationalism. Specifically, democratic pluralism in its Jewish guise relied on the formulation of Zionism articulated by Louis Brandeis during the years of World War I. Brandeis argued that "there is no inconsistency between loyalty to America and loyalty to Jewry." The ancient Jewish teaching of "brotherhood and righteousness has, under the name of democracy and social justice, become the twentieth century striving of America." For Brandeis, these Jewish ideals, which were essentially American, found their noblest expression in Zionism. Brandeis stressed that "democracy is also a Zionist concept. Social justice is also a Zionist aim. Full and complete liberty is an essential of triumphant Zionism as it is the American ideal of the twentieth century." In his most famous aphorism, Brandeis declared that "to be good Americans we must be better Jews, and to be better Jews, we must become Zionists." Zionism embodied Jewish self-respect and represented Progressive values in action. Brandeis likened Zionism to other movements of national self-determination, arguing that "every Irish-American who contributed towards advancing home rule was a better man and a better American for the sacrifice he made." The Zionist endeavor linked American Jews to other national groups in the United States who sought to transplant American ideals to their national homelands. He expected American Jews to work for the realization of a glorious ideal in Palestine, which included a cultural regeneration linked to the rebirth of the Hebrew language. Hebrew became the spoken tongue of Jews in Palestine because, the Zionists argued, it was the repository of Jewish nationalism as well as the language of scripture. Moreover, the Hebraic heritage possessed universal significance: it was a formative element in western civilization. Thus advocates of Hebrew reinforced their parochial claim with a nonsectarian plea. Yiddish, the language of poverty and oppression in the diaspora, could not hope to compete with Hebrew in the regeneration of the Jewish people nor could it make the humanistic claim which Hebrew did, the Zionists felt. Such arguments, of course, ignored the ideas of many Yiddishist theorists associated with the Yiddish secular school movement. They saw Yiddish culture fostering the socialist regeneration of the Jewish working class.[29]

The fervent dedication to Hebrew of Progressive American Zionists also allowed them to sidestep the awkward issue of the Board of Education's explicit rejection of Yiddish. Instead they could present the Board with a means to recognize and sanction Jewish ethnic identity through the symbolically important medium of language by accepting Hebrew instruction.

The arguments developed in favor of Hebrew language instruction in the decade after World War I also relied on progressive educational theories and the concepts of cultural Zionism of the Hebrew writer Ahad Ha'am. A group of second generation Jews imbibed these theories in the years around the first World War when they simultaneously attended Columbia University's Teacher's College and the Jewish Theological Seminary's Teacher's Institute. The former, a newly established bastion of progressive education, introduced its pupils to John Dewey's theories of the individual in the community and the role of the public school as the socializing agent of democracy. The latter, recently revived under the guidance of a famous scholar, Solomon Schechter, imbued its students with a love of the Jewish people and a dedication to preserve the Jews' integrity while integrating them into American society. Under the guidance of such professors as Israel Friedlaender and Mordecai M. Kaplan at the Seminary and William Heard Kilpatrick at Columbia, these second generation Jews struggled to articulate a theory of acculturation which would allow them "to sacrifice nothing that is essential to Judaism, which shall not impoverish Judaism but enrich it." As Friedlaender urged, such a theory would also "take fully into account what the environment demands of us, and shall yet preserve and foster our Jewish distinctiveness and originality." Encouraged by their mentors, many pursued careers in Jewish education and a number of them became the leading Jewish educators of the 1920s and 1930s. These ranks included such men as Isaac Berkson, Alexander Dushkin, Samuel Dinin, Mordecai Soltes, Leo Honor, and Samuel Citron, and a number of women, among them Dvorah Lapson, Rebecca Brickner, and Libbie Berkson.[30]

Dewey's compelling vision of wholeness—of the individual and society's finding fulfillment in each other—inspired these educators to search for a way to preserve the Jews' cultural rights while enabling them to share in the common faith of America. Since the common faith, emerging from common experience and expressed in the common life, held America's diverse groups and individuals together while they pursued their individuality, American Jews needed to attend the public schools. "School and society were two sides of one coin." Democracy, as Dewey defined it, "is more than a form of government, it is primarily a mode of associated living, of conjoint communicated experience." As Berkson understood the problem in 1918, "without common interests crystallized into common purposes, without the means of communicating these purposes and relevant facts and ideas through a common language, without opportunity for general discussion of common problems and for participation in common tasks the democratic ideal of government by the people remains impossible of attainment." Certainly Jews did not want to be excluded from the commonality, and if this meant abandoning any thought of parochial education or even supernatural religion (both of which Dewey considered to be divisive factors and antithetical to the public school), then these educators were willing to accept such conditions.[31] But the more difficult task remained of making Jews a part of the commonality as Jews. Jewish educators rejected the dualism between home and school, between child and parent, between English and Yiddish. They wanted to build a strong bridge to American common experience while retaining intact their Jewish identity. Most focused their efforts on developing a system of supplementary Jewish religious education which would not detract from the centrality of the public school. But a few also strove to complement these efforts by modifying the content of the public schools' commonality and incorporating into it a distinctively Jewish, but nonetheless universal, aspect.

Kaplan especially pressed to make the public schools, high schools, and universities of America part of the "Jewish educative process." Arguing that democracy required Jews to live in two civilizations, Kaplan accepted public education as a necessary component of American life. However, he also felt that distinctively Jewish values could be incorporated into the public schools because "no culture can be complete without the principal cultural values of the Jewish civilization, especially those identified with the Bible." Although many Jewish educators supported Kaplan's forthright justification for using the public educational network to teach Jews about their Jewish culture, they shunned his nomination of the Bible. Other second generation Jews also rejected the idea of teaching the Bible as literature when it was proposed in New York City in the 1920s. The teachers' union mounted a vigorous campaign against substituting courses in religion for secular subjects. Kaplan acknowledged in 1934 that "the resistance which Jews everywhere display to the introduction of Bible reading into the schools is perfectly understandable and justified, because the spirit in which those who seek to make Bible reading a part of the school curriculum is sectarian." But Kaplan still felt that by opposing the teaching of the Bible as literature in the public schools, "the Jews allow themselves to be maneuvered into a position which prevents their own children from ever gaining a knowledge of the Bible. Obviously, Jewish children will not get to know the Bible, if they are to depend solely for that knowledge upon their religious or Hebrew schools." [32] If the Bible, subject to sectarian interpretation, were not sufficiently universal, what could Jews offer in its place?

In 1929 cultural Zionist Jewish educators chose Hebrew language instruction. As Berkson explained, to the Jew Hebrew "is an international language which symbolizes Jewish unity and through which he can communicate with Jews all over the world." For New York Jews who were rooted in Yiddish language and cul-

ture, Berkson arrogated to Hebrew one of the virtues of Yiddish.
But he went further. Hebrew linked the Jew "not only with the
Jewish past but with the Jewish present." And, he might have
added, with a Jewish future. Though Hebrew was "a national
possession," it managed "to break the barriers of time and to
cross the boundaries of countries. It has in itself," he concluded,
"a means for transcending the purely national consciousness in
the direction of the international and universal." In harking back
to the biblical, and hence universal, roots of Hebrew, Berkson
was legitimating for Jews simultaneously a Jewish and American
past. He also was engaging in a crucial second generation enterprise. By expressing ethnicity through its identification with
abstract values and ideals associated with the Hebrew language,
he symbolized for Jews their ancestral heritage.[33] Hebrew fulfilled the requirements of the common school and yet contributed
a Jewish component to its community. As a national language undeniably Jewish, it avoided religious controversy while it addressed the conflicts produced by Americanization. Unlike Yiddish, spoken by the Jewish masses in eastern Europe and New
York City, Hebrew evoked an idealized and distant Palestine.
Hebrew lacked any flesh and blood, working-class associations;
from the security of Flatbush, middle-class American Jews could
romanticize the distant Hebrew-speaking kibbutzim, ignoring
their socialism. Hebrew promised middle-class, second-generation
Jews self-esteem and an assertive secular Jewish identity. The acceptance of Hebrew by the Board of Education would validate
their progressive American Jewish synthesis.

The campaign for Hebrew as a language of instruction in the
city's public high schools began in 1929 when Superintendent of
Schools William O'Shea authorized the formation of clubs of a
semi-religious nature under faculty supervision. Jewish organizations immediately introduced into a number of schools extracurricular clubs led by local teachers. Small and scattered, linked
only tenuously to the public school structure, and dependent on
the willingness of faculty members to supervise them, the clubs
nevertheless gave Jewish students a chance to participate in Jewish activities under the aegis of the school system. In addition to
holding dances and other social events, the clubs sponsored
Jewish holiday celebrations, encouraged debates on current Jew-

ish issues, and promoted an appreciation of Jewish culture. A number of the organizations assisting the clubs (such as Avukah, a student Zionist organization, and the Menorah, a Jewish cultural society) encouraged Jewish students and parents to press for more formal recognition from the Board of Education. The Jewish Education Association and the Bureau of Jewish Education—agencies devoted largely to fostering supplementary Jewish religious education—cooperated in creating a committee to urge the Board to adopt Hebrew language instruction.[34]

The bipartisan committee, including such prominent Jewish spokesmen as Zionist leader Rabbi Stephen Wise, Bureau of Jewish Education director Samson Benderly, Democratic politician Nathan Straus Jr., Republican politician, and later president of the Board of Aldermen, Bernard Deutsch, Republican judge and Jewish philanthropist Otto Rosalsky, and Congressman Nathan Perlman took the cause of Hebrew instruction in the public high schools before the Board of Education in 1929. In a lengthy memorandum in 1930, Israel Chipkin, head of the Jewish Education Association, indicated to the Board the value of Hebrew language instruction and outlined some second-generation Jewish expectations from the public school. After emphasizing Hebrew's nonreligious aspects, Chipkin argued that "Democracy demands the recognition of all cultural values, and the free opportunity for all pupils whatever their origin, to elect the studies which prove of interest and value to them."[35]

Chipkin stressed a major concern of second generation Jews when he queried, "to what degree is the public school system helping these children towards a 'self-realization and towards the greatest contribution to society.'" The Board of Education needed to correct the injustices the public schools had perpetrated on the children of Jewish immigrants. Jewish educators, Chipkin wrote, were "repeatedly confronted with the physical and psychological maladjustments among Jewish youth which can be traced to the effects of public school education, which have estranged child from parent. The Jewish child," he continued, "has been given a new set of values and has grown up in ignorance of those of his forbears. He has frequently grown up not only to misunderstand his parents and the people from whence he sprung, but to dislike them and to consider them a burden." Hebrew in-

struction under public school auspices, it was hoped, would re-
store the Jewish child's respect for his heritage, respect for his
family, and respect for himself.[36]

The seven-member Board of Education, headed by George
Ryan, turned down the request in 1929. Although the committee
deliberately dissociated religion from any description of Jewish
ethnicity, defining it in national cultural terms (with frequent
comparisons to the Italian or German experience in the city), the
Board decided that Hebrew instruction was sectarian. Prompted
to reconsider by its Jewish member, Samuel Levy, an Orthodox
Jew and ardent supporter of Yeshiva College, in 1930 the Board
authorized two experimental classes in two new Brooklyn high
schools, Thomas Jefferson and Abraham Lincoln. The Board's
decision reflected the pervasiveness of progressive educational
thought. Under the impact of Dewey's teaching, foreign language
instruction changed focus in New York City. Foreign languages
became "vehicles for developing the student's social awareness
and for encouraging his appreciation of foreign cultures." In such
a context, "if the culture he is to study is that of his parents and
grandparents, so much the better," argued Jewish educator
Judah Lapson. "He comes more easily to accept both this culture
and himself, develops into a better integrated personality and,
hence, into a better citizen as well."[37]

The Board's choice of Lincoln and Jefferson as the site of the
experimental Hebrew classes underlined the type of influence second generation Jewish educators could exert on the public school
system. Two Jewish progressive educators (who were also
friends), Elias Lieberman and Gabriel Mason, served as principals of Jefferson and Lincoln respectively. Both came to the
newly constructed high schools with a sense of mission and both
shaped the schools in their image. Under Lieberman and Mason,
Jefferson and Lincoln rapidly acquired reputations as liberal,
progressive schools. Mason, for example, attracted to Lincoln
Jewish children from such bastions of progressive education as
the Brooklyn Ethical Culture school. Lieberman was an editor of
Puck, the literary editor of *The American Hebrew*, and editor of
numerous anthologies of poetry; he also wrote poetry and published several volumes of verse. Mason, too, loved poetry, along
with music and chess. He came to Lincoln after teaching on the

Lower East Side and combined a passion for philosophy with a
dedication to American intellectual figures. He published two volumes on Spinoza and edited a book devoted to his favorite figures, *Great American Liberals*. Fond of acting, Mason rarely let a
school production pass by without taking a part. "He would appear on stage, a ruddy and rotund man with dark, bushy eye-
brows and an ever-present circle of smoke overhead from his pipe
or cigar." Both men sympathized with the cause of Hebrew and,
by implication, Jewish ethnic recognition. They encouraged
parents to let their children attend the experimental Hebrew
classes. Lieberman opened Jefferson's doors to a large educational rally for Hebrew. Sponsored by the League of Jewish
Youth, the rally attracted almost 5000 parents who came to hear
Zionist orator Charles Cowen and Joseph Bragin, principal of the
Hebrew High School. Such efforts led the Board of Education to
declare the experiment in teaching Hebrew a success after one
probationary semester. In 1931 Hebrew entered the high school
curriculum as an elective subject.[38]

The symbolic success of Hebrew language instruction before
the Board of Education contrasted with the failure of claims advanced in behalf of Yiddish. In 1930 the recently founded Yiddish
Culture Society tried to rescue Yiddish from the public school on-
slaught. The Society lobbied unsuccessfully to have Yiddish
taught in the public schools. Yiddish language instruction would
have bridged the gap between home and school, but Yiddishists
could not rally sufficient political support for their cause. The
Yiddish school movement had been divided into bitterly opposed
right and left wings since 1926, and the creation in 1930 of the International Workers Order closed out any possibility of Yiddishist
solidarity. Contention between Communist and Socialist Yiddishists doomed any attempt to convince a wary Board of Education of the educational value of Yiddish. The active support of
such a Bronx public school principal as Dr. Hirdansky of P.S. 4
made little difference without effective external lobbying. Ambivalent about their own *mama-loshen*, Jewish politicians and educators in the city shield away from promoting Yiddish before the
Board of Education. Democratic pluralism in the public school
system, a delicate plant in 1930, could risk the taint neither of
radicalism nor of immigrant foreignness.[39]

The middle-class Progressive version of pluralism adopted by Zionist Jewish educators accommodated the promotion of a secular Jewish ethnic identity under public school auspices. But this secular Jewish ethnicity, legitimated by Hebrew language instruction, did not challenge the class bias of the public school. It did succeed in integrating Jewish values into the public schools' pantheon of American middle-class virtues, and in so doing undercut the grounds for Americanization programs conceived as Anglicization. "Americanization was simultaneously a class and an ethnic battle," Gorelick argues. "The 'leaders' were not only asserting the superiority of Western 'civilization' against 'Oriental' outlandishness; they were expressing the contempt of investment bankers, national civic figures and international merchants for petty traders, neighborhood customer peddlers, and tailors." By tying Jewish ethnicity to American middle-class values, second generation Jews resolved the conflict endemic to Jewish immigrant life produced by Americanization.[40]

The promotion of Hebrew permitted Jews to accede to the general ground rules of Americanization while laying the cornerstone of a new ethnic Jewishness. Second generation Jews yielded to the derogation of a perceived lower-class, foreign, "racial" Jewishness. The cooperative decision not to teach Yiddish in the public schools symbolically sealed this understanding between Jews and Gentile society. But by nominating Hebrew in place of Yiddish, the second generation symbolically transformed the assimilationist slide from Yiddish to American English into an affirmation of ethnic identity. Hebrew was not entirely religious, but neither was it as secular as its advocates insisted. It was something new, an ethnic insignia.

Significantly, the victory of Hebrew remained largely a symbolic one. Ten years after its initial acceptance by the Board of Education a mere 3,000 students were studying Hebrew from 33 teachers in eleven high schools and three junior high schools. Only 4 percent of the total number of Jewish high school students enrolled in Hebrew classes in 1940. And most of these students preferred to take Hebrew to fulfill their two-year language requirement, studying French or German for the three-year sequence required by most colleges. Yet by successfully lobbying for Hebrew's inclusion in the public school curriculum, Jews won establishment endorsement of a symbol which associated the new American Jew with an ethnic identity of unimpeachable credentials. Hebrew in the public schools helped anchor American Jewishness in precisely the mode most acceptable to the American civil religion. A Zionism of sentiment rooted the Jew in a religiously authenticated secular identity—American but not Christian.[41]

Yet as a secular national language, Hebrew could not help second generation Jews eradicate the professions of public piety in the schools. Second generation Jews failed to fight Christian observances, which grew adventitiously throughout the fabric of public education, as successfully as they advocated Hebrew. The subject of religion eluded any communal consensus. Unable to forge a broadly representative committee such as the one supporting Hebrew language instruction, second generation Jews of necessity acquiesced in public school celebrations of Christian holidays. At most the Board of Education granted token responses to Jewish pressures for public school respect for their religion. The Board recommended local prerogatives, which would reflect the pupil population in a neighborhood, but avoided any general policy statements.

Throughout the 1920s, Jews persistently pushed the Board of Education to recognize the Jewish calendar in its scheduling. In 1922 the Federation of Jewish Women's Organizations requested an end to Friday night graduations. The Board demurred, leaving the decision to the local district superintendents and public school principals. But Superintendent of Schools William Ettinger agreed to urge the local authorities to choose the night for graduation carefully to avoid offending the religious sensibilities of any large group in the neighborhood. This policy of localism allowed Jews to obtain some acceptance of their religious differences, but it left the issue of public school policy untouched. In 1928, for example, Rabbi Max Reichler of the Beth Sholom People's Temple delivered the commencement address at the Monday night graduation of New Utrecht High School at the Brooklyn Academy of Music. Yet earlier that year Rabbi Herbert Goldstein, president of the Union of Orthodox Jewish Congregations, had to petition the Board of Education to change the Easter vacation schedule to begin on the first day of Passover rather than on Good Friday.

Although the Board agreed to the change, it established no policy on the Jewish holidays. Two years later Jewish attempts to gain recognition for Rosh Hashanah and Yom Kippur failed.[42]

Religious issues involving the principle of the separation of church and state evoked near unanimity among New York City Jews in the 1920s. Jews consistently opposed the introduction of any religious activities into the public schools. They spoke out against released time for religious instruction, teaching the Bible in the public schools, or even daily reading of the Ten Commandments. The *American Hebrew*, the major Jewish-English weekly with a Reform inclination, rejected the latter for the interesting reason that the Decalogue "contains at least one injunction the constant mention of which is sure to arouse prurient and morbid curiousity." Jews generally did not accept the popular American attitude toward the Bible "as the primary source book for spiritual inspiration and moral guidance." Like Catholics, they usually saw the Bible as a specific document related to particular religious beliefs rather than as a universal moral and religious book.[43]

While Jews almost unanimously fought any action which might be construed as an entering wedge of religion in the public school, they rarely attempted to remove or modify school celebrations of Christmas or Easter. This is ironic because in 1906 the Orthodox, encouraged by their Yiddish mouthpiece, the *Morgen Zhurnal*, led a successful school strike to protest Christmas celebrations in the schools. Approximately 25,000 Lower East Side students stayed at home supporting Orthodox demands that these "unAmerican" activities be eliminated. But by the 1920s Jewish religious leaders could not agree on the significance of Christmas. Without a consensus on the holiday's meaning, they could not develop a programmatic response to its celebration in the public schools. Some, like Stephen Wise, reform rabbi of the Free Synagogue, thought Christmas had "become a secular rather than a religious festival." He saw no point in asking "my fellow-Jews to refrain from the notice or observance in a secular and non-religious fashion of Christmas. It certainly cannot harm Jews to get presents on Christmas or . . . to give presents," he declared in a Christmas sermon. Wise only objected to those Jews "who overdo Christmas and leave Chanukah undone." Others, like

Israel Chipkin, argued that Christmas was not at all a national holiday like Thanksgiving but a sectarian one. He felt Jewish children should not participate in Christmas celebrations. An editorial in the *Jewish Forum*, an Orthodox monthly, agreed with Chipkin and urged Jews to complain to public school principals about Christmas celebrations. Additionally, the *Jewish Forum* suggested Jews substitute Chanukah celebrations in public schools where Jewish pupils were a majority. Isaac Bildersee, a district superintendent of schools in Brownsville, objected vehemently to both Chanukah and Christmas celebrations. "He unleased a storm of controversy over the issue as to whether or not Hanukkah songs should be sung in the schools along with Christmas carols." Advocating a rigorous separation of church and state, Bildersee wanted to eliminate both.[44]

Second generation Jews' inability to generate a consensus on Christmas reflected their minority status as well as their ambivalent relationship to Christians in the public schools. Although Jewish demographic and occupational trends changed the social structure of Jewish neighborhood public schools, Jews often failed to perceive the Gentile pupils in the school. For someone like Paul Jacobs, who "grew up, nominally Jewish on Sundays and on the Jewish holidays, . . . being Jewish didn't make much of an impression on me or my friends." In retrospect Jacobs admitted that he "must have known many children who were not Jewish" at his Grand Concourse public school, for he remembered that "while I was in the first grades, I would drop my eyes to steal furtive glances at the Christian boys when they stood at the urinal next to me, for then I was still curious about how a foreskin looked." But Jacobs's awareness of otherness focused on "the Catholic boys and girls who attended parochial school." In fact, Catholic parochial schools siphoned off large numbers of non-Jewish pupils and helped to produce the relatively high percentage of Jewish students in public schools in such new neighborhoods as the Grand Concourse and Flatbush. Statistics from 1930 and 1934 show this contrast. In 1930 the eight Grand Concourse Catholic parochial schools enrolled almost 5,000 children; in 1934, the public schools' register revealed that there were 24,000 students, of whom roughly 18,000 were Jewish. In Flatbush in 1930, five local Catholic schools listed 4,000 pupils on their rolls; in 1934, there were 24,000 students in the neighborhood public schools, including approximately 15,000 Jews.[45] Jewish students thus often failed to perceive their Gentile peers in the public school, having associated Christians as a group with the Catholics in parochial schools.

Intraschool stratification made it easier for Jews to ignore their Christian fellow pupils. Schoolmates were not always classmates. "Anyone familiar with the social geography of a place like Flatbush," writer Ronald Sanders observed, "does not need any explanation as to why, in certain parts of it, such a random sampling among its brighter children as I had unwittingly made should have turned out to be composed almost entirely of this one ethnic group." Sanders discovered that Jewish-Gentile pupil differences correlated with attitudes toward academic achievement. Thus he found himself "growing up within a social environment mainly consisting of bright, high-spirited middle-class Jewish kids who were determined to make their mark upon the world and perhaps improve it a little in the process."[46]

With the confusion over the meaning of Christmas and with Jewish awareness of Christian otherness focused on Catholics attending parochial schools, the public schools in Jewish neighborhoods encountered little effective opposition to the celebration of Christmas and Easter. The schools continued to celebrate both holidays throughout the 1920s and 1930s. "There were no Christmas-Chanukah festivals when I went to grammar school," Jacobs remembered, "and even in our home Christmas was a more important holiday than Chanukah." Jacobs acknowledged that he "always hung up Christmas stockings, although we didn't have a tree." Sanders, whose awareness of the religious significance of Christmas was tempered by his parents' intermarriage, recalled that, "Christmas was celebrated far more equivocally than Thanksgiving by us—or at least by my Jewish friends." In his Flatbush public school, he continued,

> more than half of the students . . . were Jews, but there was not yet a glimmer of . . . the idea of giving equal time to Jewish and Christian holiday symbolism, much less of excusing the Jewish kids from singing praises to Christmas. It was only years later that I learned of how many of my friends had sung:

Oh, come, let us adore Him,
Mm—mm the Lord.[47]

Despite the anguish to some Jewish students caused by the
public schools' Christian character and rigid structure emphasizing the achievement of high grades, second generation Jews often
succeeded in making the public schools in their local neighborhoods responsive to Jewish concerns. The changes introduced
in the schools' personnel and the Jews' achievement of middle-
class status helped modify public school policy. As poor immigrants, most Jews confronted the public school as an alien, albeit local American institution. As middle-class Americans, many
Jews sensed the public school's potential as an agent of Jewish education. Throughout the interwar decades articulate second generation Jews tried to transform the public school, to make it
amenable to Jewish values. In the process Jews jettisoned many of
the attitudes toward public school espoused by their immigrant
parents and adopted new ones reflecting their middle-class standing. Thus, when they asked the public school to fulfill its legen-
dary promise of social mobility, second generation Jews pressed
the school to include more students on its educational ladder, not
to revise the ladder's structure. Similarly, in urging that the public schools discard Americanization construed as Anglicization,
they recast the issue of language instruction to sidestep the challenge of a socialist, immigrant Yiddish culture. Finally, the con-
frontation with the public schools over the Christian character of
their public piety spurred second generation Jews to develop Jewish religious practices to parallel Christian ones. But in the 1920s
and 1930s Jews found it difficult to promote Chanukah with
Christmas, especially at the expense of the latter. Indeed,
Christmas remained the biggest stumbling block to the synthesis
second generation Jews evolved.[48]

Through the simultaneous modification of the school and
their homes, second generation Jews succeeded in developing a
continuity of behavior and values. As parents and teachers they
changed their children's schools from agents of Americanization
into instruments of democratic pluralism. The presence of Jewish
teachers clothed with the authority of a pervasive American institution provided significant Jewish American role models for Jew-

ish students. A Jewish teacher who spouted Yiddish phrases while sporting a green tie in honor of St. Patrick's Day visibly embodied a concept of democratic pluralism Jews could appreciate. Indeed, as Jewish teachers came to teach Jewish students under the auspices of the public school system, and especially in the high schools, the schools began to foster a secular Jewish American identity.[49]

By 1938 even the Board of Education was prepared to support pluralism in the public schools. It resolved that "to renew and reaffirm our faith in American democracy," the public schools needed to devote assemblies to "making the children of our nation aware of the contributions of all races, and nationalities to the growth and development of American democracy." The Board emphasized the American context of ethnic group activity and stressed the pivotal role of democracy in encouraging expressions of pluralism. By contrast, sixteen years earlier an eager Commissioner of Accounts, David Hirschfield, had drawn only bemused publicity when he announced an investigation of public school American history textbooks because of neglect of American heroes of Jewish, Dutch, Swedish, Irish, and African descent. Hirschfield's probe came too soon. By the late 1930s, with the overt anti-Semitism of the Christian Front spreading from the city's streets to its schools, the Board of Education needed to define the public school as a bastion of tolerance.[50]

The Board of Education's commitment to democratic pluralism legitimated Jewish secular ethnicity. By 1940 second generation Jews had succeeded in redefining Jewish ethnicity as an aspect of American middle-class life. A middle-class mode of identity, Jewish ethnicity belonged inside the public schools. As Greer observed, "the quest for cultural pluralism . . . confirms the class patterns in American society." Although Greer considers "the cultural pluralism of which school people have been so proud" to be a "phenomenon of class" and hence "not the successful defense of variously indigenous people against homogenization," for New York Jews such middle-class pluralism reinforced their sense of ethnic uniqueness.[51] The public school's acceptance of secular middle-class Jewish ethnicity enabled Jews to identify with this foremost agent of American democracy.

Second generation Jews narrowed the gap between home and

school and overcame the bifurcated attitude toward education which had characterized immigrant Jewish experience. Second generation Jews looked on the public schools not only as instruments of social mobility—which they proved to be, despite the debilitating effects of the Depression—but as part of the American Jewish educational process. With pluralism in the public schools, Jews did not need to turn to Jewish schools for an antidote to the attitudes fostered in the public schools. Jewish schools increasingly provided the religious or ideological beliefs which the public schools could not teach, ideas which were seen to enhance democratic pluralism. And for the minority who cared, even Jewish religion could be harmonized with the pluralist, secular school synthesis.

5

The evidence suggests an absence of religious as distinct from ethnic commitment on the part of most nominally Orthodox immigrants to the United States. Thus, the rise of Conservative Judaism and secularism in American Jewish life did not entail a decision to opt out of traditional religion. It was, rather, a decision to substitute new social and cultural mores for the older ones, which had been intermingled with certain ritual manifestations."

Charles S. Liebman, "Orthodoxy in American Jewish Life," *American Jewish Year Book* (Philadelphia: Jewish Publication Society, 1965), p. 30.

From Chevra
to Center

Facing the public schools, the preeminent symbol of American culture in the neighborhood, stood the synagogues. Jewish religion, institutionalized in the synagogue, epitomized American Judaism. Although the synagogue enrolled only a minority of New York City Jews as members, lack of formal affiliation with one did not destroy its symbolic importance. It served as the Jewish home which Jews conveniently could take for granted and ignore. A neighborhood synagogue announced not merely the presence of Jews, but their commitment to group survival. Activities carried out under its auspices bore the stamp of Jewish authenticity. As Marshall Sklare observed, "the local synagogue becomes the Jewish badge of identification to the neighborhood at large."[1] In America Judaism became associated preeminently with the synagogue; religiously observant Jews joined a congregation. Yet as the repository of traditional Jewish religious culture, the synagogue did not remain an unchanging institution. Immigrant Jews transformed the traditional synagogue when they transplanted it in New York and second generation Jews remodeled it once again when they moved to new neighborhoods.

The synagogue's changing character reflected the redefinition of Jewish ethnicity wrought by the second generation. In the United States, voluntary religious affiliation also articulated class and ethnicity. Under the impact of American conditions, eastern European Jews introduced class and ethnic concerns into the synagogue. As observant Jews adjusted their religion to their new situation, first as poor immigrants and then as middle-class Americans, the synagogue progressively embodied their ethnic concerns. The changing context of Judaism, from immigrant chevra

to synagogue center, modified the content of its ethnicity. Yet the
American synagogue's enduringly ethnic character also underscored the centrality of religion for Jewish identity in America.
Even as Jews Americanized the synagogue into a synagogue
center, they posited it as a bulwark against assimilation. The
synagogue center's program expressed the intention of second
generation Jews to perpetuate Jewish group life under religious
auspices and to delimit their own acculturation.[2]

Second generation Jews built their synagogue center as the
antithesis of the immigrant chevra. A generation removed from
the Jewish *shul* of eastern Europe, they saw the immigrant type of
synagogue as the embodiment of traditional Judaism. Yet the immigrant chevra itself represented an innovation in response to
American conditions. East European Jews arriving in New York
City took advantage of the voluntary character of American religious life to create a new type of Jewish religious institution.
Rejecting the upper-middle-class religious synthesis of American
Reform Jews, Jewish immigrants developed their own version of
the shtetl *shul*. The immigrants' synagogue catered to their social
welfare and religious needs; it fostered "friendly ties among
former neighbors" and kept alive "local customs and precious
personal memories" of ancestral homes. "That the new immigrants founded countless small synagogues almost immediately
upon arrival was not in itself evidence of religiosity," argues social scientist Charles Liebman. "If the function of the synagogue
was primarily for worship there was no need for such multiplication whereas if the primary purpose of the synagogue was to meet
the social and cultural needs of small groups originating in the
same European community, the multiplication is more understandable." An organization of *landslayt*—of Jews who emigrated
from the same town or locality—the immigrant chevra defined
ethnicity "based very strictly on kinship and shtetl of origin."
While the chevra manifestly was "organized primarily for religious purposes and always constitutes itself as a congregation,"
it subordinated these functions to ethnic needs. Liebman characterizes these synagogues as "social forums and benevolent societies adapted to the requirements of poor, unacculturated people."
The chevra's "meticulous preservation of the traditional Orthodox service" articulated immigrant Jews' ethnic ties with their

place of origin. Abraham Cahan's prototypical immigrant, David Levinsky, "spent many an evening at the Antomir Synagogue, reading Talmud passionately. This would bring me in touch with my old home," Levinsky admitted. The chevra of *landslayt* served the needs of immigrant Jewish men and expressed their religious culture.[3]

In Brownsville, "the Jerusalem of America," the chevra emerged as the norm. All of Brownsville's synagogues followed Orthodox Jewish ritual and varied little from each other in their general manner of worship. Despite the pressures of earning a living at a time when work on Saturday was still required, a survey of 34 chevras in Brownsville in 1916 found that all of them barred a deliberate violator of the Sabbath and holidays from membership. These chevras provided a place of worship for a daily *minyan* in the morning and evening as well as on Sabbaths and festivals. Since Jewish law prohibited extensive traveling or the use of vehicles for transportation on the Sabbath, observant Jews lived within easy walking distance of their synagogue. Nevertheless, many chevra constitutions also reflected the impact of American middle-class decorum in matters of public prayer. The Kletzker society, which maintained its own synagogue building, insisted that: "Every member is required to conduct himself quietly, and not to wander about the synagogue during services. During such services he must also refrain from conversation with others." And it added: "It is up to the trustees to see that this rule is enforced to the letter."[4]

The majority of Brownsville's synagogues lacked any aesthetic attractiveness. Only the larger congregations maintained a separate structure. The smaller ones generally met in such rented quarters as basements, halls, or lofts. Some chevras conducted worship services in the homes of rabbis or private Hebrew teachers. Of 71 synagogues surveyed in Brownsville in 1926, only 20 had their own buildings. Moreover, the Brownsville Jews who supported synagogues did not lavish money on their physical appearance. Small synagogues dotted the neighborhood, and few streets were without at least one; many blocks housed two or three. The synagogue's pervasive presence contributed to Brownsville's Jewish character, making the neighborhood into a visibly Jewish enclave.[5]

Yet Brownsville's synagogues served immigrant Jewish men
almost exclusively. "The old type of synagogue that prevail [*sic*]
in this district," noted a survey of Brownsville in 1925, "have the
usual structures devoted to worship primarily and at times to
religious instruction for the children. They offer few or no attractive facilities or activities for Jewish youth." Many synagogues
conducted study groups in the Talmud, but they rarely sponsored
supplementary Hebrew schools for the children. In his memoir,
Alfred Kazin juxtaposed Brownsville's synagogues to its movie
houses. Like the movies, the synagogue

> was dark enough, but without any illusion or indulgence for a boy;
> and it had a permanently stale smell of snuff, of vinegar, of beaten
> and scarred wood in the pews, of the *rebbetsin*'s cooking from the
> kitchen next door. . . . old as the synagogue was, old as it looked
> and smelled in its every worn and wooden corner, it seemed to me
> even older through its ties to that ancestral world I had never seen.

However, boys regularly appeared in the synagogues to celebrate
their Bar Mitzvah, and with them came their mothers. A Sabbath
survey of Brownsville's synagogues in 1926 discovered approximately 5,000 people attending services. Of these 900 were women
and 560 were boys aged ten to sixteen. These participants in the
rites of passage came to the synagogue only occasionally. But for
their members, Brownsville's synagogues reinforced social bonds.
Jewish customs and holidays provided occasions for festivities and
social gatherings. Members rejoiced together upon the completion
of a tractate of Talmud by the synagogue's study group or they
enjoyed a *kiddush* of liquor and cake on the Sabbath.[6]
 Because of the personal *landslayt* ties which brought religious Jewish immigrants into a particular synagogue, there was
no need for ideological unanimity among members. The chevras
expressed their purposes in their constitutions: to unify all
members to live in a spirit of brotherhood, to support a member
fallen on bad days, and to bury members according to Jewish law.
"To die, or not to die," philosophized one chevra president.
"Each person strives not to 'die away,' strives that his memory
may survive on this earth as long as possible." Thus the chevra
filled religious and social welfare needs through membership in a
meaningful community. What secular Jewish immigrants found in

landsmanshaftn and fraternal lodges, religiously observant immigrants obtained in their chevras. Members and their families
received sick benefits, including the nursing services of a night at-
tendant or cash relief. Upon the death of a member, the chevra
helped to pay funeral expenses, contributing to cover the cost of a
hearse, a tombstone allowance, and a cash payment to the sur-
vivor. Many chevras also offered interest-free loans to members
to help them in emergencies.[7]

Modest membership fees, ranging from six to twelve dollars
annually, covered more than just the cost of upkeep of the synagogue; they also helped to support the chevra's social welfare programs. The chevras raised extra funds for charitable purposes
through High Holiday appeals, the sale of seats and honors during worship, and at special occasions in the lives of members. So
important were the Rosh Hashanah and Yom Kippur appeals that
Congregation Ohab Shalom, one of Brownsville's largest and oldest synagogues, taxed members who absented themselves on the
High Holidays an extra three dollars to make up for the money
they would have contributed if present.[8]

Brownsville reflected a pattern of Jewish religious behavior
characteristic of New York Jews. Its synagogues regularly attracted a mere 8 percent of the neighborhood's adult Jewish
males. Most Brownsville Jews did not follow Jewish religious practices and ignored the synagogue and its activities. Only on Rosh
Hashanah and Yom Kippur did Brownsville Jews flock to the synagogues. On those holidays, Brownsville's synagogues could not accommodate all worshippers, so individual rabbis and cantors
transformed movie theaters and private halls into makeshift synagogues. In these improvised quarters they conducted services for
a modest fee to the overflow crowds.[9]

Religious leadership devolved upon both rabbis and laymen.
The rabbi (in most Brownsville synagogues which could afford to
hire one) acted as judge and communal arbiter, counselor to
members on religious issues, and teacher of classes in Talmud. In
some synagogues rabbis preached sermons (in Yiddish; prayers
were recited in Hebrew), an American innovation. Rabbis' salaries tended to be meager, and occasionally they received no
stipend at all from their congregations. Most rabbis supplemented
their income by supervising *kashruth*, performing marriages and

divorces, and conducting other religious ceremonies. Prominent Brownsville rabbis who served the larger synagogues received a more substantial and secure income, and could afford to partici- pate in Jewish communal affairs. Rabbi Morris Tomashev of Con- gregation Beth Israel, for example, helped to edit a monthly jour- nal of Hebrew law, belonged to the executive board of the Union of Orthodox Rabbis, and served as president of the Rabbinical Board of Brownsville and East New York.

Laymen supervised the synagogue's mundane affairs and led the worship services. Since congregations usually consisted of no more than 100 members, conversation sufficed to convey informa- tion and carry on the chevra's activities. Indeed, often only a few individuals constituted the synagogue's executive board and de- cided whatever matters of import arose regarding the expenditure of money. A devotion to Yiddish underscored the chevra's *lands- layt*, particularist ethnicity and suggested its leaders' concern for their future control of the chevra. Many constitutions stipulated Yiddish as the language of communication as an indication of the commitment to *Yidishkayt*.[10]

In 1914 Brownsville Jews established the first synagogue, a Conservative one, to depart substantially from the chevra pat- tern. Located on the outskirts of the neighborhood at Lincoln Place and Rochester Avenue, Temple Petach Tikvah appealed for members through its nonreligious programs. It sponsored a Men's Club and a Sisterhood, and tried to attract children through clubs and a Junior Congregation. The Junior Congregation con- ducted Friday night services and social affairs, and promoted cul- tural activities. In 1919 a branch of Young Israel, a modern Or- thodox movement, opened in Brownsville. It, too, expanded the range of synagogue activities. Young Israel held occasional dances at hotels and offered classes in Jewish history, philosophy, ethics, and music. However, most Brownsville synagogues declined to compete for young members and women, or to expand their pro- gram. While Zionist activity flourished in Brownsville, Zionists only occasionally channeled appeals for funds or members through the synagogues. Similarly, local politicians made it a practice to visit the larger synagogues, but most Brownsville syna- gogues refused to participate directly in such activities.[11]

The establishment of Temple Petach Tikvah and Young

Israel in Brownsville augured a change in the synagogue structure
which would culminate in the synagogue centers of second generation Jews. As they moved to new neighborhoods, second generation Jews sought to transform the synagogue once again. They did
not recognize the immigrant chevra as a novel American variant
of a traditional form, but saw it as old world orthodoxy incar-
nate.

If the chevra were a foreign institution, second generation
Jews would build an American synagogue that would answer their
middle-class needs while ignoring the social welfare activities
required by working-class immigrants. Second generation Jews
would design a synagogue center that would serve families, not
immigrant men. Rabbis of such centers would become communal
leaders, largely leaving behind the intensive scholarship of their
immigrant predecessors. In place of *landslayt* ethnicity and its
ties to *Yidishkayt*, second generation Jews would substitute a secular form of ethnic identification linked to American culture and
the English language. Instead of creating an institution which
looked back longingly on a world left behind, they would build a
synagogue aggressively oriented toward the neighborhood and its
concerns. Rather than closing the door on most Jewish communal
activities, the synagogue center would welcome as many organizations under its roof as possible. Most importantly, cultural Zionism would find a home there. Second generation Jews would lay
down the rules on how to start (and end) an event: with the sing-
ing of "Hatikva" and the National Anthem.[12] As they developed
these changes of content and structure, second generation Jews
reconstructed the synagogue into an institutional bulwark of middle-class ethnicity, but no longer an ethnicity based on town of
origin.

Committed to building the symbolic Jewish institution in a
new neighborhood like Flatbush, second generation Jews first
faced the problem of coping with the relatively dispersed character of the population. Under such circumstances they saw "a
burning need to provide the community with an institution which
would do something more than attract Flatbush Jews to the Synagogue three times a year." As Israel H. Levinthal, rabbi of the pioneer Brooklyn Jewish Center argued, "if the Synagogue as a
Beth Hatefilah has lost its hold upon the masses, some institution

would have to be created that could and would attract the people
so that the group consciousness of the Jew might be maintained."
Rabbis and laymen alike found that "social opportunities . . .
to promote the commingling of the various Jewish families"
answered both Jewish group needs and institutional requirements.
According to the anonymous historian of the Jewish Communal
Center of Flatbush, the decision "to erect a type of building
which would satisfy the needs of adult and youth . . . gradually
developed into an idea that a Jewish center should include all activities, be they Jewish, religious, intellectual or recreational."
"The name center," Levinthal wrote with a touch of irony,
worked "magic with thousands who would not be attracted to the
place if we simply called it Synagogue or Temple." Thus the synagogue center was born.[13]

Second generation Jews wanted to create an institution to ensure ethnic group survival. Their financial need to have Jews use
the synagogue regularly complemented their concern to find a
Jewish locale for their secular activities. By bringing these activities under the auspices of the primary Jewish institution, the synagogue, second generation Jews succeeded in domesticating their
American values. Samuel Rottenberg, president of the Brooklyn
Jewish Center for its first ten years, stressed this coincidence. The
Jewish Center, he wrote, "will show the world the ideal that you
can be a Jew and enjoy life, and will express in everything you do
that the same thing can be done in a Jewish way." The movement
drew Jews committed to Judaism who wanted Jewish religion to
nourish their middle-class familial ties.[14]

Harry Seinfel, one of the founders of the Brooklyn Jewish
Center, listed first the aim of uniting "the fathers and mothers of
Israel with their children" in the dedication number of the Cen-
ter's bulletin. The other purposes enhanced this primary focus:

> to provide a common meeting place, under Jewish auspices—for all
> of the members and their families—to give the best in spiritual
> guidance—to establish a place for recreation and play—to encour-
> age thought—to help the members in the art of self-expression—to
> bring out the best in each of us.

"In all," he concluded, "to reinterpret Jewish life so that it may
continue to be a living force."[15]

Indeed, the ideological justification for the reconstruction of the synagogue actually predated the heyday of the synagogue center. Although he influenced directly few of the laymen who threw themselves into fund raising and synagogue building, Rabbi Mordecai M. Kaplan first articulated the concept. "One of the earliest among his group to study the works of Durkheim, Cooley, and other social scientists with care," writes Sklare, Kaplan integrated "a functionalist approach with his pragmatic leanings." Using sociological concepts Kaplan argued that "whatever helps to produce creative social interaction among Jews belongs to the category of Jewish religion, because it contributes to the salvation of the Jew." In an article in the *American Hebrew* in 1918 Kaplan proposed four activities for the synagogue center: worship, study, social service, and recreation. In Kaplan's view, the synagogue could not afford the luxury of religious specialization in America. Because the traditional ghetto no longer existed, he argued, the synagogue had to provide a center for sociability and recreation. Because America was an open, democratic society, Jews needed to implement their ideas of social justice and to work for the upbuilding of Palestine as a spiritual center through the synagogue. "To live Judaism as a civilization," Kaplan wrote in 1934, "is not only to pray as a Jew, but to work and to play as a Jew, that is, to carry on, as a Jew, activities which answer to fundamental human wants."[16]

Kaplan saw the synagogue center as a Jewish neighborhood institution, by which he meant that it "must not be monopolized by a particular congregation. It must belong to the entire Jewish community," he stressed, and "all Jews to whom it is accessible should resort [to it] for all religious, cultural, social and recreational purposes." Kaplan's vision resembled some of the aims of the Protestant institutional church, specifically its intention to abolish the distinction between the religious and the secular and to serve the entire community, regardless of class, through its social services. "This mode of reintegrating church and community," writes historian Robert Cross, "became celebrated as the institutional church."[17]

Using Jewish criteria, Kaplan legitimated such a synthesis for the synagogue. As Liebman observes, Kaplan expressed in his philosophy of Reconstructionism the folk religion of the American

Mordecai M. Kaplan, theoretician of the Jewish center movement. *Courtesy of the Reconstructionist Rabbinical College.*

Jewish masses. According to Liebman, "Reconstructionism comes closer than any other . . . school of thought to articulating the meaning of Judaism for American Jews." As a teacher at the Jewish Theological Seminary, Kaplan also reached other rabbis, who often served as leaders for the new synagogue centers. Not content to delineate ideology, Kaplan attempted to put his ideas into practice in 1918, when he founded the model Jewish Center on West 86th Street in Manhattan. Kaplan's philosophy filtered through the Jewish Center, although he left it over a policy dispute with the membership before the big spurt of synagogue building began.[18]

Middle-class Jews moving to the Grand Concourse and Flatbush, neighborhoods which contained the largest number of synagogue centers in New York City by 1930, wanted the synagogue to serve their own religious, educational, social, and recreational needs. In fact, a number of synagogue center presidents resented the philanthropic energies directed at improving the lot of poor immigrant Jews. They frankly voiced the sentiment that "the New York Jewish community, up to recent years, has devoted too much attention to the needs of a small dependent group entirely to the neglect of those normal Jewish families who make up the New York Jewish population." These second generation Jews modified Kaplan's vision of social service and its assumption that synagogue center membership, reflecting a neighborhood in which both workers and bourgeoisie lived, would cross class boundaries. Thus lay leaders dismissed one of the key characteristics of the institutional church in favor of the single class community accepted by the neighborhood church.[19]

Defining the Jewish community as coextensive with the middle-class neighborhood, the synagogue center departed both from the traditional synagogue, "a place of worship for all—rich and poor, educated and uneducated," and the immigrant chevra. Instead of the *landslayt* ethnicity of the chevra, the synagogue centers posited an American ethnicity rooted in the neighborhood. "Because most synagogues . . . are neighborhood institutions," sociologist Eli Ginzberg observed, "and because neighborhoods tend to differ sharply from each other on the basis of average family income, radical class differences can be found" separating one congregation from another. The lay leaders ignored Kaplan's vision of a multi-class Jewish community and the corresponding concept of social service as an integral part of the synagogue center's program.[20]

The growing synagogue center movement signaled the maturity of a new generation of local Jewish leaders. Previously these Jews "had occupied no role in Jewish communal leadership." The rapid construction of synagogue centers announced their "economic and social arrival." Many synagogue centers "owe their origin to an augmentation of the Jewish middle class since the war," observed a contemporary survey. This group, "who had not heretofore supported large-scale philanthropic programs," turned "to the erection of synagogue centers as a mode of community expression."[21]

Jewish community centers, the hallmark of second generation Jews' social and economic arrival in smaller communities, also took a back seat to the synagogue centers. The large numbers of Jews in New York reduced the need for cooperative efforts to create community centers but stimulated the growth of religiously diverse synagogue centers. Middle-class, second generation Jews devoted their money and energies to establishing synagogue centers. They chose to identify as Jews through contributions supporting synagogue centers instead of Y's, settlement houses, or community centers. They rejected the philanthropic model offered by their German Jewish predecessors as decisively as had immigrant Jews. Few second generation Jews combined membership in a Reform synagogue with philanthropy in order to identify with the Jewish community. Furthermore, second generation Jews viewed the synagogue center not as a charitable enterprise, but as a self-sufficient, nonprofit organization with balanced books. The synagogue center program also reflected the needs and values of middle-class, second generation Jewish families. It ignored completely the most prominent feature of the Y's and settlement houses—their Americanization activities. It also shunned the emphasis of the Jewish community center on character building and self-development through recreational programs and group work. Instead synagogue centers emphasized the importance of preserving and transmitting Jewish religious and cultural traditions. Synagogue center leaders took for granted their American identity and psychosocial health. As one observer noted, "we may consider the synagogue center building as a physical monument to the completion of the Americanization of the New York Jew."[22]

The new Jewish middle class spent lavishly to build these imposing examples of "community expression." In 1919, before the fever of synagogue-center-building spread, there were over 670 synagogues in the United States with a total value of approximately $31 million. Between 1924 and 1927, American Jews invested over $40 million on 162 new synagogues, and New York City Jews expended roughly $12 million. Yet the synagogue center building spree did not reach its height until 1929, when twelve centers were under construction in New York City alone. By that year New York City's synagogue center distribution reflected the new location of its religious-minded middle-class Jews. Manhattan contained 28 percent of the city's synagogue centers, all of them located uptown. These accounted for 46 percent of the capitalization. In the less affluent and less religiously oriented Bronx, the total investment reached only 13 percent for 23 percent of the city's synagogue centers. But the ideal borough for synagogue centers was Brooklyn. It contained 32 percent of the capitalization lavished on 33 percent of the buildings. While the median cost of a New York synagogue center building was $155,000, in neighborhoods like Flatbush costs usually ranged from $250,000 to $500,000. A particularly elegant synagogue center, such as the Brooklyn Jewish Center on Eastern Parkway or the East Midwood Jewish Center on Ocean Avenue, cost over a million dollars to build.[23]

The synagogue center's architecture reflected its program, earning it the humorous epithet of "a pool with a school and a shul." The Jacob H. Schiff Center, on Valentine Avenue just off the Grand Concourse, comprised three unconnected structures: a synagogue, a school, and a combined gym and swimming pool. The Brooklyn Jewish Center, the largest synagogue center in the borough, stacked its three components. The Center had a swimming pool and gym in the basement, an auditorium on the main floor, and a huge, two-story synagogue, reached by a marble staircase, above. Synagogue centers often hired the same architects. Louis Abramson, who designed Kaplan's prototype, the Jewish Center, also drew the plans for the Brooklyn Jewish Center, the Jewish Communal Center of Flatbush, and the East Midwood Jewish Center.[24]

The lavish synagogue centers arising on the streets of Brooklyn and the Bronx elicited some sharp criticism. Examining the

Brooklyn Jewish Center on Eastern Parkway in 1924. *Courtesy of the Museum of the City of New York.*

motives behind the building boom, social statistician Uriah Engelman assessed the synagogue center skeptically. The synagogue center "is no longer the old-fashioned place of worship," he wrote. "It has become the rich man's club. The synagogue has ceased to be a place to commune with the Maker. Like the exclusive club its purpose is to provide the proper background on which to set off the changing economic status of the American Jew." Engelman's perceptive analogy, which correctly underlined the upper-middle-class character of most synagogue centers, missed the larger point: the laymen who built synagogue centers chose not to create elite social clubs. Departing from the precedent of wealthy American Jews of German descent, who did establish exclusive social clubs, second generation Jews developed an institution which visibly proclaimed their Jewish identity. Choosing to socialize under the auspices of the synagogue, they made their Jewishness central to their secular activity. Indeed, Brooklyn Jewish Center leaders proudly compared its facilities with the best of clubs. From their point of view, in addition to its luxuriously appointed rooms, its excellent kosher restaurant, and its fine recreation facilities, the Brooklyn Jewish Center offered a genuine Jewish atmosphere. Here was the best of both worlds.[25]

Some Jews who looked at the synagogue centers found in their synthesis of sacred and secular the possibility of sacralizing the secular. Nathan Krass, rabbi of the Reform Temple Emanu-El, asserted in a speech dedicating the new Park Avenue Synagogue in 1927: "Israel may be busy building apartment houses on Park Avenue, but it has not forgotten to build a house for God—not a house within which to enclose Him and His teachings but rather a tabernacle from which He may go forth and be among His people." Other observers viewed the synagogue center in the more pragmatic terms "of geographic location, a department store with all merchandise under one roof to save the customer expenditure of energy, and, to provide the management greater economic efficiency." Rabbi Abraham Heller considered this rational structure a positive virtue. The synagogue center, he wrote in 1946, brought "back under the influence of the House of God

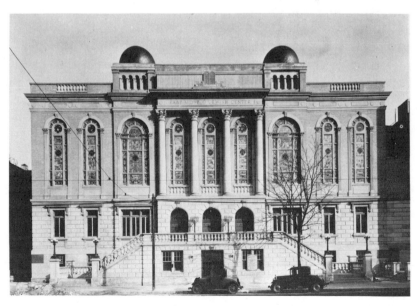

East Midwood Jewish Center on Ocean Avenue between Avenues K and L in 1929. *Courtesy of the Museum of the City of New York.*

those elements in Jewish life, spiritual in origin . . . which have been secularized in an age of specialization."[26]

Yet for all its emphasis on secular American Jewish ethnicity, the synagogue center originated in a concern with religion. As a religious organization, the synagogue center focused first on the needs of its adult Jewish members and then on the educational requirements their children. The laymen who started such an organization as the Brooklyn Jewish Center had received solid Hebrew educations and were religiously committed Jews. They also were Zionists, considered themselves a nationality. From their perspective, the secular activities pursued in the synagogue center reflected the Jews' national character. They saw secularism through Zionist lenses. To build a gym under the synagogue meant introducing into a religious structure an expression of Jewish peoplehood, not American ethnicity. Nevertheless, concern with religion took precedence over ethnic or national ties.[27]

Theological issues and religious practices divided congregations from one another. The extent to which Jewish ritual laws and customs were observed and the degree and type of concessions made to American norms generated conflict. When a congregation found it impossible to alter religious practices with unanimity, the segment whose ideas were not accepted seceded and reconstituted itself as a separate group. In the 1920s, the national Jewish congregational organizations attempted to give this localized process direction and cohesion. They urged synagogues to affiliate with either the Reform, Conservative, or Orthodox unions of congregations, thus making explicit their religious position. Most synagogue centers in the Grand Concourse and Flatbush joined the Conservative union of congregations, the United Synagogue of America. "Conservatism mediates between the demands of the Jewish tradition," notes Sklare, "and the norms of middle class worship."[28]

The synagogue centers' religious activities varied, but they usually kept the spirit of tradition while introducing new forms. The chevra's nascent concern with decorum during worship blossomed into a major obsession in the synagogue center. The decline in familiarity with the traditional *siddur* and adoption of a standardized prayer book in the late 1930s facilitated the maintenance of decorum, encouraging the congregation to rely on the rabbi to lead the services. An irregular feature of chevra services, the sermon in the English language became a central component of synagogue center worship. Second generation Jews introduced other liturgical modifications on the grounds of aesthetics, a criterion rarely employed by chevra members. Aesthetic worship mandated both a mixed choir and responsive readings in English.[29]

But perhaps the most extensive innovation came with the creation of a Friday night service to supplement the traditional Sabbath services. The Friday night service, along with mixed seating of men and women, clearly distinguished Conservative from Orthodox centers. Speaking before the second annual convention of the Rabbinical Association of the Orthodox yeshiva, the Rabbi Isaac Elchanan Theological Seminary, Brooklyn Rabbi Nachman Ebin vehemently attacked late Friday night services. As a religious activity, it represented an unwarranted innovation. But Ebin supported secular Friday night lectures held in the synagogue as a legitimate American activity which did not threaten traditional patterns of religious worship. By contrast, Reform synagogue centers made Friday night their major Sabbath service, ignoring Saturday morning. Such an emphasis underlined for second generation Jews the substantial break with tradition Reform represented. Reform synagogue centers also eschewed daily services continued by both Conservative and Orthodox and curtailed their festival celebrations to one day.[30]

Yet American middle-class norms most strikingly shaped the nonreligious aspects of the synagogue center program. As each synagogue center grew, the primacy of its religious origins receded. The expanding synagogue center added a Hebrew school as its second major activity and often sponsored both a weekday school as well as a one-day-a-week, or Sunday, school. Occasionally an ambitious synagogue center like the Brooklyn Jewish Center established a day school, designed to synthesize Progressive and Hebraic (but not religious) education. The schools reflected second generation Jews' concern with Jewish ethnic persistence. The cultural Zionist outlook of most synagogue centers appeared in their school curricula in the emphasis on the solidarity of a world-wide Jewish people, and in the stress laid on learning Hebrew language and literature. But in conjunction with the

school, the synagogue centers usually supported junior congregations designed to foster a pattern of worship among the children.[31]

Ultimately, the complete synagogue center program divided
into thirds: one third to the synagogue itself, another third to
Jewish education and such cultural activities as lectures, and the
final third to secular activities. The latter generally comprised
physical recreation and social events. Social service rarely appeared on the synagogue center calendar. Sociability replaced it.[32]

Despite a three-pronged synagogue center program, the religious activities generated the largest amount of money. At the
Schiff Center in 1927, over 65 percent of the annual budget came
from synagogue-related sources. Synagogue centers raised funds
through contributions, usually solicited within the context of such
religious events as the High Holidays, weddings, or Bar Mitzvah
ceremonies. Although synagogue centers dropped the public auc-
tion of worship honors, they retained the practice of selling seats
for Rosh Hashanah and Yom Kippur, and the Kol Nidre night appeal. Joseph Goldberg, executive director of the Brooklyn Jewish
Center, saw the problem as "how to *spiritualize* and how to remove the obnoxious elements from the Kol Nidre appeal." Goldberg recognized that at the New Year "the Jew is imbued with the
spirit of giving in order to maintain his house of worship," and
the synagogue center could not afford to forego such an opportunity to raise funds. "The income derived from the sale of tickets
and donations reached high sums," observed a contemporary
journalist, and afforded many congregations "the possibility of
paying off their mortgages, increasing the Hebrew schools, raising
the salaries of the officiating rabbis and constructing new buildings."[33]

The campaign waged by leaders of New York City's synagogue centers throughout the early years of the Depression
against "mushroom" synagogues—temporary synagogues created
to serve the large number of High Holiday worshippers—suggests
the importance of synagogue fund raising. Hyman Reit, chairman
of the United Synagogue's mushroom synagogue committee, in-
veighed against the individuals who profited from the sale of seats
to mushroom synagogues. He noted pointedly that, "unburdened
by the heavy expenses and upkeep which legitimate synagogues

and temples must carry, these individuals are enabled to sell seats for the so-called high holy day services at a price below that which regular temples must charge.'' Mushroom synagogues underpriced the synagogue centers and lay leaders resented it. Proposals to combat the mushroom synagogue menace ranged from prosecution by local district attorneys to expansion of neighborhood synagogues. Ultimately most synagogue centers adopted the latter approach, sponsoring additional services on the High Holidays.[34]

Although most synagogue centers planned each department to be self-supporting, the synagogue often subsidized the school. In fact, educational activities usually produced the least income. Synagogue centers with restaurants or catering facilities, like the Schiff and Brooklyn Jewish Centers and Temple Adath Israel in the Grand Concourse, received substantial income from that source. The median annual expenditures of New York City synagogue centers in 1929 approached $29,000. But most of the larger ones budgeted more than twice as much each year. In 1927 the Schiff Center spent over $70,000, while the following year the Brooklyn Jewish Center spent almost $115,000. In 1929, the East Midwood Jewish Center budgeted $55,000 for its manifold activities.[35]

Such large budgets required substantial membership fees which effectively restricted membership of the lower middle class. Annual dues ranged from a modest $15 to $100 per family, but active members often paid more for the multitude of special services provided, such as the Hebrew school or gym privileges. As a middle-class institution, synagogue centers offered neither the insurance nor mutual aid benefits of the immigrant chevras. Despite such high fees, the larger synagogue centers in Flatbush and the Grand Concourse had an average of 250 heads of family per center. Indeed, most active members chose the most comprehensive and expensive membership by joining the synagogue, not the center. For example, the Ocean Parkway Jewish Center in 1935 had 255 active members of its congregation compared to 51 members of its center; similarly, the Schiff Center in 1927 had 166 participating members of its synagogue and 51 members of its center. The recreation facilities alone exerted only a limited appeal. After the first ten years of operation, Brooklyn Jewish Center President

Rottenberg lamented that "we have not yet found something that
will attract the member to spend his leisure time at the Center
when he is not anxious to pray, be lectured to, or to be educated."[36]

Synagogue centers in the Grand Concourse and Flatbush
drew their middle-class members from a greater distance than the
synagogues in Brownsville. Centrally situated, synagogue centers
reached a larger and more dispersed Jewish population. Yet the
majority of members came from the neighborhood. In 1935 the
Ocean Parkway Jewish Center drew 94 percent of its members
from an area only seven blocks square in the center of Flatbush,
bounded by Church, Foster, and Ocean Avenues and 13th Street.
Similarly, the Schiff Center's membership in 1937 came predominantly from the immediate neighborhood, a district defined by
Mosholu Parkway, the Harlem River, Tremont, and Webster Avenues. Despite the local character of the membership, the physical intimacy of neighboring contact did not dominate the environment. The American Jewish ethnicity of the neighborhood
fostered a different sense of community than that generated by
the *landslayt* ethnicity of the chevra. The center substituted a
newsletter for the face-to-face contact and gossip of the chevra.
The newsletter listed the activities of the month, announced
happy or sad occasions in the lives of members, and tried to keep
its community informed of center and communal events. In the
process, the newsletter redefined the scope of the community's
concerns.[37]

Most often the synagogue centers synthesized local interests
with Zionist activities. The large Schiff Center served as head-
quarters for Junior Hadassah, Concourse Hadassah, Keren
Hayesod of the Bronx, Ivriah, and Zionists of the West Bronx.
But it also rented its facilities to neighboring people for weddings.
In Brooklyn, Young Israel of Flatbush found space for Hadassah,
Mizrachi, and Zionist organization meetings while accommodating
Jewish family circle gatherings. The latter represented a second
generation alternative to the immigrant *landsmanshaftn*. Joseph
Goldberg boasted that "the Eastern Parkway Zionist District be-
came synonymous with" the Brooklyn Jewish Center.[38]

While the synthesis of Zionism with localism characterized its
concept of community, the synagogue center persistently worked

to bring most middle-class Jewish activities under its auspices. In addition to the program of classes, clubs, lectures, dances, and recreation directly sponsored by the synagogue center or one of its constituent bodies (Men's Club, Sisterhood, Young Folk's League, Parent's Association) it opened its doors to Jewish agencies and invited them to use its facilities and to meet under its aegis. In the Bronx the Concourse Center of Israel provided space for boy and girl scout troops and a Young Judaea club, while the Kingsbridge Heights Jewish Center offered its rooms to the Jewish War Veterans and Einson Food Donors. In Brooklyn, the East Midwood Jewish Center included on its calendar the gatherings of several fraternal lodges, family circles, philanthropic societies, and boy scout troops. Writing in the Jubilee Book celebrating the twenty-fifth anniversary of the Brooklyn Jewish Center, Goldberg enthusiastically described how "the building itself became the center of nearly all important activities in the Borough. . . . The Keren Hayesod, Federation of Jewish Charities, United Jewish Appeal and many other campaigns received powerful support from the Center leadership and membership."[39]

The synagogue center rabbi functioned as an executive, with a comfortable income. A survey in the late 1930s estimated the modern rabbi's median annual income at $3,700. The rabbi actively participated in decisions regarding financing, priorities, and program. A popular rabbi's influence extended beyond the institution's walls. Under Rabbi Levinthal's leadership, rabbis of various Brooklyn synagogue centers prevailed upon the Brooklyn Jewish Hospital's board of trustees to reverse its 26-year policy and install a kosher kitchen. Synagogue center rabbis who ministered to second generation Jews spoke English fluently, for English was the language of conversation and preaching. The larger synagogue centers employed assistants to help the rabbi supervise the mundane and secular aspects of the program. Activist rabbis of synagogue centers in Flatbush and the Grand Concourse accepted an additional role of Jewish representative to the Gentiles. In 1925 Rabbi Alexander Basel of the Schiff Center helped to sponsor an inter-religious rally at the center, which generated support for the removal of the prestigious DeWitt Clinton High School from Manhattan to the Bronx. Rabbi Levinthal assisted in the organization of the Brooklyn Jewish Community Council in

1940. Fifty-five synagogues created this central organization to
deal with increasing anti-Semitism in Brooklyn and chose Rabbi
Levinthal as the first president. These activities reflected the rabbis' interest in acting as local communal leaders, lending validity
to the synagogue center's claim to serve the entire neighborhood.[40]

Lay leaders made up only a small proportion of the synagogue center's membership. Excluded from participation in the
chevra, women occasionally joined the leadership of the center.
While a few served on the boards of directors, most women channeled their active involvement through the sisterhood organization.[41]

Despite the multi-faceted synagogue center program and active rabbinic leadership, the percentage of second generation Jews
participating in Sabbath services approximated the low level of
Brownsville's Jews. Here, too, the turnout rose for the High Holidays. The synagogue centers in Flatbush and the Grand Concourse each averaged 1,200 High Holiday worshippers. Again, the
large synagogue centers drew even greater numbers. In 1927 the
Schiff Center accommodated 4,000 people at High Holiday services. From the crowds drawn on Rosh Hashanah and Yom Kippur, statisticians estimated that the city's synagogue centers collectively reached a potential membership of 181,000 Jews, or 10
percent of the city's Jewish population. Yet if few second generation Jews returned to regular Sabbath worship at the synagogue
center, many came to the building for the secular activities it
sponsored. The synagogue centers' popular events steadily drew
substantial numbers. Friday night forums at the Brooklyn Jewish
Center regularly attracted crowds of a thousand people; other
synagogue centers' Friday night lectures drew an average of five
hundred people per lecture. Visiting the Schiff Center in 1940,
writer Doris Glassman found the gym and pool to be the busiest
spots in the summer. The young people especially frequented the
pool; their elders attended services. Some rabbis of synagogue
centers felt that the educational, recreational, and social activities
sponsored by the synagogue center were "back-door methods" to
win members' children to the synagogue. Rabbi Levinthal admitted that "it is true that many will come for other purposes than to
meet God. But let them come," he urged. Others who defended

the synagogue centers' secular activities argued that the institution aimed to organize middle-class Jews "so that their normal recreational and cultural needs may be served and so that they may be part of their Jewish heritage." As for the members, they clearly wanted to keep their recreational and cultural activities within a Jewish milieu. Since the neighborhood no longer adequately provided that milieu, they sought it within the more formal structure of the synagogue center.[42]

Looking back in retrospect, Kaplan argued that "the function of the Jewish center would have to be the all-inclusive one of developing around the leisure interests a sense of social solidarity through face-to-face association and friendship."[43] The new Jewish neighborhoods did not provide a sufficiently Jewish environment or sense of community for those Jews who built synagogue centers. They created the synagogue center as a greenhouse to nourish the primary contacts vital to Jewish group preservation. These second generation Jews erected the synagogue center to guarantee Jewish structural segregation from American society even as it exemplified Jewish absorption of American middle-class norms. Yet the advent of the synagogue center stemmed from a concern for Jewish religion. Only as second generation Jews faced the realities of their new neighborhoods did the center concept emerge to enhance and ultimately to transform the religious impulse. With the center idea second generation Jews found a symbol which persuasively posited the synagogue and Jewish religion as the core of American Jewish life. Reaching out to Jewish activities in the neighborhood, the center brought them within its orbit and connected them to Jewish tradition.

With its blend of religion and recreation, sociability and education, the synagogue center was sustained by the hope that the synagogue would sacralize the center's secular activities. Rabbi Heller called the synagogue center "the saving institution of Jewish life in America. . . . With the Center idea, American Israel began to develop Jewish Jews who became concerned with the wholeness of the Jewish people and Judaism." The synagogue center, Heller felt, "made possible the fulfillment of the promise of the synthetic integration of a worldly life with Jewish loyalties— Judaism within an atmosphere of freedom." But others disagreed. Rabbi Israel Goldstein of B'nai Jeshurun in Manhattan assessed the synagogue centers' compromises and found them to be inadequate. "Whereas the hope of the Synagogue Center was to Synagogize the tone of the secular activities of the family, the effect has been the secularization of the Synagogue."[44]

Yet the synagogue center could never have reconciled completely the competing claims of the sacred and secular. Indeed, this ambivalence also plagued the synagogue centers' lay directors. In the 1920s the Schiff Center's board of trustees debated the relative merits of building a bowling alley versus a Beth Hamidrash, a room for daily prayer and Talmud study. But what criteria could mediate between a bowling alley and a Beth Hamidrash? Certain issues the synagogue center faced could never be resolved. When the board opted for the Beth Hamidrash did their decision reflect the triumph of religion or did it merely indicate a choice in favor of an adult male constituency? The synthesis of middle-class secular ethnicity and Jewish religion necessarily would remain in flux even as it proved to be an enduring institutional structure.[45]

The synagogue center succeeded in transforming a local vision into a communal one. Within the neighborhood it became the central communal institution. It defined the Jewish community it served as a middle-class ethnic one, to which it brought an ideological message of Judaism and cultural Zionism. Building on Jews' associational patterns, the synagogue center incorporated American ethnic and middle-class values under undeniably Jewish auspices. By developing the center as a family institution—a place where primary relations predominated—second generation Jews established the synagogue center as a preserver of Jewish separateness even while they fashioned it as a model of acculturation. By keeping the changes within the neighborhood, second generation Jews usually avoided conflict with other ethnic groups and with militantly secularist Jews who created their own local Jewish institutions. And by fostering a synthesis of religious identity with Zionist ideology, second generation Jews designed a means to transcend parochial concern with local community.

The synagogue center forged a powerful metaphor for community. The heart of an organic Jewish group, the center mediated the manifold activities of the neighborhood. The center metaphor endowed a local congregational leadership with authority and prominence; it suggested that religion lay at the core of Jewish ethnicity. Yet despite the vigor of its vision, the synagogue center failed to embrace secularist Jews. Furthermore, the center's very success within the neighborhood inhibited it from crossing those boundaries. Defining Jewish community as coextensive with the neighborhood, the center neglected the possibility of establishing a city-wide Jewish community. From the Grand Concourse and Flatbush, the Jewish solidarity nourished in the centers extended to Jews throughout the world, bypassing New York Jews conceptually and institutionally. Successful as the synagogue center was, it could not develop an institutional community broader than the neighborhood. Its congregationalism meant that any effort to build a city-wide community would have to rest on a nonsectarian foundation.

6

The Federation originated as a very pragmatic—one is moved to say typically American—response to a set of needs. Yet the form of the response was fully consonant with Jewish political culture as well as the American environment. Perhaps it was that combination that led to the development of a "federation perspective," a justification of the federation approach that was something less than a coherent ideology but had certain articulated theoretical premises of its own, which emphasized the necessity to seek Jewish unity, communal responsibility, organizational efficiency, and comprehensive community planning within the context of the inevitably loose matrix of organized Jewish life.

Daniel J. Elazar, *Community and Polity*
(Philadelphia: Jewish Publication Society, 1976), p. 165.

A Collective
Enterprise

The limitations of the synagogue center left room for the city's
German Jewish elite to assert its leadership over New York Jews.
But to legitimate their claims, wealthy German Jews had to confront and secure the assent of the vast majority—Jews from eastern Europe and their descendants. They also faced the problem
of defining the boundaries of the group they desired to lead. In
short, wealthy New York Jews intent on becoming communal
leaders necessarily embarked on the Progressive American quest:
the simultaneous search for community and social control.[1] Ignoring Jewish neighborhood life, they defined New York Jews as a
physical entity and potential moral community. When wealthy
Jews asked themselves what ties bound them to other Jews in the
city, they answered: philanthropy. The bonds of charity linked
Jews together.

Seen as communal cement, philanthropy opened new vistas
on American society. Philanthropy appealed to wealthy New York
Jews because it connected them to both American and Jewish
traditions. Philanthropy provided an arena for a new Jewish-
American synthesis. Building on nineteenth-century foundations,
affluent New York Jewish leaders developed a Jewish nonsectarian rationale for philanthropy. They institutionalized their
ideology in the Federation for the Support of Jewish Philanthropic Societies of New York City, as they reconstructed Jewish
philanthropy in the city. From a social activity of wealthy individuals, philanthropy became a communal endeavor. As a collective
enterprise, Jewish philanthropy tried to reach across class lines to
unite Jews into a nonsectarian community of interest with moral
dimensions.[2]

The passage from *zedakah*, what Jews had called charity for centuries, to philanthropy occurred in the 19th century. The European Jewish religious tradition of *zedakah* emphasized "the moral worth of charity." An integral part of Jewish religion, the obligations of *zedakah* often were fulfilled through autonomous associations which nonetheless maintained informal ties to the kehillah, the independent Jewish community. In the nineteenth century American Jews transformed *zedakah* into philanthropy even as they splintered the synagogue which had been coextensive with the monolithic Jewish community in the United States. The trend toward fragmentation revealed in the establishment of autonomous nonreligious agencies reflected similar developments in American society. As a separate institution Jewish charity fit into the pattern of American voluntary organizational activity and became amenable to the influence of the nonsectarian American philanthropic ideal.[3]

The American nonsectarian justification for charity stemmed from the Protestant concept of stewardship. Secularized into the Gospel of Wealth and popularized by millionaire steel magnate Andrew Carnegie, nonsectarian philanthropy legitimated the wealthy individual's elite position. Carnegie argued that a person's money, obtained from the competitive struggle to survive, was entrusted to him so that he might oversee its beneficent distribution. The Gospel of Wealth required rich individuals to spend their money—preferably in their own lifetime—to endow all of society. As the elect of society, wealthy individuals assumed the burden of philanthropy. Carnegie characterized the ideal philanthropic impulse as strictly nonsectarian. "Churches as fields for the use of surplus wealth . . . are sectarian," he wrote. Carnegie saw gifts to churches not as "gifts to the community at large, but to special classes." Jewish philanthropists, even those who prided themselves on their Orthodoxy, often agreed with aspects of Carnegie's gospel. "I have no desire to accumulate a fortune merely with the idea of bequeathing it to charity at my death," wrote wealthy builder Harry Fischel. "It is rather my intention to give while I am living and while I may have the opportunity of exercising a controlling influence over my gifts, to the end that they may most fully accomplish their purpose."[4]

The ideological harmony of American Protestantism with the

industrializing America of the late nineteenth century found its secular expression in the Gospel of Wealth. Emotionally identified with the growing bourgeois society and its free enterprise system, American Protestantism accepted its values, thus giving sanctity to the American social order. Thus, nonsectarian charity appeared to American Jews not only as the ideal American rationale for philanthropy but also as one of the dogmas of American civil religion. To use the Gospel of Wealth to justify Jewish separateness on philanthropic grounds was an attempt to integrate Jews into the blessings of the civil religion. Like the melting-pot image, nonsectarian philanthropy could be shared with all Americans, and thus promised Jews social acceptance.[5]

The transformation of the Jewish religious tradition of *zedakah* into the ideology of American Jewish community provided the framework for the philanthropists' encounter with east European Jews in the city. Federation leaders who asserted the nonsectarian value of philanthropy ignored the class conflict that charity engendered between the donors and the beneficiaries. Instead they argued that philanthropy was not controversial; everyone could agree that those in need deserved to be helped. Philanthropy avoided ideological disputes, especially if fund-raising rather than fund-distribution were stressed. From this perspective, philanthropy became the basis for a new type of Jewish politics derived from the American model. For its advocates, New York Federation served simultaneously as the religious expression and as the political structure of the New York Jewish community. Federation leaders' insistence that philanthropy avoid religious issues stemmed not merely from practical concerns (a desire to sidestep the problems of religious dissension) but from the American ideal of separation of church and state. As the "state" of New York Jews, Federation had no right to meddle in Jewish "church" affairs. Thus supporters of philanthropy as a communal ideology could hold out a hand of cooperation to religious Jews and secularist Jews alike and invite them to participate in Federation's new Jewish polity.[6]

The Federation community that wealthy Jews created also reflected their experience with the New York Kehillah. In New York City in the years before World War I, the Kehillah mediated the acute struggle between Downtown Jews and Uptown Jews, between the beneficiaries of Jewish charity and the donors, between the working class and the upper class, between Russian Jew and German Jew. The New York Kehillah drew its strength from east European Jewish traditions of community (still vivid in the memories of immigrants) and from the city's German Jews' elite communal heritage of philanthropy and defending Jews from attack. The Kehillah linked this Jewish inheritance to the American traditions of democracy, voluntarism, and cultural pluralism. The Kehillah aimed to serve as an "authoritative influence sustained by the 'democratic sanction' of the community."[7] In their decision to create Federation in 1917 while supporting the Kehillah, wealthy philanthropists like Felix Warburg expressed their basic distrust and impatience with the inefficiency of a democratic, pluralist community.

The possibility that a sense of solidarity might grow from the routine of fund raising dawned upon the city's wealthy philanthropists as they watched all Americans respond to the mass appeals for wartime relief. An elusive ideal until World War I, nonsectarian philanthropy suddenly became immensely popular as a realistic, businesslike cause. Voluntarism acquired new esteem as the war catapulted philanthropy, especially overseas aid, into the forefront of American Jewish concerns. The war launched Jews into mass fund-raising campaigns as serious business. "The federation, as the corporation, was conceived as a vehicle for the more efficient use of the means of production—in one case, production of goods and in the other, production of services." As sociologist Kenneth Roseman notes, "Jewish communal enterprise thus adapted for social service a form which was proving to be successful in the economic sphere." The wartime experience also showed wealthy Jews how to maintain class differences and elite control in mass fund raising. Rabbi Judah Magnes's plea for the support of the Kehillah in 1908 ("an army without leaders is almost as absurd as leaders without an army") was now relevant. Suddenly the opportunity was "at hand for leaders and soldiers to recognize the need they have of each other and to join ranks," but in support of philanthropy, not of the Kehillah.[8] Wealthy New York Jews realized that philanthropy and the machinery of fund-raising could express American Jews' sense of community more effectively and congenially than religious activity. While philanthropy continued to reflect personal religious responsibilities, philanthropic organization could serve as a substitute for the Kehillah.

Philanthropy promised New York City Jews an unexpected bonus from their charity: a sense of identity and a basis for community. The possibilities for organized American philanthropy seemed limitless and New York Jews shared in the exhilaration of successful fund raising. Though the Kehillah had floundered and drowned in the war-engendered tides of Jewish particularism, charity would become the ark of a reorganized Jewish community in the city. Fund-raiser Henry Rosenfelt, in his book praising *This Thing of Giving*, boasted that "Jews today are closer together than ever before. . . . We are no longer orthodox and reform, conservative and radical—all are becoming united, bound together by that ancient formula, 'I am a Jew!' " Numerous Jewish orators (speaking in Yiddish or English) shared the platform at the huge fund-raising events of the time, where they articulated this glorious vision.[9] With prestige from public giving at its acme, various Jewish spokesmen endorsed the idea that a new institutional Jewish community, based on American sanctioned philanthropy like Federation, would arise from the debris of the Kehillah.

The war relief drives also held out the chance that the east European Jews would, by their support, lend credence to the claims of wealthy Federation leaders that they were at the head of the New York Jewish community. The war relief drives tapped the resources of Jews who only recently had acquired their affluence. In return for their contributions, the drives gave these Jews prestige and a sense of solidarity with other Jews and other Americans. But the campaigns also ranked the newcomers, many of them second generation Jews. In December 1917, the Jews' War Relief Campaign hierarchy evoked military analogies. The next month "a great many of the same captains and same lieutenants" followed their "General," Felix Warburg, and "threw themselves heart and soul into the Federation campaign." In this fund-raising drive Federation reached 50,000 new member contributors. The following year I. Edwin Goldwasser, executive director of the Federation, determined to capitalize on the success of the War

Relief Fund Drive. With Warburg's assistance he launched the
Business Men's Council as an independent organization to raise
money for Federation.[10]

With the creation of the Business Men's Council, Federation
leaders made clear their intention to acquire the Kehillah's
mantle. In 1918, one year after its establishment, Goldwasser
credited Federation with uniting New York Jews into "a solid
unit." Ignoring the Brooklyn Federation of Jewish Charities, an
independent organization founded in 1909, Goldwasser announced that Federation committees were "considering the general problems of community welfare, and for the first time in the
history of the Jewish community in New York City giving full con-
sideration to the problems affecting its institutions."[11] Goldwasser complemented his extravagant claims for Federation with
extensive efforts to mobilize the support of east European Jews
through the Business Men's Council.

The Council helped to bring east European Jews into Federation. The Council reached out to the emerging middle-class
stratum of second generation Jews and invited them to join Federation as Council members. If successful in its appeal, the Council
would justify Federation's claim to represent the Jewish community of New York.

As a fund-raising mechanism, the hierarchical Business
Men's Council recognized class differences but stressed mass participation as the way to harmonize democracy with plutocracy.
The Council ranked members according to the size of their contributions to Federation. Therefore, ambitious and affluent east
European Jews could aspire to stand with the city's German Jewish leadership. To reach the Council's acme required a contribution of $50,000, although some councillors gave only $5,000 annually. Those who could not afford such largesse could achieve
the rank of division heads. A $2,000 contribution secured such a
position. Beneath the division heads were the trade chairmen
while on the bottom appeared the individual or collective donors.
By 1925, when the Council was established securely, it contained
approximately 500 trade chairmen under 80 division heads who
were supervised by 43 councillors.[12]

The Business Men's Council also expressed the Federation's
ideology in its approach to fund raising. According to Goldwas-

ser, the Council's purpose would be "to devise a system of more or less voluntary organization of the firms listed within each industry so that there shall be an equitable, a fair and a reasonable distribution of the burden in supplying the funds to meet communal needs." The Council must be, he elaborated, "not merely an agency for securing equitable distribution of giving, it must be an agency for educating the people themselves so that they shall realize the justice of giving."[13] Goldwasser proposed that the Business Men's Council solicit the individual Jew in his office rather than in his home. The American marketplace provided the secular, business setting in which the Jew would affirm his solidarity with his people by contributing to Federation. And, if necessary, the Council would teach Jews "the justice of giving," that is, the importance of identifying with the Jewish community through membership in the Business Men's Council. Soliciting in the American marketplace also encouraged Federation fund-raisers to employ an American nonsectarian philanthropic appeal. Giving to Federation not only expressed Jewish ethnic sentiment but fulfilled the requirements of American civil religion.

As the Council thrived in the 1920s, the Federation's leaders quickly recognized that its social activities contributed to its successful fund raising. Relying on volunteer solicitors, the Business Men's Council carefully cultivated these social aspects, and in the process introduced second generation Jews to the sociocultural world of the American upper middle class. From monthly luncheons, the Council expanded its social calendar to include annual golf tournaments at the Fenimore Country Club in White Plains.[14] But the Council's campaign "opening event"—generally a lavish dinner without any solicitation of funds—proved to be most popular. Here volunteers of all ranks mixed freely. "The social implications, are, therefore, tremendously important," observed an anonymous Federation member.[15]

The Council's successful social program also registered in the world of exclusive Jewish clubs. In 1933 wealthy philanthropist Felix Warburg wrote Federation treasurer Walter Beer that one $5,000 per year contributor "feels that he has been maltreated by his co-religionists" because he was denied membership in one of the elite Jewish social clubs. As a result, he was withholding his annual contribution to Federation. Warburg went on to assure

Beer that since the club had promised to elect the dissatisfied con-
tributor "we will probably regain his good will. I am sorry," he
concluded, "that these matters, which have nothing to do with
Federation, interfere with Federation, but human beings are
human beings." Warburg's assessment of the situation missed the
underlying issue. Certainly Federation, when it created the Business Men's Council as the instrument to implement its concept of
community, recognized its implicit offer to east European Jews to
join the society of affluent American Jews. Goldwasser's original
statement had promised that the only qualification for leadership
in the Business Men's Council would be the "men who have
shown real open-mindedness, direction and guidance." A generous contribution to Federation paved the way to admission to the
circle of New York Jewish communal leaders.[16]

But Federation leaders refused to restructure completely the
city's Jewish community, even along the hierarchical lines developed by the Business Men's Council. While they fraternized with
east European Jews at the Council's social events, uptown Jews
usually drew a line around their private lives and social institutions. Typically, the prestigious architect and builder G. Richard
Davis rejected overtures from aggressive builders Nathan Wilson
and Benjamin Winter about establishing a club for Jews in real
estate and building. While Davis sanctioned a Real Estate Club as
part of Federation, he explained to Wilson and Winter that Federation "permits me and you and all of us to sacrifice all our personal likes and dislikes, so as to help the cause in which we are all
interested. A regular club, as opposed to a Federation club," he
argued, "would be full of factional troubles, clashings of interest
and a lack of social unity."[17] Often wealthy uptown Jews did not
even view their clubs as within the framework of the Jewish community. Thus they rebuffed the attempts of east European Jews
to gain admission as irrelevant to the noble project of uniting
Jews into a single community.

But if New York's wealthy elite refrained from excessive frat-
ernizing with upwardly mobile second generation Jewish businessmen, Federation leaders saw the value of accommodating
within it east European members of the Business Men's Council.
In 1925, with Warburg's encouragement, Federation expanded its
Board of Trustees to admit more Trustees-at-large, men or

women who were not affiliated with any of the Federation's charitable agencies. Originally, the Trustees of the charitable societies served by Federation, largely German Jews, dominated the Board of Trustees. With the expansion of the number of Trustees-at-large, Federation honored the new money contributed by individuals in the Business Men's Council. The Federation further implemented its concept of community by accepting second-generation Jewish businessmen as communal leaders. With the recognition that the basis of membership need not be the support of a specific charitable agency, the Business Men's Council removed pressure on Federation to admit any more organizations. The Council appealed to individuals as contributors, not as institutional representatives. The expansion of Federation's Board of Trustees measured the Council's amazing success in reaching the city's east European Jews and their money. Federation's other fund-raising divisions, notably its Women's Division, did not receive such recognition, although "as a token of appreciation" of its work in the 1918 fund-raising drive a woman had been placed on the list of Federation officers.[18]

Rewarded in its initial efforts in the 1920s, the Council extended the implications of its concept of a secular, voluntary Jewish community united by philanthropic bonds and activated in America's free capitalist arena. The secular principle behind the Council's trade approach suggested "that if philanthropy was to be given substance and reality in our complex, modern world, it must become an intimate part of the life of office and shop and showroom, and find organized expression in keeping with the pattern of each business and professional grouping." The Council assumed that Jews could be reached most effectively through their business associates. Its solicitation practices located Jews through their ethnic occupational distribution. Proceeding from the premise that in a given trade a handful of Jews would know all of the other Jews engaged in the field, the Council proposed to transform fund raising largely into a process of identifying Jews in their work. Once tabbed, the prospective donor and future member of the Jewish community need only be told how much to give and why. In a plan submitted in 1926, merchant and Federation councillor Herman Lissner presented such a method whereby each individual contribution could be calculated. Lissner computed a donation based on the percentage the Council established in the various trades and on the individual's rated wealth. He conceived of this contribution as the donor's "duty to the community"—the way he purchased membership in the Jewish community of New York. Lissner considered charity only as what a person might give beyond the assessed amount.[19]

Lissner's logical extension of the Council's concept of community mandated the organization of its trade councils into independent units that would be responsible for soliciting in its own industry. The Business Men's Council would simply establish the amount required from each industry by the Federation Jewish community. This plan to decentralize the Jewish community and establish industries as Jewish subcommunities stemmed from the Council's initial approach to fund raising. Throughout the 1920s Federation fund raising created cohesive Jewish groups in a variety of businesses and professions, even unifying Reform, Conservative, and Orthodox rabbis. Once given form by Federation's philanthropic appeal, these groups often took on an independent life of their own. In the Fur Industry, where a Jewish subcommunity was established, the Business Men's Council accurately anticipated increased contributions and closer associational ties among Jews. Alex Bernstein, chairman of the Distribution Committee of the Fur Industry Charity Chest, underscored the greater efficiency of the industry solicitation. "There is no clouding of issues," he asserted. "The Charity Chest, because of its control, influences people to give more than they ever gave before its establishment." Bernstein characterized the Fur Industry as "an organized community where everyone knows everyone else." In such a community, he concluded, "the non-giver cannot escape his duties and the generous giver will not be hounded by solicitors." True to the same nonsectarian American ideal as Federation, the Fur Chest distributed its funds to charitable agencies without regard to race or religion.[20]

Federation leaders used the nonsectarian philanthropic principle not only to justify Federation's existence as a separate Jewish institution, but also to guide its internal decisions. The nonsectarian argument was effective within the Jewish community. An observant Jew, Harry Fischel, repeatedly lobbied for nonsectarian luncheons at Jewish philanthropic meetings. He explained that "a non-sectarian luncheon means that the Orthodox Jew can eat it, the Conservative Jew will not spoil his stomach by it and even the Reform Jew will not die from it." But if nonsectarianism could be used to support demands for *kashrut*, it found its fullest expression in fund-raising rhetoric. In 1928 Federation president Sol Stroock pointed out that "while Federation is itself essentially Jewish and while all of the affiliated societies are themselves Jewish, it must be borne in mind that in their philanthropic activities . . . a large number of persons who are not Jews receive care, attention and relief."[21]

In demonstrating Federation's nonsectarian distribution of funds via its affiliated agencies, its leaders legitimated Federation's position within what they considered to be the mainstream of the American philanthropic tradition. But such rhetoric also could lead Federation spokesmen to the brink of denying the Jewish nature of Federation in their desire to emphasize its American attributes. In 1931 newspaper magnate Paul Block accepted the chairmanship of New York Federation's deficit campaign, announcing that he was "especially pleased to be chairman of a campaign which raises funds for institutions so much of whose work is non-sectarian. They extend their humanitarian help to the people of all races, creeds and colors," he added. "In fact, at some of the clinics which we support there are more Gentiles treated than those of Jewish faith." In his zeal to proclaim Federation's inherent American values, Block obscured Federation's Jewish function of uniting its members into a Jewish community.[22]

The euphoria produced by the Business Men's Council's early triumphs and by Federation's success in supplanting the Kehillah collapsed in the 1930s under the impact of the Depression. In the face of mass poverty, voluntarism declined. The government's increasing involvement in unemployment and welfare relief implicitly challenged the validity of private philanthropy. At that point more sober assessments of such organizations as Federation observed that they had "the limitations of their origins. Sponsored chiefly by wealthy givers, they had to reflect their conceptions of Jewish communal work, although they proposed to represent the whole community," wrote Frank Sulzberger and Ben Selekman. Yet the Federation "proved an efficient money-

raising mechanism." Furthermore it "became the means of linking the growing prosperity and status of American Jewry, with
recognized community responsibility for the underprivileged."
The Business Men's Council's success lay within this tradition.
While at its peak of the decade in 1926 New York Federation
enrolled only 34,000 members compared to 76,000 contributors to
the United Palestine Appeal of the same year, its Business Men's
Council managed to reach the more affluent Jewish businessmen
in the city. With less than half as many donors as U.P.A., Federation raised the same sum. Federation's leadership, in the opinion
of its professional workers, also cut across "many of the groups
which constitute the Jewish community of New York." As an effort at cooptation, the Council achieved unqualified success despite the Depression.[23]

The Depression did reduce contributions drastically and
spurred the Business Men's Council to address the problem of the
tremendous variation in amounts it secured from donors. While
the Council's methods succeeded in providing Federation with
ever larger annual sums throughout the 1920s, they failed to
reach upper and middle class Jews consistently. Among the
wealthiest Jews (those earning over $2 million annually), yearly
donations ranged from $1,000 to $76,000. Similarly, among those
earning $1 million annually, yearly giving ran the gamut from $50
to $4,000. Such discrepancies prodded Joseph Willen, director of
the Council, to suggest that Federation find a new basis for fund
raising.[24]

Inspired by the collective industrial organization the New
Deal introduced into American economic life, Willen proposed in
1935 that the group become the basic unit of Jewish philanthropy.
Willen urged Federation to replace its individualistic fund-raising
with a genuine effort to involve the Jewish masses through the
workers' organizations. Although Federation often received contributions from such working class organizations as the *Forward*
association and the United Neckwear Makers Union, it did not
work with these agencies systematically. Willen attacked the current Federation practice of soliciting workers for quarters and
dollars in shops and factories. Such an individualistic approach
usually involved pressure from the employer, and the worker's
contribution appeared insignificant in relation to the sum to be

raised. "The past has seen many proclamations of interest in the masses on the part of community leadership," he declared, "but too often 'mass support' has been thought of in terms of the old utility corporation technique which considered it good business to secure as many consumer stockholders as possible to ward off undesirable legislation. No relationship with labor or any other group will mean anything," he concluded, "unless we are prepared to deal with it as an organized group, and to give it a share not only in support, but in control and management." Willen admitted that such an effort would disturb the tight knot of "sociability and humanitarianism" previously established by the Business Men's Council, but he insisted that the times demanded change: "Of course, this approach has its dangers. One cannot hope to bring basic groups of such diverse character around one table without inviting disagreement and conflict. The peace, harmony, and complete accord so characteristic of our board meetings today might disappear." But the increase in funds and permanent support for Federation warranted the risk of conflict. For Willen, Depression-sponsored difficulties suggested the need to extend the Council's model of cooptation to include other groups.[25]

Willen's proposals and Federation's economic difficulties encouraged the creation of another independent council, the Council of Fraternal and Benevolent Organizations. Ironically, Goldwasser initiated this Council and served as its first president too. Federation leaders hoped this new group would draw lower-middle-class Jews into Federation, much as the Business Men's Council had attracted those higher on the economic ladder. The Council of Fraternal and Benevolent Organizations, however, emphasized the importance of Jewish tradition in philanthropy. In "Closing the Ranks in Jewish Life," an appropriately titled pamphlet advertising the Council, Federation admitted that the Council's member organizations "know in a deep sense what the Jewish charitable tradition means." The new Council also complemented the Business Men's Council in its solicitation, since it asked for contributions from mutual aid societies organized on an ethnic basis. These societies represented the grass-roots efforts of thousands of immigrant Jews to cope with the distress produced by sickness, unemployment, and death. The estimated 3,000 societies in the city reached a vast membership, approximately 500,000

people (roughly one out of every four Jews in New York City).[26]
Bringing these groups within the orbit of Federation involved
bridging the gap between generations—immigrant and American
—without using the social-class escalator.

Yet the Council of Fraternal and Benevolent Organizations
did not threaten Federation's fundamental philanthropic ideology. As the only city-wide organization with claims to represent
the Jewish community, Federation pursued its course of cooptation without substantial compromise. Even those committed to
more traditional expressions of Jewishness than nonsectarian
philanthropy admitted that "Federation is at present the only
agency through which . . . organizing and planning can be facilitated. Through its fund-raising and service functions," wrote
Bureau of Jewish Education Director Samson Benderly, "Federation provides the members of the Jewish group an opportunity to
assert themselves as Jews. Being representative of all of the diverse elements and interests of the Jewish community," he
concluded, "Federation is logically the agency that can help
in bringing about the desired integration of Jewishness with
Americanism."[27]

Benderly's conclusions revealed how Federation had pre-
empted the position of the representative Jewish communal institution in the city. Federation's nonsectarian ideology and its
subtle use of American political norms made competing organizations appear parochial and partisan. As early as 1924 the American Jewish Congress was rebuffed when it called for the creation
of a Jewish Council of Greater New York because of the "urgent
need for the consolidation of the forces working for the solution of
Jewish communal problems in New York City." New York City
did not need a new Kehillah, it was claimed. Federation existed
and Jews would not cooperate on religious matters. If not for
charity and religion, what do you need a Kehillah for?[28] The implicit Zionism of the Congress appeared to be too narrow a
ground for all Jews to share. Yet Federation's advocates knew
that its authority rested on the ability to convince Jews of the validity of its definition of community. Alone, the Business Men's
Council did not suffice. Federation needed a more comprehensive
vision of community, one extending beyond a hierarchy of affluent Jews voluntarily engaged in fund-raising. To that end, Feder-

ation leaders turned to the ideals of the social science survey to find a tool with which to forge a moral community embracing all the city's Jews.

The concept of a scientific survey conducted by a community in search of its self drew its inspiration from the ideas of Progressive American urban reformers and philanthropists who established bureaus of municipal research in the early decades of the twentieth century. Unable and unwilling to compete with urban political machines, the bureaus of municipal research "sought to represent the interests of the city as a whole and have appealed to a sentiment and opinion neither local nor personal. These agencies," wrote sociologist Robert Park, tried to achieve their aims "by the education of the voter, that is to say, by investigating and publishing the facts regarding the government. In this way publicity has come to be a recognized form of social control," he concluded. The bureaus of municipal research and the philanthropic social welfare foundations pioneered in developing the large-scale social survey as a scientific instrument. The social survey provided a new method of civic education and presented a new means to promote collective action. The large-scale survey did not restrict itself to a particular problem but attempted to transform the entire city into a community of shared values. The survey technique extensively developed by the Russell Sage Foundation, especially in its landmark Pittsburgh Survey, promised that community consciousness lost through urban industrialization could be replaced through the scientific communication of knowledge.[29]

Behind the practice of the social survey lay a theory of communication. Social scientists expected the self-survey to create community-mindedness among anonymous city dwellers. These social scientists associated with the University of Chicago contrasted the impersonal, anonymous life of city residents with the intimate, secure environment of the small town. In their view, urbanization and industrialization were destroying "a social organization based on family, neighborhood, and small-town solidarity." Although physical unity and economic interdependence existed in the city, moral unity and shared values needed to be recreated. For these Progressive social scientists, the technology of communication assumed potent powers. Seeing the city as a

psycho-physical organism, they contended that communication
strengthened the psychic sources of unity. In historian Jean
Quandt's words, "through the new means of communications, the
values of intimacy and immediacy would permeate the whole
structure of organized society." Although secondary impersonal
relationships now characterized urban society, these relationships
could be transcended and a "quasi-religious notion of commu-
nion, with its qualities of intensity and fellowship" could be attained. While the newspaper served as one of the most effective
agencies of communication in the impersonal urban setting, the
most potent force for cohesion came from publicity itself. The
self-survey in this context provided a giant looking-glass for a
community; it mirrored the community's physical existence and in
the process painted a psychic portrait. The collective self-
knowledge produced by the survey would therefore create consensus. Thus scientifically guided communication effected through
the mirror of the self-survey became the source of communal
unity, even as it functioned as an instrument of social control.[30]

In turning to a survey of New York Jews for a vision of community, Federation leaders linked their search for consensus with
a desire to control those Jews untouched by the deferential Business Men's Council. When Federation leaders, flushed with their
success at coordinating Jewish charitable activities in the city,
called a meeting of Jewish communal representatives in 1926 to
consider the prospect of surveying the Jews of New York, the
need for a survey appeared obvious. Never before had so many
Jews lived together in a single city. The magnitude of New York's
Jewish world seemed to defy comprehension, let alone control. No
one even knew just how many Jews were living in the city or
where they lived. The last population study, ten years out of date,
had portrayed a Jewish group largely immigrant in character.
Since Congress had sharply reduced the volume of immigration to
the United States, New York Jews faced a new era in 1925. But
how were they to chart their future when they did not know who
they were? This absence of information particularly vexed those
Federation leaders who wanted to plan for the future. They saw
in the social survey a potential guide as well as a collective portrait. Recognizing the ambitious character of such an undertaking, they looked for the cooperation and tacit endorsement of

most of the city's Jewish constituencies. Federation addressed its
initial letter "to Jewish citizens who represent all phases of organized Jewish philanthropic and communal effort in Greater New
York" and invited these representatives to discuss the concept of
a self-survey. The first conference fulfilled the Federation's expectations. The meeting brought together philanthropists and union-
ists, Zionists and Yiddishists, Reform and Orthodox, educators
and social workers from Brooklyn, Manhattan, and the Bronx.
This gathering endorsed Federation's proposal to conduct a Jewish Communal Survey of Greater New York, launching an experiment in using social science to create communal consensus.[31]

Behind the manifest purpose of the Survey lay a larger vision: its sponsors saw in the process of accumulating and communicating information about New York Jews a scientific tool to
create a Jewish community where before there had been only
Jews. Like an individual undergoing psychoanalysis, the Jewish
community would find self-knowledge through the intervention of
scientific experts. Through the Survey, leading Jewish philanthropists joined hands with a progressive group of Jewish social
workers to develop an instrument which would simultaneously
forge a common consensus among New York Jews and transform
them into an institutional community under the aegis of Federation. The survey held the key to collective self-knowledge. At Federation's victory dinner Frederick Brown, a wealthy real estate
man and chairman of Federation's 1925 fund-raising campaign,
justified a study of the entire Jewish situation in New York City as
the only way "the Jewish community of New York can achieve
conscious self-knowledge and organization." Samuel Goldsmith,
executive director of the Bureau of Jewish Social Research which
conducted the Survey, agreed in retrospect that it had been "conceived as an instrument . . . for community organization."[32]
Collective self-knowledge, community organization, social consensus—the Jewish Communal Survey of Greater New York contained those components of an American Jewish community miss-
ing from the Business Men's Council.

Proponents of the Survey argued that it offered a solution to
partisan squabbling among New York Jews. In providing vital
knowledge about Jews and their organizations in the city, the Survey would establish the framework for cooperation. Its scientific

findings would be objective and above partisanship. Goldsmith underscored these arguments in his defense of pragmatic social science. "I feel that our efforts are useless and our so-called expert assistance practically valueless unless we are willing to actually show communities . . . how they can put into practice the findings of our surveys," he wrote. "I do not believe that this is propaganda," he reiterated, "unless the spreading of authentic, scientific knowledge can be called propaganda."[33] The Survey's supporters believed in social science and felt that it alone could supply the basis for genuine unity among New York Jews. Such unity derived not from ethnic or national or even religious attachments but stemmed from shared values. Actually, the Survey's advocates expected that the evidence produced would generate objective communal sentiment sufficient to override dissension, perhaps even obliterate it entirely. Ultimately, the Survey would be the key to unlock the door obstructing New York Jews' quest for community, because it would fashion a community along objective scientific principles suited to American conditions.

Like the Business Men's Council, the Jewish Communal Survey found its precedent in the New York Kehillah. In 1916 the Kehillah published the *Jewish Communal Register* as a preliminary to a plan for communal reorganization. The historian of the Kehillah characterized the *Register* as "a comprehensive, demographic, economic, and institutional survey of New York Jewry. This massive 1,600-page inventory," he continued, represented for its sponsors "the application of scientific method to the building of the 'Good Community.' " The editors of the *Register* considered the "first task" of those who wanted to shape future Jewish communal policy that of helping "the community to know itself as it is at present."[34] In spite of the *Register*'s fate to have recorded the peak of Kehillah accomplishment rather than to have charted its future triumphs, the central vision of creating a community through scientific knowledge remained potent enough to inspire Federation leaders ten years later to essay an even more monumental survey. Like their Kehillah predecessors, the Jewish leaders who manned the citizen committees directing the work of the Jewish Communal Survey shared a desire to control Jewish life in New York City and to shape Jews into a legitimately American community. The Survey promised to fulfill both expectations.

True to its sponsors' values, the Survey conceived of the New York Jewish community in philanthropic terms. The supervisory Citizen's Committee organized in January 1926 outlined the field of a survey of the Jewish Community of Greater New York as a study of Jewish population, Jewish philanthropic communal activities, other communal activities, and coordinating activities. Under the rubric of Jewish population, the Survey examined Jewish physical mobility in the city as well as fertility and morbidity patterns. Subsequently, the Survey intended to expand its demographic inquiry to include the economic and social life of New York Jews, comprising Jewish membership in trade unions, trade associations, professional groups, synagogues, and country clubs. Within this category the Survey also placed an estimate of Jewish occupational distribution in the city. All of these important topics the Survey treated as only a necessary preliminary to the essential study of Jewish communal activities. The Survey divided its heart, the study of Jewish communal activities, into two unequal halves. The larger half included philanthropic agencies, and as the Survey progressed these achieved primacy. The Survey understood philanthropy to comprise nonsectarian organizations founded by Jews, among them agencies involved in child care, welfare, delinquency, health, and leisure. In the category of "other communal activities" (the other side of the Survey's heart) the Survey lumped all intrinsically Jewish activities, both religious and educational. The fourth category recognized the importance of New York City as the headquarters of American Jewry and it examined the work of national organizations alongside of the New York and Brooklyn Federations. But the Citizen's Committee supervised an Executive Committee, in the hands of Federation supporters, which directed the actual progress of the Survey. In May 1926 the Executive Committee, chaired by Lee K. Frankel, set up six subcommittees dealing with child care, family welfare, medical services, recreation, Jewish education, and allied fields. These six subdivisions emphasized the nature of a philanthropically defined community; except for Jewish education all of the subcommittees concerned themselves with nonsectarian activities conducted under Jewish auspices.[35]

The Survey's structure neglected traditional Jewish communal activities. Initially the Survey reduced Jewish education and religion to a quarter of Jewish life. Under the Executive Committee, religion disappeared as a category completely. Ironically, the Survey's most significant examination of Jewish religious practices in the city took place under the rubric of recreation. There it discovered the synagogue center, which it described as "the antithesis of the traditional YMHA community organization." To begin with, the Survey noted, "the synagogue centers start from their Jewish origin." Furthermore, "the synagogue centers concern themselves only with the middle-class." This participating membership also controlled the synagogue center's policies and programs. The Survey went on to observe that "the synagogue centers are Jewish not only in origin but almost entirely in interest as well." Yet these religious organizations contained new physical facilities for recreation, often outstripping the Y's and settlement houses. Tempted by the wealth of untapped resources in the synagogue centers, the Survey tried to incorporate them into a recreational framework, arguing that such a nonsectarian perspective was needed because "despite great facilities for work along extra-synagogue lines, the synagogue centers of New York still remain synagogues in their religious sense and . . . their chief efforts center in the purely Jewish aspects of their program."[36] Even when it faced a new religious movement in New York Jewish life, the Survey refused to deal with it as an integral part of Jewish community concerns.

By contrast, the Survey comprehensively analyzed the work of more than 1,000 Jewish agencies dealing with family welfare, delinquency, medical care, child care, recreation, and Jewish education. The Survey dealt with these fields objectively, including in its extensive report on Jewish education both Jewish secular and religious schools. Occasionally in its analysis, the Survey even questioned basic assumptions behind a charitable organization. Thus it reviewed the arguments for supporting Jewish hospitals (the need to have hospitals which offered kosher food, the desire to maintain a haven for Jewish doctors who suffered from discrimination, and the general feeling that Jews prefer their own institution when sick), and found none of these arguments compelling. It recommended as a result a moratorium on hospital expansion. The Survey also brought a new level of sophistication to its analysis of Jewish population trends, fertility, and morbidity. Its demographic report revealed "the really dramatic and vital . . . march of the Jewish population into Brooklyn and into the Bronx." The Survey correctly anticipated new developments in Jewish population shifts, concluding that the "intra-city migration must have a tremendous effect on the reallocation of the philanthropic and communal organizations among the Jewish community."[37] Yet compared with the Kehillah's *Jewish Communal Register*, the Survey slighted the religious, economic, and cultural aspects of Jewish life. Skimming over such controversial subjects, the Survey emphasized studies of health facilities and family relief, both central components of Jewish philanthropy. Thus the Survey played down the traditional concerns of Jewish communal life in its desire to evoke consensus.

The Survey's conclusions spoke in terms of all the Jews of New York. Its sponsors published only two volumes, a summary executive report and the study of Jewish demography. The bulk of the material remained in typescript, awaiting the funding needed for publication. In the published volumes, the theme of acculturation permeated the conclusions while the scientific ideal of rationalization shaped the recommendations. The executive committee wrote that the Survey revealed "a population, social conditions and sociological ideas in flux," and called for "alertness, openmindedness and adaptation of methods." The overall picture of New York Jews portrayed "an economically poor, but young, vigorous and ambitious group, who [sic] has taken advantage of its opportunities in a new country, has struggled up to a considerably higher scale of living than it enjoyed when it first came, and has shown a disposition to bear an increasing share of communal responsibility." Given these conclusions, the executive committee recommended the consolidation of Jewish social work agencies in virtually every area studied and the development of a single overarching organization to give form to the emerging trends. In the report's words: "The organization of future Jewish social work should be looked at from the standpoint, not simply of the individual boroughs, but of the Greater City." Thus the single most important recommendation to come out of the monumental Survey which took over two years to complete and cost $250,000 suggested that the Brooklyn and New York Federations merge and that, in addition to raising funds, Federation take on the task of setting communal priorities.[38]

Hardly innovative or original, this idea confirmed the initial intent of the philanthropic sponsors of the first meeting. Clearly New York Federation leaders could not proceed to set communal priorities for all of New York's Jews when its activities were limited to Manhattan and the Bronx. In fact, opponents of the founding of New York Federation in 1917 originally argued that it represented an "attempt to gain control of all Jewish philanthropy in New York." While Federation leaders denied these charges at the time, the nonpartisan Survey gave them a mandate to absorb Brooklyn's Federation on scientific grounds. In addition, they expected the Survey to generate the consensus to effect the consolidation. To that end, James Brooke, a member of Brooklyn Federation's Board of Directors, precipitated a public debate on the same query contained in the January letter calling the first meeting to launch the Survey. Anticipating its publication, Brooke asked whether New York and Brooklyn Federations should consolidate and whether other charitable agencies ought to be admitted into the new city-wide Federation. Brooke's case in favor of consolidation combined an appeal to New York Jews' ethnic ties and to the logic of American business efficiency with an attack on localism. The existence of "two organizations engaged in the same charitable activities" he blamed on "local pride and narrow provincialism. . . . It matters little from what side of the East River the cry for help emanates," he urged. "Cooperation is the keynote of our business enterprises and we should therefore take a leaf from the experiences of commercial enterprises as a guide for our activities in philanthropic endeavor."[39]

The recommendations for consolidation denigrated as parochial the strong ties Jews had to their neighborhoods, local associations, and small organizations. Ignoring the network of primary relationships Jews had structured throughout the city, the Survey's scientific perspective assumed that Jews lived anonymous, isolated lives in need of membership in a city-wide community. These scientific premises supported Federation's desire to control the effervescent Jewish community life evident throughout the city. Consolidation implied control, a control legitimated by the communal consensus evoked by the Survey. Federation leaders hoped the Survey would provide the social cement of personal feeling that would allow Jews to become part of a philanthropically structured community based on the secondary relationships appropriate to the American urban milieu. The Survey would transform an instrumental community into a moral one capable of superseding the communal associations characteristic of immigrant Jewish life.

But while the Survey sparked widespread debate among Jews, it failed to generate the consensus required to override dissension. The representative of socialist labor on the Survey's citizen committee, Baruch Charney Vladeck, balked at the idea of enlarging the number of Federation constitutent societies. He contended that "the present mode of representation of either the New York or Brooklyn Federation does not encompass the elements of the Jewish community and unless a new form of representation is carried out, it would be unhealthy to have all philanthropic organizations managed from one office." Vladeck went along with proposals for consolidation of New York and Brooklyn Federations, arguing that "one organization would be in a better position to reach all Jews who can afford to contribute to charity than two separate federations can." But the Survey did not convince him of the need to submit the socialist and secularist Jewish organizations to the supervision of wealthy philanthropists. Joseph Barondess, a labor leader, Zionist, and lawyer, opposed even the consolidation proposal, arguing that Brooklyn Federation encouraged greater intimacy among its members and was more democratically organized than its New York counterpart. Barondess also attacked New York Federation for wanting "to be relieved of the burden of supporting" Jewish schools. "I am a firm believer in the old well-established principle of Israel, the Torah and God are one," he declared, "and while it is very praiseworthy to minister to the physical needs of the poor, indigent, and afflicted, I deem it is . . . even more important to minister to their Jewish educational needs."[40] In short, Barondess rejected the concept of a philanthropic Jewish community.

Such critical opposition overwhelmed the enthusiasm generated by Federation-sponsored conferences and by the Survey itself. Its first published report received loud acclaim in the Jewish and Gentile English language press. Characteristically, an editorial in the New York *Evening Post* praised the Survey "as an ex-

ample of the kind of activity that renders modern philanthropy a
new thing under the sun—a combination of sympathy and efficiency which, if anything can, will some day reduce poverty to
the vanishing point." The *Post* editorial placed Federation in the
mainstream of American charity of the 1920s. The moderate Yiddish daily *The Day* also expressed sentiments of approval, following a successful Federation conference of fraternal orders, neighborhood groups, shops, factories, and offices. *The Day* urged
Federation to bridge the economic differences among New York
Jews, to encourage the wealthy to accept the fact that the masses
could contribute both money and ideas. It pointed out that if the
masses could be involved in helping the poor, they might be de-
flected from dreams of revolutionary solutions. The collective enterprise, *The Day* editorialized, could unite rich and working
class Jews, give New York Jews a sense of identity, and serve as
their communal representative.[41]

Such expectations for Jewish philanthropy in the city pointed
both to Federation's success in developing a nonsectarian ideology
of Jewish community and to the vacuum Federation occupied.
Federation offered to lead New York Jews; it developed an ideology which stressed a minimum number of shared values as the
basis for collective Jewish endeavor, and it elaborated an institutional structure reflecting the American political model. Few Jewish groups could present an alternative to this program, but many
could refuse to cooperate or to assent to Federation's communal
consensus. Federation leaders sensed this dilemma when they
turned to the Survey, but the Survey failed to spark the hoped-
for consensus. The onset of the Depression the year after the Survey published its second and final report only aggravated the
fragmentation of New York Jewish communal efforts. No plan of
consolidation was able to override the objections of entrenched
interests or the practical economic difficulties until more than a
decade passed. Throughout the 1930s Brooklyn Federation
leaders regularly pleaded for money from New York Federation's
Board of Trustees to support Brooklyn's Jewish needy. Only after
six years of joint fund-raising did the two Federations merge and
the combined New York Federation implement the Survey's recommendations.[42]

Though the Depression spurred a reassessment of ends and

means in Jewish philanthropy, Federation succeeded in preserving its ideology intact. The creation of the Council of Fraternal and Benevolent Organizations did not essentially compromise the Business Men's Council. Rather, the second Council complemented the Business Men's Council, as did Federation's Women's Division and neighborhood network, by providing the vital membership figures which validated Federation's claim to represent New York Jews. By 1942 Federation had enrolled 265,000 individuals, over 10 percent of the city's Jewish population. Yet the Council's trades organization continued to be "the bulwark and mainstay of the annual fund-raising campaign."[43]

Similarly, although the Jewish Communal Survey failed to achieve its larger goal of consensus through self-knowledge, it did forestall any attempt to supplant the concept of a philanthropic community as the scientifically appropriate one for New York Jews. New York Federation's leaders succeeded in winning acceptance for their nonsectarian ideology of community in part because American society legitimated it. The Gospel of Wealth endorsed nonsectarian philanthropy as a dogma of American civil religion. Jews shared in this civil religious fellowship when they joined a Jewish philanthropic community dedicated to helping all without regard to race or creed. Similarly, the American ideal of the separation of church and state validated Federation's refusal to support Jewish religious organizations. Within this ideological framework Federation leaders pursued their Progressive American quest for community and social control. While they attained neither the philanthropic community they imagined nor the social control they desired, Federation leaders did acquire recognized authority and influence. Federation's nonsectarian ideology brought together a wider spectrum of New York Jews than any neighborhood organization. Furthermore, through the Business Men's Council, Federation succeeded in integrating a significant minority of second generation east European Jews into its leadership structure, patching the split between Uptown and Downtown Jews. If Federation failed to weld all Jews into a collective unit, the fault lay with the limits of its view of community.

New York City Federation leaders discovered in fund raising a source of moral community which emphasized the American character of Jewish distinctiveness. Federation's community embraced even the most nominal Jew and did not promote any substantial barrier to assimilation. For those Jews oriented toward Jewish tradition and concerned with cultural continuity, the Federation ideology lacked adequate roots in a Jewish past. What kind of heritage did Federation offer future generations of Jews? Such a question implied a concern with education as a vehicle of cultural transmission. The various Jewish constituencies participating in Federation's philanthropic community contended over the issue of education. Their contention spelled dissent from Federation's larger claims of leadership.

7

Orthodox Judaism must be taken out of the ghettos where it is now hidden and confined. It must stand conspicuously before American Jews as a challenge and an invitation. This will be accomplished through the building of a great educational institution, grounded in the ancient faith of Israel and at the same time thoroughly American and in complete sympathy and understanding with the spirit of the day.

Judge Otto Rosalsky,
Jewish Daily Bulletin, December 23, 1924.

Yeshiva College:
Orthodox Hedge

In December 1923 the Board of Directors of the Orthodox Rabbi Isaac Elchanan Theological Seminary launched a $5 million fund-raising campaign for the Yeshiva and a new school of higher education, the Yeshiva College.[1] An effort to lift the Yeshiva out of the Lower East Side, the fund-raising drive stimulated Orthodox Jews to redefine their relationship to the American environment. The proposal to establish a Yeshiva College, a liberal arts college sponsored by a yeshiva, sparked a debate on the goals of American Orthodox Judaism. A Yeshiva College combined American and Jewish institutions of higher education into an original synthesis. Thus, through the process of compromise, Orthodox Jews erected a hedge around traditional Judaism which enhanced and protected it, much as the law the rabbis had once constructed as a hedge around the Torah.

The fund-raising network organized by Yeshiva College unified second generation Orthodox Jews in New York City and generated among them a communal self-consciousness surmounting the localized concerns of disparate city neighborhoods. The fund-raising campaign also encouraged the emergence of new spokesmen for Orthodox Judaism in America. When the drive appeared to be successful in 1928, it heightened the stature of New York City's Orthodox leadership. The campaign linked Zionist and non-Zionist educational institutions and provided an arena where immigrant and second generation Jews could define a common program for second generation Orthodox youth. Just as the New York Federation fund-raising during the 1920s tried to locate a consensus for Jewish communal action, so the Yeshiva College drive uncovered a discrete ideological constituency.

The decision to establish a Yeshiva College came on the heels of acrid debate over the restriction of Jewish students at Harvard and Columbia. The fund-raising publicity extended the discussion of the relationship of American Jews to secular institutions of higher education. The Yeshiva College proposal not only brought into focus the problems faced by Jewish students who desired college degrees but it raised as well the larger issue of the status of Jewish culture in the United States. For the Yeshiva College combined a view of Jewish learning and its place in a program of higher education with a pragmatic concern for Jewish group continuity. The Yeshiva College idea attracted a variety of interpretations, each one refracting a vision of American society and of the Jews' role within it. Oriented toward the future, the debate over a Jewish university in general and a Yeshiva College in particular produced several paradigms of Jewish education in a democratic society. Ultimately the Yeshiva College crystallized a relationship of Jewish culture to the Jewish people in its educational program, which defined the identity of American Orthodox Judaism.

The concept of a Yeshiva College developed among Yeshiva directors partly in response to the success in the early 1920s of the Talmudical Academy for boys sponsored by the Rabbi Isaac Elchanan Theological Seminary (RIETS). Founded in 1916, the Academy combined Talmud study with a secular high school curriculum mandated by New York State law. The course of instruction led to a high school diploma upon graduation, while the level of the Talmud classes surpassed those offered in any Jewish supplementary afternoon school. In establishing a liberal arts college, the Directors of the Rabbi Isaac Elchanan Theological Seminary proposed to let young Jewish men continue their religious studies in the Yeshiva without interruption for college. The Yeshiva College would eliminate competition between the pursuit of secular and religious education, since both could be obtained under one roof. In addition, a Yeshiva College would help keep students in the Yeshiva and would draw to RIETS students who intended to enter other vocations than the rabbinate. As Harry Fischel, wealthy builder and ardent supporter of RIETS, explained: "It is our aim to produce educated rabbis, yet we are mindful of the fact that in order to produce ten rabbis it is necessary to educate at least one hundred young boys, so as to have material from which to select those who are eligible to take up the study of rabbinical culture."[2] By making RIETS more attractive to a larger number of students, the Yeshiva College would help it achieve its stated purpose of being a center of Jewish study for rabbis and devoted laymen alike.

Most of the lay leaders of RIETS enthusiastically supported this idea of a Yeshiva College. On the Board of Directors were such successful, upper-class immigrants as banker Mendel Gottesman, builder Harry Fischel, and real estate merchant Nathan Lamport. They recognized the value of higher education in America and expected to send their own children to college. The Yeshiva College they envisioned represented an Orthodox synthesis of Jewish and American values designed to perpetuate traditional Judaism in the United States by producing a dedicated laity and a new rabbinical leadership. These rabbis would "be able to deliver sermons in English so that they may appeal to the hearts of the younger generation" and still decide ritual questions authoritatively. Such leaders would assure Jewish cultural continuity.[3]

The idea of a Jewish college stemmed also from the changing educational situation of New York Jews. Reform Rabbi Louis I. Newman astutely observed that "fifteen years ago a Jewish University in America would have been virtually unthinkable. Jews in colleges and universities either in number or influence presented no problems." In the years immediately following the first World War the numbers of Jewish students desiring to go to college increased substantially as more Jews acquired the income to support their children in school. But this upsurge in Jews attending college collided with the decision of colleges to reduce their enrollments in the postwar period. The colleges' shift in interest from expansion and the structural reforms of the past two decades—trends which had encouraged Jews to take advantage of new collegiate opportunities—coincided with an ugly mood of nativism, anti-Semitism, and anti-radicalism. The imposition of selective admissions reduced the percentage of Jewish students entering Columbia University from 40 percent to 22 percent in a two year period from 1919 to 1921. The following year Harvard's announcement of its intention to restrict Jewish admission opened a bitter debate on anti-Semitism in higher education.[4]

Rabbi Newman argued that efforts to bar the Jew "from liberal and professional colleges is in reality designed to banish him from the field of competition with Gentile professional men. If the Jew loses his fight to gain admission to the college campus," he continued, "he is defeated in a far more significant battle, namely, the right to entrance into higher spheres of the professions and commerce." Jews and Gentiles countered Newman's argument by suggesting that "indiscriminate discrimination" was at fault. Such prejudice forced "the more liberal institutions," in Felix Warburg's words, to become "quickly surcharged with Hebrews, which made these places undesirable even for Gentiles generally welcoming associations with Jews . . . and as such, unsatisfactory to the modern Jews themselves, who strongly object to being thrown back upon themselves, thereby losing the opportunity, sought particularly for their children, of a healthy and thorough Americanization." Warburg's argument meshed with that of Harvard president A. Lawrence Lowell, who claimed that restricting Jewish students would reduce anti-Semitism and encourage assimilation. According to Lowell, limiting the number of Jewish students to a proportion acceptable to Gentiles would enhance Harvard's "democratic, national" character and would promote "a sympathetic understanding" among its students.[5]

The "advocates of quotas did not question the right of Jews to a college education," sociologist Stephen Steinberg points out. "Rather the issue was the right of certain Eastern colleges to preserve their unique character, which was Protestant and upper-class." As one dean put it, "we do not want to make our college a Ghetto." While Newman might object that "it is a fallacy to believe that Gentiles have a monopoly on gentility, and that Jews learn breeding and cultivation only through association with them," the popular reputation of colleges with a majority of Jewish students, such as the City College of New York, reflected these assumptions.[6]

Newman proposed a Jewish University as an alternative to exclusion, "not because we desire to be tribal," he wrote, "but because we refuse to allow restriction to stifle our talents and deprive us of the privilege of freely expressing our native energies on behalf of ourselves and the community of which we are part." Newman first published his suggestion in the pages of the *Jewish Tribune* in October 1922, several months after Harvard's announcement of restriction. The proposal to establish a Jewish university elicited a wide-ranging debate. Those who opposed Newman argued that a Jewish university evaded the problem of exclusion and that it would accentuate the evils of Jewish separateness and lead to greater segregation. Some accepted Newman's analysis of the situation but thought that the appropriate response would be for Jews to encourage the expansion of state or municipal colleges. Zionists agreed that a Jewish university was needed, but pointed out that it would be futile to erect one in the United States. The only hope lay in the recently established Hebrew University in Palestine. Newman's supporters generally underscored one or another of his points. A few, like writer Waldo Frank, extended Newman's argument and elaborated the positive premises for a Jewish university. "As I take it, a University is a sort of flower growing naturally from the cultural impulses of a group," Frank wrote. "If the impulse is strong, if the means are adequate, the University must follow." Frank thought the establishment of a Jewish university would require a shift from the process of material acquisition and possession currently characteristic of American Jewish life to a new posture of spiritual and cultural creation. "If our ethnic wealth is to become cultural wealth, there must be cultural institutions to effect the change," he argued. The Jewish university was just such a cultural institution.[7]

Frank agreed with Newman's description of the university's curriculum as " 'universal,' liberal and free." At the Jewish University, Newman explained, "no attempt would be made to 'Judaize' the students or their work." The University would be open to all students, regardless of race, color, or religion, although the bulk of the students would come from the Jewish masses who faced difficulties obtaining a college education. Frank elaborated on this theme, pointing out that "such a University would function beyond Judaism just as Harvard has long functioned beyond Unitarianism." Yet because Frank saw the Jewish University as an American Jewish "cultural expression," he also accepted the

argument that the elite private universities "had their sources in
the Anglo-Saxon culture that came to dominate our colonial expansion." Furthermore, Frank observed, "they remain true to
their source. They should do so. It is in the retainment of this cultural individuality that they alone can function," he concluded.
Frank's pluralist stance led him to endorse the argument of those
who upheld the need for restriction, but he indicated that alone
this view was inadequate. "What is needed is not to make over
Harvard and Yale and Princeton . . . , but to supplement them
with other cultural expressions."[8] Frank's analysis completed the
circle of argumentation initiated by Harvard's decision to restrict
Jewish enrollment. The entire debate on a Jewish university set in
motion by Newman brought before New York Jews a wide range
of arguments for Jewish cultural expression through higher education and foreshadowed public discussion of the Yeshiva College
proposal.

A $5 million building fund campaign carried on for five years
made possible the actual creation of Yeshiva College. In December 1923 Rabbi Herbert Goldstein, Harry Fischel's son-in-law
and head of the Union of Orthodox Jewish Congregations, announced the plan. The drive continued through December 1928,
when the new buildings were dedicated. The Yeshiva's Board of
Directors chose a prominent businessman and observant Brooklyn Jew, Harris Selig, to head the campaign. Selig previously had
organized a successful $1 million drive for the Beth Israel hospital
of Boston. He designed the initial Yeshiva campaign around several dinners. In December 1924 the first dinner celebrated the
acquisition of a site for the Yeshiva and raised $800,000 from rel-
atively few individuals—such stalwart supporters of RIETS as
Fischel, Lamport, and Judge Otto Rosalsky. Republican politician Samuel Levy enthusiastically described the event as "a red
letter day in Jewish life in America." At that time, he went on,
"Orthodox Jewry was reborn, revitalized in America." Although
Yeshiva leaders expected to raise only $100,000 from the 125 peo-
ple who attended the dinner, "the magnitude of the proposed institution—the arresting significance of this movement, heretofore
considered as a nebulous dream—the responsibility resting upon
this small group of earnest men and women for their children and
their children's children," Levy wrote effusively, "all these emo-

tions crystallized and before the meeting was over nearly $1,000,000 had been pledged." Even the *New York Times* was moved to comment editorially: "We did not think it possible to squeeze another thrill out of a drive for funds, but at the dinner," it admitted, "things happened. . . . Orthodox Jews had never before raised such an amount for so stupendous an undertaking," the editorial observed, "and no such ambitious project had ever before been attempted on behalf of any educational institution."[9]

Fired by such dramatic success, a year later Selig promoted a $1,000-a-plate dinner to secure the second million dollars. Despite the unusually high cover charge, this dinner drew approximately 1,200 participants to the Hotel Astor. In December 1926, after construction had started, Selig sponsored a 70th birthday testimo-

Laying the cornerstone of RIETS's new home on Amsterdam Avenue and 186th Street in Washington Heights in 1927: Harry Fischel (center figure left), Nathan Lamport (center figure right, leaning), Mendel Gottesman (behind Lamport to the right, facing camera). *Courtesy of Yeshiva University Photo Library.*

nial dinner for Nathan Lamport, a man who viewed the Yeshiva as his life's project. The only significant mass fund-raising event Selig planned, a music festival at Madison Square Garden in May 1926, proved to be a source of conflict. Thus, as soon as the $5 million goal appeared to be within reach, Selig resigned as Executive Director of the Yeshiva campaign.[10]

The fund-raising drive brought the Yeshiva out of obscurity. Its seemingly endless publicity linked the campaign for the college with a number of important trends prevalent among second generation Jews in the 1920s. Yeshiva College spokesmen struggled to overcome the dualism inherent in the immigrant Jewish experience. Preeminently, the drive for Yeshiva College embodied the efforts of second generation Orthodox Jews to accommodate traditional Judaism to American life. Modern Orthodox leaders like Goldstein hoped that the creation of Yeshiva College would make "Jewish learning self-sustaining in America." The incorporation of secular liberal arts college studies into the Jewish yeshiva framework would crown their effort to adapt Jewish religious study to the American environment.[11]

The Yeshiva College campaign illustrated the power of philanthropic fund raising to strengthen the bonds of religious unity. While other Jewish organizations conducted national campaigns for comparable sums, these drives usually appealed to all American Jews, not to an ideologically defined segment. Orthodox Jewry found itself in the Yeshiva College campaign. Never before had Orthodox Jews united to achieve anything big for themselves until the drive. It recruited second generation Orthodox Jews into the fund-raising network and promoted their acceptance as Orthodox Jewish leaders. In New York City the activity surmounted neighborhood barriers. The Building Committee brought together Manhattan and Brooklyn builders and realtors. Despite the participation of second generation Jews, the largest sums raised by the Yeshiva came from a coterie of immigrants. The first two dinners, which generated approximately 40 percent of the total sum, appealed to a compact group of Orthodox Jews, but the dinners highlighted their new fund-raising methods. Extensive publicity afterward emphasized their philanthropic achievements: Yeshiva supporters adopted modern American mechanisms. They es-

chewed the house-to-house canvass, the highly paid staff, the
elaborate organization of earlier Orthodox fund raising.[12]

Because the creation of the college was linked inexorably
with the success of the building fund campaign, choice of the
physical site for the buildings assumed unusual importance. Fischel, who took over the chairmanship of the Building Committee
upon the death of Samuel Greenstein, expanded its original plans
and doubled the number of city lots purchased. He also emphasized the significance of the future location of Yeshiva College on
Amsterdam Avenue and West 186th Street, in the second generation middle class neighborhood of Washington Heights, instead of
in the Lower East Side, where RIETS had been situated since its
inception. Fischel felt that the Yeshiva College of America could
not claim exclusive national status as an organization situated on
the Lower East Side. The new Yeshiva needs "surroundings more
befitting the character of the proposed great institution," he
wrote. The Washington Heights site "is one of the most desirable
in the city. . . . It is near Columbia, City College and New York
University, situated on a hill three hundred feet above a beautiful
bend in the Harlem River and surrounded with parks on two
sides." For Fischel, these strategic considerations helped to define
the Yeshiva College's character. Judge Otto Rosalsky, New York
Jewish communal leader, agreed with Fischel's assessment. "Orthodox Judaism must be taken out of the ghettos where it is now
hidden and confined," he declared at the 1924 Chanukah dinner
for the Yeshiva. Orthodox Judaism, he went on, "must stand conspicuously before American Jews as a challenge and an invitation." Privately both lay and rabbinic leaders agreed on the importance of dissociating the Yeshiva and its College from the
immigrant Lower East Side.[13] Even the Yiddish-speaking Union
of Orthodox Rabbis, the Agudath Harabanim, pointed out the
status of the Yeshiva's new surroundings. The Agudath Harabanim announced in the Yiddish press that "beautiful buildings
have been constructed for the Yeshiva and they represent the
pride and glory of Orthodox American Jewry. These buildings
have been constructed in the uptown section of New York and it
represents the successful arrival of Orthodoxy in the mainstream
of American Jewry." The Agudath Harabanim concluded with a

Opening of the Main Building of Yeshiva College in 1929. *Courtesy of Yeshiva University Photo Library.*

celebration "of the victory of traditional Judaism over the spirit of reform and secularism that exists in our land" which the Yeshiva embodied.[14] With the emphasis on physical size, beautiful surroundings, a high status neighborhood, and the proximity of other prestigious American colleges, Orthodox Jewry unhesitantly entered the "mainstream" of American Jewish life.

In the process of moving the Yeshiva out of the Lower East Side and onto the Heights, lay and rabbinic spokesmen articulated conflicting visions of the future college's purposes. The personal enthusiasms of those involved in the undertaking brought before the public some of the differences between the secular and religious orientations of second generation New York City Orthodox Jews in the 1920s. A respected lay leader like Rosalsky could define the Yeshiva College as "grounded in the ancient faith of Israel and at the same time thoroughly American and in complete sympathy and understanding with the spirit of the day" without provoking objections. But such a definition lacked clarity and invited interpretation. And as the campaign picked up momentum, new supporters brought to the Orthodox bandwagon their own versions of the College's goals. The image of a Yeshiva College stimulated the imagination of many second generation Orthodox Jews. Morris White, a wealthy realtor and industrialist and chairman of the Yeshiva College Dedication Dinner in 1928, proclaimed proudly that "with the establishment of the Yeshiva College, we are building a tower of strength for Jewish learning in America. An institution like the Yeshiva College will build a line of defense against the inroads of indifference and desertion, which is noticeable among our young in this country." Commenting that America "knows of the magnificent buildings built and erected by the Jews of our country," White pointed out that the Yeshiva would inspire similar sentiments as an "edifice for Jewish learning. . . . The Yeshiva College will be the arsenal of the Jewish people in America," he concluded, the building "where the spiritual equipment for the defense of our existence will be stored and treasured."[15]

Rabbi Bernard Revel, head of the Yeshiva since 1915, articulated a less heady vision of the college. Unlike White, Revel saw Yeshiva College as a necessary compromise with the demands of the American environment, rather than as the vanguard of a new movement in American Jewish life. Revel recognized that although the traditional Jewish world view did not necessarily include advanced secular study, American society valued it. Given the impact of American attitudes on the second generation, Revel chose to modify Jewish tradition to accommodate the higher secular education eagerly sought by college-age Jews. Instead of di-

vorcing Jewish religious learning from the pursuit of advanced
secular knowledge, Revel opted for a synthesis of Jewish and
American values as more desirable than separation. Yet he continued to argue that the primary purpose of the college would be
to promote Jewish ideals. Revel emphasized that Yeshiva College
was intended mainly for RIETS students, to give these men who
were dedicated to pursuing a career in the rabbinate, Jewish
teaching, Jewish social service, or Jewish scholarship an opportunity also to acquire the higher secular education desired by Jews
in America. "Such a college will help bridge the chasm between
intellectualism and faith," Revel wrote. "It will present to at least
a portion of our academic youth, in a proper setting the spirit and
vital message of Judaism, and make it a potent force in their
lives." The Yeshiva aimed to "help bring back the days when our
great thinkers and intellectual giants were at the same time our
religious guides," Revel explained.[16]

Revel and the leaders of RIETS responded to the problem of
promoting Jewish higher education in America by leaving the substance of Jewish learning intact while changing the context. What
New York State law mandated on the elementary and high school
level (namely, that parochial schools provide under their auspices
a minimum of secular studies) evolved into a creative accommodation to the Jewish demand for secular knowledge on the college
level. Even more than Catholic parochial colleges, the secondary
school yeshiva in New York City provided an accessible and acceptable model for the builders of Yeshiva College. The structural
familiarity of this synthesis adopted by the Yeshiva College in
part made its innovation appear to be only one of degree, and
therefore less threatening. Yet for Orthodox Jews who sensed the
radical change in Jewish education embodied in the Yeshiva College, the proposal stirred qualms for the future. Pondering the establishment of the College in 1926 in the context of the "Problem
of Higher Jewish Education in America," Peter Wiernik, editor of
the Orthodox Yiddish daily *Morning Journal*, admitted that "we
are . . . at sea even in that part of the Vineyard of Israel where
conformity to our great past is mostly stressed."[17]

The articulation of an Orthodox American Jewish educational synthesis provoked widespread debate among New York
City Jews. While Revel never lost his power to shape the college,

the challenges presented by laymen and rabbis suggest the many tensions that beset Orthodox Jews in New York in the 1920s. Especially during the five years of the building fund campaign, College leaders hammered out several alternative definitions of the nature and purpose of Jewish learning and the extent of adaptation required to perpetuate traditional Judaism in America.

The debate over the specific character of Yeshiva College revolved about two institutional reference points: the eastern European yeshivas and the American liberal arts colleges. In both cases, the models lacked the combination of elements which was to make Yeshiva College distinctive. Few European yeshivas offered any secular studies, although in the 1920s the Berlin Yeshiva and the Lida Yeshiva introduced secular subjects into their curriculum. Similarly, few American liberal arts colleges or universities included courses on Jewish studies. Although several prestigious universities created departments of Semitics in the late nineteenth century, these rarely appeared to be Jewish cultural expressions. Indeed, the endowment of the first university chair in Jewish thought and philosophy at Harvard by Lucius Littauer revealed the extent to which Jewish learning had been ignored by American universities. Littauer admitted that he endowed the chair in 1925 "not from a religious but from a secular standpoint; that true enlightenment may result from the contribution throughout the ages of the Jews to the humanities; that they may become more fully and clearly understood." Rabbi Hyman Enelow of the Reform Temple Emanu-El, who encouraged both Littauer's initial gift and Linda Miller's subsequent endowment of a chair in Jewish history at Columbia, went further than Littauer in his analysis of the importance of Jewish learning in secular universities. Enelow argued that beyond a "contribution to general enlightenment" and the increase in "respect for Judasim," the secular study of Jewish history and literature "would increase the self-respect of Jewish students at our universities, who . . . often feel humiliated that their own tradition and heritage enjoys no academic recognition" and it "would diminish, if not destroy, the ignorance of Jewish experience and ideals, which so often is the source of suspicion and antagonism." Despite Enelow's cogent reasoning, designed to appeal to wealthy congregants who worried about anti-Semitism and yearned for Gentile acceptance, the Miller and

Littauer chairs remained singularly conspicuous. Efforts to bridge
the gulf between Jewish and American learning—to obtain recognition for the former in secular institutions or to incorporate the
latter in Jewish institutions—were confined to a handful of prominent examples. In the 1920s few schools existed where higher Jewish education could be obtained in a secular context or advanced
secular studies pursued under Jewish organizational auspices.[18]

Some colleges, it is true, seemed "Jewish" because of the
number of Jewish students attending them. City College of New
York, with an enrollment 85 percent Jewish, acquired the nick-
name "the cheder on the Hill" in the 1920s. While CCNY graduate A. L. Shands admitted that "the nearest thing to a secular
Jewish college in New York is often named as CCNY," he also
noted that "the Jews of New York take this designation with a
sense of humor. They are well aware of the minority of Jewish
teachers in that school, and the complete absence of any studies
dealing with the Jewish religion." Although in the 1930s New
York University and the newly established Brooklyn College offered instruction in Hebrew, the paths of Jewish and secular studies in the realm of higher education rarely converged. Attempts to
unite the two produced dissension.[19]

As head of the Yeshiva College, Revel grasped the dimensions
of this dilemma. In 1928 he indicated the scope of the problem by
describing what he considered to be the proper relationship of
Torah learning to general knowledge. "The Torah is to us not a
discipline among disciplines," Revel wrote, "but the crux of our
moral and spiritual existence, the test of ultimate truth. We hold
that truth in all its phases can but strengthen and deepen our understanding of and adherance to the Torah, its demands of life,
and its ideals." Yet his own faith in the primacy of Jewish learning did not diminish his commitment to an unfettered, secular liberal arts college. Revel placed his synthesis within a pluralist understanding of American society and culture. At the 1926
commencement exercises of the Yeshiva he invoked ideas associated with the Jewish philosopher of cultural pluralism,
Horace Kallen. "All serious minded Americans recognize that
American culture is enriched and advanced not by the sub-
mergence of all the cultural forms and phases of its varied and
component parts into one cultural melting pot," Revel urged,

"but by each group contributing its best to American cultural values." Revel saw "the unique contribution of America to civilization" as the "dwelling and working together of diverse cultural groups in harmonious blending, all united by mutual fervent devotion to the fundamental ideals and traditions of the Republic."[20]

Revel implemented this understanding of the proper relationship of Jewish and secular studies by dividing college class time proportionately. Students at Yeshiva College spent the mornings and each afternoon until 3:00 P.M. engaged in talmudic study. The liberal arts program, including the study of Jewish history, literature, and philosophy, absorbed the remainder of the afternoon and evenings. In spite of the heavy class schedule and the precedence given to Talmud over the liberal arts curriculum, Revel also introduced in 1934 such extracurricular activities as intercollegiate sports, which were associated with American college life but foreign to traditional Yeshiva study. Revel maintained the compromise evolved in the apportionment of class time in the division of honors given by Yeshiva College. Before the establishment of the College, Revel had made it a custom to invite learned rabbinic scholars visiting in America to give an exposition of the Talmud, or *shiur*, at the Yeshiva. After the college was created he continued this practice. But when Yeshiva College celebrated its first graduations in the early 1930s, Revel chose to bestow honorary degrees from the College upon Jews and Gentiles who had gained renown in the secular world, and thus uphold the liberal arts values of the college. In 1933 Yeshiva College awarded its first honorary degree to New York Governor Herbert Lehman (himself a Reform Jew), and John Finley, editor of the *New York Times*.[21]

This policy drew heated criticism from some Orthodox Jews. They challenged the legitimacy of the distinctive forms Revel employed to honor traditional Jews and secular individuals. For such Orthodox Jews as Nathan Isaacs, Harvard law professor and staunch supporter of the college, any recognition accorded by Yeshiva College to non-Orthodox Jews—especially to Reform Jews—was tantamount to honoring lax Jewish religious behavior. In 1934 Isaacs wrote Revel to complain that the disposition of the honorary degrees were "a declaration to the student body that

success in politics, business or science will win the approval of
their *alma mater*, even if they disregard the Judaism that she has
taught them." Nevertheless, over the opposition's protestations,
Yeshiva College in 1934 gave an honorary degree to Albert Einstein.[22]

Lay leaders in charge of fund-raising also challenged Revel's
synthesis, but from a secular perspective. They introduced into

Conferring an honorary degree on Albert Einstein at Yeshiva College graduation, 1934. Bernard Revel, head of the Yeshiva, stands second from the left.
Courtesy of Yeshiva University Photo Library.

the publicity for the Yeshiva their own concepts regarding the
college's functions which reflected their acute sensitivity to Gentile
American values. As public enthusiasm for the Yeshiva College
campaign increased, some lay leaders posited a response to anti-
Semitism as part of the Yeshiva College rationale. Aware of the
debate at Harvard University over restriction of Jewish students,
the outcry over alleged quotas at several New York City schools,
and allegations of discrimination against Jewish professors, Jewish publicists argued that Yeshiva College constituted an apt re-
buttal to these intolerant acts. At a publicity luncheon preceding
the Yeshiva's Madison Square Garden music festival, its one
large-scale popular fund-raising event, Gustavus Rogers, a wealthy
Brooklyn lawyer, asserted that the Yeshiva College would pro-

vide a haven where Jews could study. By implication, the college also would refute anti-Semitic charges that Jews contributed nothing to higher education in the United States. Harris Selig also saw Yeshiva College in the context of the American collegiate environment. He compared its founding with the original religious establishment of Harvard, Princeton, or Brown. In time, Selig expected, Yeshiva College would become a nonsectarian institution open to everyone.[23]

Such fund-raising publicity soon produced public dispute between the Yeshiva's rabbinic and lay leaders regarding the college's purposes. Speaking to its rabbinical supporters, Revel indignantly contradicted both Rogers and Selig. A religious impulse lay behind the creation of the college; ethnic and cultural concerns were subordinate. "The chief purpose of the college department of the Yeshiva," he declared, was "to afford those students of the Torah who are continuing their studies in an atmosphere of love and loyalty to the Torah and Jewish ideals, an opportunity to acquire the learning and culture of the modern world, in addition to the learning of the culture of Israel." But even so consistent a lay supporter of the Yeshiva as Samuel Levy, later Borough President of Manhattan, envisioned a less parochial role for the college than Revel. Speaking at the Madison Square Garden music festival, he remarked that "such an institution is not for Orthodox Jews alone. It is for all scholars, Jews and gentiles." Levy saw the Yeshiva College validating Jewish learning for Gentiles in addition to legitimating secular study for Orthodox Jews.[24]

Reactions to the establishment of Yeshiva College reflected different ideas of the proper relationship of Jews and Judaism to American society and culture. In the ensuing debates, Jewish learning acquired symbolic structure; its form and content defined the Jews themselves. Conversely, the definition of the Jews as a religious, ethnic, or national group implied an ideal of Jewish learning and a setting for Jewish study. American Jews impressed Jewish learning into the service of their ideological battles.

The positive attitude of Reform Jews toward contact between Jews and Gentiles led them to oppose vigorously any Jewish organization which appeared to set up barriers to that social interaction. Concerned with fighting the discriminatory social restrictions established by Gentiles, such men as Louis Marshall and his associates on the American Jewish Committee kept a close watch on Jewish behavior which suggested exclusivity or separateness. Marshall denounced any Jewish university as a "glorified Ghetto." He saw the critical issue as Jewish separateness and, by implication, the perpetuation of immigrant traditions. Taking a slightly different tack, the English language weekly *American Hebrew* derogatorially compared Yeshiva College to Catholic parochial schools, imputing to both an un-American character. Newspaperman Charles Joseph, writing in the local *Brooklyn Review*, questioned "the wisdom of establishing Jewish universities if limited to the teaching of modern subjects." Joseph worried that "it may make it more difficult for Jews to get into other universities. Further, it seems to me to intensify the spirit of separatism of which there is already too much."[25] Most Reform Jews associated Jewish parochialism with the immigrant generation and its traditions. They felt that the second generation should aim to free itself from immigrant Jewish social and educational patterns in order to fit into the Reform definition of the Jews as a religious group.

But Reform Jews deemed Jewish learning pursued under religious auspices appropriate. Indeed, many equated advanced Jewish study with rabbinical training. Rabbi Samuel Schulman of the prestigious Reform Temple Beth-El in Manhattan endorsed the plan for Yeshiva College as a legitimate one "for strictly Orthodox Rabbis." He interpreted the creation of the College as the recognition by a segment of Orthodox Jews of the "indispensableness of secular education." Nevertheless, Rabbi Schulman's "ideal for the education of our Jewish youth" was "to bring to bear upon them all the Jewish influences we can, but to have them go for their secular education to the American colleges in which they can and should mingle freely with their Christian fellow-students."[26]

Other elements within the orbit of Reform Judaism actually defended the Yeshiva College concept. Joseph Shipley countered the attacks by decrying specialization, the "one great evil of Jewish life today." Encouraging an educated Jewish laity, Yeshiva College will help to reverse the prevalent viewpoint associated with Reform Jews that only rabbis need Jewish learning. He also observed pragmatically that "especially in metropolitan colleges, there is little of the campus life that helps give the college student 'social grace,' and the ability to mix in any society; where this does exist, it is doubtful that the college atmosphere is free from segregation and prejudice." The *B'nai B'rith Magazine* published a similar response. "There are those who will at once protest against such an institution," it observed. "They will say that a Jewish college serves to build a ghetto wall about the Jewish student." But the article rebutted these objections by referring not to Catholic institutions, but to "colleges conducted by the Methodists," whose purposes were "similar to those that animate the Yeshiva. Are the students of these institutions cut off from participation in the common life because they are being educated within their communions?" it queried. "Why are we Jews forever afraid of any expression of ourselves as Jews?"[27] While these analyses shared a common assumption that the Jews were a religious group, they differed in their interpretation of American society and hence of the Jews' place in that society.

Radical Jews, such as the editors of the Communist Yiddish daily *Freiheit*, objected to the perpetuation of Orthodox Judaism as anachronistic. They found distasteful any major effort to strengthen it. Communist Jews had little room in their world outlook for Jewish religion or Jewish education. But Cahan, a Socialist, encouraged an attitude of tolerance toward Orthodox efforts to perpetuate a distinctive Jewish culture. Nevertheless, many Jewish radicals considered the fund raising for Yeshiva College a colossal waste of money. They condemned the priorities of Orthodox Jews which placed religious education ahead of material relief for Jews overseas. The liberal Yiddish daily, *The Day*, expressed a more moderate attitude. Commenting on the placing of the Yeshiva College cornerstone, it remarked:

> The new Yeshiva College is the best proof that Orthodoxy has come to the conviction that it must combine the Jewish traditions with American education, that it must find a way of harmonizing the old Judaism with American conditions; that our pious Jews have finally realized that they can expect to perpetuate the old Jewish life-forms, not by ignoring the new conditions, but on the contrary, precisely by recognizing powerful factors in the American environment, and that only in this way can the further existence and development of Orthodoxy in America be assured.

The Day charitably concluded that "this is an important gain for the whole American Jewry. There is room in American Jewry for all tendencies which seek to preserve Judaism." By contrast, the Yiddishists within the socialist camp advocated a secular and radical Jewish education which used Yiddish language and culture as a source of generational continuity.[28] Such learning fit the Jews' character as a national, or at least an ethnic, group.

The Yiddish-speaking Orthodox rabbis, led by the presidents of the Agudath Harabanim, such as Rabbis Joseph Konwitz and Eliezer Silver, failed to see anything in the American environment to warrant the radical changes in traditional Jewish education Yeshiva College was effecting. From their viewpoint, traditional Judaism would survive by the time-tested mechanisms established in Europe. They opposed the acculturation of second generation Jews. Spurning innovation and accommodation, they sought to strengthen traditional Jewish education. These rabbis criticized the concept of a Yeshiva College: Orthodox rabbis did not need a secular college education. Drawing their inspiration from the eastern European yeshivas in which they had studied, they found no reason to compromise with the American environment. Yeshiva College was setting a dangerous precedent. Indeed, the Yeshiva's publication of scholarly articles challenging traditional Jewish interpretations of sacred texts confirmed these fears. And when money was scarce in the 1930s, the immigrant rabbis considered it extremely foolish to waste dollars on secular studies at the college, as these precious funds could have been spent on religious learning at the Yeshiva. Many of these rabbis had found an institutional home in the Yeshiva Torah Vodaath in Williamsburg when it added a Mesifta High School and expanded its program in the late 1920s. Antagonistic to advanced secular knowledge, the Mesifta offered only the subjects required by state law. The Mesifta's atmosphere resembled that of the European yeshivas and many members of the Agudath Harabanim found it a more congenial setting. Usually lacking secular education themselves, they did not understand the collegiate milieu and felt uncomfortable with the spirit on the Yeshiva College campus.[29]

Ironically, even some of its own lay leaders did not fully grasp the implications of the Yeshiva College synthesis. While new members were joining the fund-raising campaign, several second generation lay directors of the Yeshiva, including Samuel Levy, Samuel Lamport, and Otto Rosalsky, pursued the possibility of merging RIETS with the Jewish Theological Seminary. That lay leaders seriously contemplated the amalgamation of the two organizations which represented, respectively, Orthodox and Conservative Judaism indicated how much secular demands influenced their perceptions. For wealthy individuals faced with the task of raising huge sums in a building campaign—and the Jewish Theological Seminary also intended to launch a building-fund drive— the theological differences between the two schools were of merely academic significance. Many Seminary faculty members followed traditional Jewish ritual in their personal religious practices, pointing to the apparent similarity of the schools. Additionally, as the need to Americanize east European Jewish immigrants declined, the importance of the Seminary's work suffered a parallel decline in the eyes of its wealthy supporters. But for the rabbinic leaders of each school, important differences separated Yeshiva and Seminary.[30]

In defending the uniqueness of Yeshiva and Seminary, Revel clarified the purpose and functions of the former. Revel insisted in an extensive memorandum on the proposed merger that the Yeshiva's intentions to be a house of learning as well as to represent the Orthodox ideal of Torah differed radically from those of the Seminary, which primarily were to train rabbis. Unlike the Yeshiva, the Seminary attracted students who often lacked training in Talmud; in fact, because the Seminary required a Bachelor's Degree for entrance, it virtually mandated a weak Jewish religious education. Indeed, Revel argued, the work in each school reflected the disparate educational backgrounds of the students: Seminary students learned about the Talmud while Yeshiva students mastered the Talmud and Codes. Revel measured the results of Seminary training by pointing to the fact that Seminary rabbis served in synagogues without a *mehitza*, or barrier, separating the men and women during worship. According to Revel this departure from tradition reflected the type of education offered by the Seminary. Yeshiva rabbis who officiated in synagogues without a *mehitza* lost their rabbinical ordination privileges from RIETS.[31]

Revel's assessment accurately reflected the distinguishing

characteristics of each school. According to Marshall Sklare, the Seminary's "essential characteristics" included "its role as a rabbinical training school, its stress on the English language, the compromise character of the religious observance which it has exacted from the student body, and its cultivation of the 'science of Judaism.' "[32] While the Yeshiva College combined American secular education with traditional Jewish learning, its synthesis left each sphere intact. The Seminary compromised with the American environment through the professionalization of Jewish learning and the adoption of the secular methodology of critical scholarship.

Yet the laymen failed to perceive these significant differences. In sharp contrast to Revel's view, banker Felix Warburg, who was marginally involved in the merger, thought that the failure to amalgamate the schools stemmed from "too many vanities." Louis Marshall, a director of the Seminary who admitted that "for several years I worked very hard with others in trying to bring about a consolidation between the Yeshiva and the Jewish Theological Seminary of America," also blamed "a few wilful men." These Reform Jews, the lay directors of the Seminary, perceived east European Jews "as a homogeneous group" religiously and they deplored the rabbinical distinctions between Orthodox and Conservative.[33]

Despite the difficult Depression years which followed shortly after the failed merger efforts, the separate existence of the Seminary and Yeshiva allowed each to consolidate its different constituencies. The collapse of the proposed merger permitted Orthodox supporters of the Yeshiva College to clarify their own synthesis of Jewish values with the American environment. Throughout the 1930s Yeshiva leaders maintained the primacy of Jewish study over secular education. They also emphasized the traditional Jewish ideal of learning for its own sake, rather than accepting the American emphasis on education for vocational purposes. From such a perspective, the separation of Jew and Gentile mandated by the former's devotion to Jewish life mattered very little.

Given the commitment of Orthodox Jews to the explicit perpetuation of Jewish religious tradition—and not to the evolution of a new form of Jewishness compatible with American urban life—the creation of Yeshiva College indicates that even first and second generation Jews were attracted to American values. The establishment of the college suggests that Orthodox Jews, too, saw their future bound up with America. As early as 1926 Revel commented on the historical significance of building an Orthodox Jewish institution of higher education in the United States. "With the doors of our country closed," he noted, "we no more can draw upon the spiritual reservoirs of the Jewish centers in Europe. The stream of Jewish idealism from abroad, which has been enriching American Jewish life, is drying up. We are entrusted by Providence with the task of creating in this land a Jewish life," he concluded. In the decade dominated by Nazi persecution, the college became "our answer to a hostile world," Levy observed. "Yeshiva College is our expression of the will to live," he proclaimed.[34]

Accepting the demands of second generation Orthodox youth for a secular college education which prepared them for white collar and professional careers, Yeshiva leaders modified the traditional structure of Jewish education to include a liberal arts curriculum. The college also sustained the ideal of Jewishly knowledgeable laymen. The process of establishing Yeshiva College brought a new self-awareness and a sense of purpose to New York City Orthodox Jews. By lessening the identification of Orthodoxy exclusively with immigrant Jewish life, Yeshiva College shaped the character of American Orthodox Jewry. But the college's very success in defining its constituency precluded a broad appeal. Revel and his rabbinic supporters rejected the lay vision of an unencumbered liberal arts institution. They did not seek to build a Jewish Harvard. The Yeshiva College concept assumed a pluralist American society, but envisioned a Jewish contribution to American culture in terms of religious tradition. The Yeshiva College represented the possibilities and limits of modern Orthodox Judaism in the United States. Its synthesis of Jewish and American learning gave New York Jews a religious alternative to the secular ethnicity flourishing in the city's neighborhoods.

8

Some East European Jews followed the German Jews into the Republican party, and some, like other immigrants, went into the Democratic party. But at least as many become strong Socialists. . . .

What attracts Jews is liberalism, using the term to refer to the entire range of leftist positions, from the mildest to the most extreme. The Jewish vote is primarily an "ideological" rather than a party or even an ethnic one.

Nathan Glazer and Daniel Patrick Moynihan,
Beyond the Melting Pot (Cambridge: The M.I.T. Press and Harvard University Press, 1963), pp. 169, 167.

The Rise of the Jewish Democrat

Second generation Jews were ardent participants in the American political process. Democracy appeared to be the real religion of America and second generation Jews embraced the new faith. Norman Salit, a lawyer and rabbi of the Jewish Center of Far Rockaway, rhetorically observed in a radio speech before the 'presidential elections of 1928 "that if there is any shrine of America's liberties that shrine is the Polling Booth. If there is any sanctuary of the genius of our people, that sanctuary is the Voting House. If there is any altar, any rite, any Holy of Holies of American life," he intoned, "that altar is the Ballot Box, that rite is the vote, that Holy of Holies is the place wherein the unfettered American citizen steps for his sovereign moment, to stand . . . as High Priest and steward of his country's destinies, before his conscience and his God."[1]

Second generation Jews concurred with Rabbi Salit's invocation. Through the voting booths in their secure middle-class neighborhoods, Jews would enter into the blessings of American democracy. Participation in New York City's inter-ethnic politics inducted Jews into the mainstream of American life. Responding to their urban experience, their group interests, and their reception by established city politicians, second generation Jews evolved an American political style, affiliation, and program which was distinctively Jewish. Rooted in the neighborhood, second generation Jewish politics influenced city, state, and, with the advent of the New Deal, national political activity. Jews developed ethnic voting patterns even as they rejected the concept of a Jewish vote. Their success in local politics gave New York Jews an institutional anchor against assimilation while it promoted a common ideological outlook.[2]

Potential Jewish candidates sensed a problem in the emerging political style of the second generation. They worried that excessive exposure might arouse anti-Semitism. They weighed the benefits of public power against the dangers of public recognition, and also tried to balance support for "Jewish" political issues with a nonethnic stance. Yet the local ethnic nature of New York politics encouraged the blurring of these distinctions. Paying debts to one's constituents often meant emphasizing ethnic issues. Aware of the manner in which political debts were paid, Jewish politicians demanded their just rewards—nomination to public office and legislation on Jewish issues. Fortunately, local politics provided a way to mediate the conflicting claims generated by ethnic political practices in the city. Through the clubhouse, second generation Jews succeeded in wedding the Jewish style of ethnic politics to the local machine.

The growth of New York Jewish ethnic politics coincided with the development of Jewish liberalism among second generation Jews. Conventional ethnic politics held little attraction for New York Jewish leaders before 1920; they shunned the idea of bloc voting. Most Jewish candidates refused to emphasize their Jewishness. Many New York Jews even declined to label local or national political issues as Jewish. A factious group, Jews were found among the supporters of virtually all political parties, including the Socialists (and nascent Communists) on the left. Yet because New York City politics rested on an ethnic neighborhood base, Jews necessarily confronted the system as it existed. Their approach to New York's ethnic political culture led them to adopt an ideological style of ethnic politics. Jewish political activity demonstrated that ethnic groups exert influence because they share similar antecedents, group consciousness, and cultural traditions which "enable them to view developing issues from a common point of view." Yet New York Jews developed neither "an affinity for one party . . . which cannot be explained solely as a result of other demographic characteristics" nor the tendency to "cross party lines to vote for—or against—a candidate belonging to a particular ethnic group."[3] Such a conventional analysis of ethnic politics did not describe New York Jews' emerging political style.

Second generation Jews' ethnic liberal politics also represented a rejection of the model of political assimilation offered by established German Jews in the city. An upper class group, German Jews generally supported the Republican party—both its regular and progressive wings. A small handful voted with the independent anti-Tammany Democrats in city and state elections. Immigrant Jews, before 1905, usually followed Uptown's lead. They supported Republicans in national elections, Teddy Roosevelt being a particular favorite. Locally, immigrant Jews went along with Tammany except during some Fusion campaigns. After 1905 and the arrival of large numbers of radical immigrants, especially Bundists who supported the separate Jewish Socialist worker's party in Russia (General League of Jewish Workers), Jewish immigrants increasingly refused to defer to German Jewish leadership. Instead they adopted the class politics of German Jews. As lower-class workers, radical immigrants vociferously supported the Socialist party. But Jewish immigrants' support for the Socialist party stemmed not only from the experience of Russian revolutionary politics. "A good part of their employment," historian Ben Halpern notes, "was provided by other Jews among the older, established community," rather than by the city government or the political machine. "This situation not only made them far less dependent on local politics," Halpern points out, "it also made intracommunal issues . . . far more important in developing their political attitudes." Immigrant Jewish institutions—including the Yiddish Socialist press, the garment unions, and the Workmen's Circle—nurtured a political consciousness "at odds with the Irish politicians, as well as the Irish police" and opposed on economic and ideological grounds to the German Jewish employers.[4] In this context there existed neither a sense of a Jewish vote nor a set of issues which could be categorized as Jewish and which evoked unanimity among Jews, except for opposition to Russian anti-Semitism. As second generation Jews came of age politically, there was every reason to suppose that, being acculturated and middle class, they too would follow a class politics.

But the 1920s transformed the politics of New York Jews.

After World War I, Republicans and Democrats launched a concerted bipartisan attack on the Socialist party in the city. In 1921 the New York State Assembly refused to seat five Socialist Assemblymen from New York City. The following year legislators gerrymandered Meyer London's Lower East Side Congressional district out of existence, effectively denying the top Jewish Socialist officeholder his position. Baruch Charney Vladeck, a Socialist Alderman from Williamsburg, also lost his seat to fusion. The bipartisan campaign, coupled with rancorous dissension within the Socialist party after the formation of the Third International, ended Socialist victories in New York. A "Socialist stronghold" in 1920, immigrant Jewish Brownsville succumbed to Democratic and Republican fusion politics the following year.[5] Democrats and Republicans united on Joseph Ricca, an Italian, as their candidate for the State Assembly. Running against the popular Jewish Socialist Abraham Shiplacoff, Ricca needed that bipartisan support to win. In 1923 Socialist party dissension led Shiplacoff not to attempt to regain the Assembly seat. As the candidate only of the Democrats that year, Ricca easily defeated his Socialist opponent Charles Brower, receiving 58 percent of the vote.[6]

Ricca's victory strengthened the position of Brownsville Democratic district leader Hymie Schorenstein. Schorenstein, whose "Yiddish accent was as thick as good sour cream," subsequently

Victorious socialist candidates in New York City in 1917. From left to right: (upper row) Beckerman, Wolff, Braunstein, Lee, Vladeck, Held, Calman; (lower row) Claessens, Feigenbaum, Rosenberg, Waldman, Whitehorn, Panken, Shiplacoff, Karlin, Orr, Garfinkle, Gitlow, and Weil.
Courtesy of the YIVO Institute of Jewish Research.

"ran his district with the traditional iron hand." Brought in during the war as a temporary replacement for James Power, Schorenstein "upset the apple cart." He built a political following and pushed for legislation Brownsville Jews desired, such as workmen's compensation. Schorenstein welcomed Irwin Steingut, who would eventually become Speaker of the New York State Assembly, into the Democratic party and supported his candidacy as Assemblyman from the neighboring 18th A.D. in 1921. The following year he guided Emanuel Celler in his first successful bid for Congress, where he would remain for half a century. Schorenstein stayed the typical machine district leader and a source of many apocryphal stories.[7] Democratic politician Edward Costikyan relates how one year Schorenstein

nominated a young man, who was making his first run for office, for the assembly. Elated, the young man began preparing speeches and practicing them. On club nights he rushed up to the club expecting to be called on to say a few words, but his presence was ignored. Posters went up, literature was distributed, rallies were held—but he was neither mentioned in the posters and literature nor called upon at the rallies.

In desperation he tried to meet Schorenstein, without any luck. Finally, on a club night, he joined the long line of constituents sitting in chairs along the side of the room who were waiting to see the leader. Finally, his turn came, and he was ushered into Schorenstein's cubbyhole office.

"Mr. Schorenstein," he began, "do you remember me?"

"Sure," came the reply.

"I'm running for the assembly," explained the candidate.

"I know," grunted Schorenstein. "I picked you."

"But I've been running for six weeks," pleaded the candidate, "and nobody knows it. No speeches, no rallies, no literature, no nothing. What should I do?"

"Go home," said Schorenstein.

As the young man, dismissed, rose and started out the door, Schorenstein relented.

"Young man," he said. The candidate stopped and turned.

"Come back," said Schorenstein with a wave of the hand.

"You ever been to the East River?"

"Yes," came the answer.

"You see the ferryboats come in?" asked Schorenstein.

"Yes."

"And when the water sucks in behind the ferryboat, all kinds
of dirty garbage comes smack into the slip with the ferryboat?"

"Yes."

"So go home and relax. Al Smith is the ferryboat. This year
you're the garbage."[8]

Schorenstein's version of machine politics marked a transition
from immigrant class politics to the second generation's ideology
of liberalism. After 1923 Brownsville's voting patterns increasingly resembled those of its middle-class Jewish neighbor, Flatbush. Both voted overwhelmingly for Al Smith as governor
throughout the 1920s. In national politics, however, Brownsville
voters declined to support Republican presidential candidates as
Flatbush did, preferring the Socialist nominee to Calvin Coolidge
in 1924. But when Smith ran for the presidency in 1928, Brownsville's allegiance to the Democratic party extended to the national
level. Brownsville also endorsed the mayoral campaign of Jimmy
Walker, the gubernatorial compaigns of Franklin D. Roosevelt
and Herbert Lehman, and the Senatorial campaign of Robert F.
Wagner Sr. By 1930 immigrant Jewish voting patterns did not differ substantially from those of the second generation. Norman
Thomas, running for Mayor on the Socialist ticket in 1929, gathered 23 percent of Brownsville's votes and 24 percent of those in
north Flatbush. Even Morris Hillquit, once the hero of Socialist
Jewish immigrants, received 26 percent of Brownsville's vote in
the 1932 mayoral election and 30 percent of north Flatbush's
vote. The figures from Brownsville and north Flatbush also indicate that voters in those districts were twice as ready to support
Hillquit than were those throughout the city as a whole.[9]

The growing allegiance of Jewish immigrants in Brownsville
during the 1920s to the Democratic party paralleled the voting
patterns among second generation Jews. "As the tomato fields
and potato patches gave way to two-family dwellings," political
journalist Warren Moscow observed, the changing composition of
Brooklyn's population registered in the polling booths. In the
early 1920s, Brooklyn often voted Republican; indeed, Brooklyn
was known as a New York City Republican stronghold. South
Flatbush, although it gave Al Smith a slim plurality in the 1922
governorship race, continued to vote Republican in national and
congressional elections until 1926. Not until 1929 did Democrats

The three popular governors of New York State who helped to bring Jews
into the Democratic fold: President-Elect Franklin D. Roosevelt,
Herbert H. Lehman, and former Governor Alfred E. Smith, on the
occasion of Lehman's inauguration as Governor of New York, January 1933.
Wide World photograph courtesy of the Herbert H. Lehman Archives.

start to carry the district by comfortable margins. The change in
north Flatbush voting patterns occurred earlier. The allegiance of
north Flatbush Jews to the Democratic party dated symbolically
from 1921 when Irwin Steingut won election to the Assembly for

the first time. But it took Al Smith to break the district's tradition of voting for Republican presidents. Smith garnered 60 percent of the district's vote in 1928. Presaging the future, in 1927 the Brooklyn Democratic party scored its first clean sweep of Kings County offices. That year John McCooey, head of the Brooklyn Democrats, won his crown as "King of Kings." After 1927 Brooklyn's fame spread as a banner Democratic county.[10]

The shift in immigrant and second generation Jewish votes to the Democratic party registered first at the local level in the 1920s and reflected the entrance of second generation Jews into local politics through the clubhouse. The political club characterized party district organization. During the 1920s thousands of regular and ethnic, political and quasi-political clubs thrived in New York City's heterogeneous neighborhoods. Democratic district leader Edward Costikyan characterized the political club as a "semi-autonomous political institution—the leader's political home." Second generation Jews discovered that local political organizations were congenial for developing an American Jewish political style. The clubs' synthesis of sociability and politics facilitated ethnic identification. After surveying thousands of New York City political clubs in the late 1920s, Roy Peel, a professor of politics, described the "political club classified as a *nationality* or racial club" as embodying "two contradictory forces. As an organization aiming at the inclusion of a large segment of the citizenry into a . . . political party, it performs a useful service in uniting heterogeneous blocs of citizens," Peel observed. "In this respect it is an integrating force." But as an organization catering to one ethnic group and their "peculiar characteristics . . . , it is a disintegrating, disruptive force."[11]

Jews found their way to the political clubs through various paths. A few, like Irwin Steingut, followed their fathers into politics. The elder Steingut's interest in civic affairs and Democratic politics spurred Irwin to seek out the local district leader when he moved from the Lower East Side to Brooklyn. Steingut received a ready reception from Brownsville leader Hymie Schorenstein. Others took a more indirect route. Judge Nathan Sobel discovered politics fortuitously. Enjoying the beach at Coney Island in a one-piece bathing suit, Sobel got a ticket for indecent exposure. Uncertain what to do about the summons, Sobel was advised to seek help from his local club. He went to the Madison Club on Eastern Parkway and liked what he saw. An aspiring young lawyer, Sobel joined the club after being told that membership was the best way "to get ahead." As a young man Judge George Abrams had worked for an Irish lawyer, who gave him the same advice; Abrams too joined the Democrats' prestigious Madison Club. Indeed, many second generation Jews were encouraged to become members of political clubs by the local Irish and Jewish politicians who preceded them.[12]

Yet joining an established club often failed to satisfy second generation Jews. A number of ambitious politicians started their own clubs where the camaraderie essential to building political loyalties could flourish. After discovering politics in the early 1920s, Nathan Sobel set up his own club in Eastern Parkway with Ira Schlossberg, a popular Jewish prize fighter. Sobel's motivation stemmed in part from the fact that "no one talked to him" at the predominantly Irish Madison Club. Nevertheless, Sobel prudently maintained his Madison Club membership and encouraged other Jewish lawyers to join the club. Irwin Steingut also ran his own social political club in addition to being a member of the Madison Club. Both Steingut's and Sobel's clubs attracted an almost exclusively Jewish membership. Yet by the time George Abrams joined the Madison Club in the late 1920s, it had many Jewish members. Abrams felt comfortable there and had no desire to set up his own club. Through the Jewish clubs, some part of the regular Democratic organization, other insurgent or quasi-political clubs, aspiring politicians developed the network of contacts and built the friendships which helped to ensure victories at the polls. For the political leader, "the club is the symbol of his district," Costikyan observed. "It is his headquarters, his meeting place, his responsibility, his ticket of admission to the meetings where candidates are selected and political policy made." Jewish leaders sought these opportunities through their clubs.[13]

The local nature of clubhouse politics permitted a great variety of political styles to flourish. New York City Jewish politicians gave away free matzos to the Jewish needy on Passover and supported a kosher soup kitchen during the bleak winter of 1930–31. They also spoke at fund-raising dinners for worthy Jewish causes. Most Jewish politicos spent two or three nights a week at their clubs, where they played their favorite card games, pinochle and gin rummy. While sociability provided the mainstay of club activity, the diversity of clubs even allowed for ideological politics. During the Depression, some Brooklyn clubs resounded to debates on the merits of socialism. But if Jews introduced a polemical style into some clubs, the clubs also inducted Jews into other aspects of American political culture. Sobel tasted clam chowder for the first time on the annual boat trip sponsored by the Madison Club. Jews came to recognize that "the game of politics is not just for election day," as Jewish Republican politician Walter Mack Jr. recalled. Local politics, he continued, is "really a method by which the people within a group in a big city can get to know each other and know what their mutual problems and desires are." Seeing themselves as community leaders, many Jewish politicians joined the local synagogue and Zionist group. Charles Breitbart, long-term Assemblyman from south Flatbush, chaired the membership committee of the Ocean Parkway Jewish Center in 1927. Irwin Steingut served on the Brooklyn Jewish Center's Board of Trustees. Sobel and many of the local district captains, like Ray Feiden, joined Temple Petach Tikvah.[14]

But the line separating legitimate community leadership from the manipulation of ethnic loyalties was blurred, and occasionally Jewish politicians stepped over its vague boundaries. In 1930 an insurgent politician, Maurice Biederman, started the Judea Democratic Club in Eastern Parkway. Known as a "fixer," Biederman planned to use the club to advance his political ambitions. Peel claimed the club catered to antisocial appetites. Aware of Biederman's unsavory reputation, the Brooklyn Jewish Ministers Association objected to his use of "Judea." While Biederman argued that it was legitimate to band together as a "racial" group to promote good government and that "Judea" had nothing to do with religion, he submitted to rabbinical pressure and changed the club's name.[15]

The widespread neighborhood political activity of second generation Jews reflected the prevailing brand of New York City politics. In the 1920s New York's political structure linked ethnic groups to their neighborhoods and apportioned political rewards along these lines. According to political scientist Theodore Lowi, it was "the large *social*, not economic, substrata, the numerous

ethno-religious subcultures, in the vast City that give its politics
its flavor. In New York, 'class consciousness' never appears so
strongly as ethnic awareness." Most New York City politicians
thought in terms of a "Jewish vote" and balanced their tickets
accordingly. Reuben Lazarus, Mayor Fiorello LaGuardia's representative in Albany, regarding Depression decade politics in
New York, noted that "there are several racial or religious voting
blocs that professional politicians consider when selecting candidates for party slates. There is the Jewish bloc, the Italian bloc,
the German bloc, and the Irish bloc." Through the technique of
the balanced ticket politicians reinforced the awareness of ethnicity. "Appointment of a group representative is also a reaffirma-
tion of group identity," Lowi observed. "Ethnic and religious
stereotypes are part of the currency of political transactions; in
political hands they function as symbols of status and influence,
characteristics that are used by the ethnic components of the
community to judge their treatment by the powerful."[16]

While "recognition of a group representative serves to make
the group more cohesive," Jews often rejected such rewards.
Socialist Alderman Baruch Charney Vladeck curtly reminded his
fellow politicians in 1920 that he never considered the *tfillin*
(phylacteries) a political symbol. The Jews' rejection of the traditional style of ethnic politics troubled politicians, especially
Jewish ones. As Lazarus reflected, "there's a curious thing about
the Jewish vote—it doesn't cohere." Lazarus referred both to the
Jews' unwillingness to cross party lines to vote for a candidate
who was a fellow ethnic and to their willingness to split their tickets. But in other respects, the Jews' vote increasingly did cohere.
Instead of responding to the ethnicity of the person heading the
ticket and accepting the symbolic recognition accorded them, New
York Jews voted for a constellation of values they thought a
politician represented. As the "Jazz Age" gave way to the Depression years, more and more of the city's Jews came to share a
common political outlook. Beginning with Alfred E. Smith's
gubernatorial campaigns, and followed by those of Franklin D.
Roosevelt and Herbert H. Lehman and the senatorial campaigns
of Robert F. Wagner Sr., Jews found the liberal Democratic
blend of social reform and internationalism a compelling combination. When faced with the choice between a conservative Re-

publican like Albert Ottinger and a liberal Democrat like F.D.R. in the 1928 gubernatorial race; or between the wealthy Jewish philanthropist George Medalie and Wagner in the 1932 senatorial contest, many Jews, ignoring the appeal of traditional ethnic politics, voted for the Gentile candidates whose values they supported. Thus Jews forged their own brand of ethnic politics, adopting it as the American mode.[17]

Nevertheless, some Jews remained reluctant to vote for fellow Jews on any ticket. What has been characterized as "the ghetto mentality" often appeared in Jewish preference for non-Jewish representatives.[18] Such Jews shied away from any form of ethnic politics, fearing anti-Semitic repercussions. Jewish politicians eager to hold office responded in varying ways to the conflict between the practices of ethnic politics and Jewish voters' fear of anti-Semitism generated by Jewish office-holders' visibility.

In 1928 Louis Marshall, a prominent Republican lawyer, told a Brooklyn Jew, Democratic Congressman Emanuel Celler: "Nobody has objected more strenuously and consistently than I have to the recognition of a Jewish vote, for there is none. I am happy to say that the Jews have always exhibited independence in politics." True to his words, Marshall consistently denied the legitimacy of ethnic appeals and denounced requests for balanced tickets and other forms of ethnic recognition. In 1927 he tried to dissuade a group of men from forming a political club to advance the interests of "Jewish young men who are deserving of recognition." "You are playing with fire and with edged tools when you announce this as the ultimate purpose of your organization," he wrote. "This idea of getting political recognition because one is a Jew is, to me, unspeakably shameful. Men will get their just desserts without that kind of boosting." Marshall recommended that "the Jewish young men become good citizens, perform their public and private duties, gain a reputation for integrity and ability and modesty, and it will not be necessary to form a club to hoist them into public office."[19]

Even after Marshall's death in 1929, other influential members of the American Jewish Committee which he had headed—such men as scholar Cyrus Adler, Judge Joseph Proskauer, and wealthy banker Felix Warburg—resisted ethnic politics. In 1940, after another election characterized by extravagant emotional appeals to Jews (Democratic Governor Herbert Lehman had equated a vote for Republican presidential candidate Wendell Wilkie with a vote for Hitler), Democrat and Judge Samuel Rosenman prepared a resolution for the American Jewish Committee affirming an individualistic interpretation of American politics:

> Differences in religion, race or nationality have no part in an American political campaign. Elections should be determined exclusively on an American basis rather than on the basis of the alleged separate interests of any religious or racial group. No member of any religion or any race or any nationality has any right to vote on any basis other than his belief as what is best for the United States alone.

Rosenman characterized the "isolated instances where attempts were made on both sides to influence the votes of these groups on racial or religious or national lines" as "contrary to American democracy." He concluded: "now that the campaign is over, we express the hope that this un-American form of campaigning will not again appear in American politics."[20]

Other Jews argued that to participate in American politics in New York City meant to engage in ethnic politics. The liberal, Democratic Yiddish paper, *The Day*, looked at eastern European Jewish politics, where legal Jewish parties ran candidates for office in multi-national states; it saw a host of problems in ethnic Jewish politics in America: "Jewish public opinion must consider clearly the significance of a 'Jewish vote' for the Jews, not less than for America." Since there was no such thing as a Jewish vote, the Jews had the option of creating it. "It must also be conceded that if a Jew is nominated as a candidate because he is a Jew," the paper continued, "Jewish public opinion has the right to inquire into the Jewishness of the Jewish candidate. Jewish public opinion may say: 'If you do give us a Jewish candidate because he is a Jew, then let us have a Jew who is genuinely Jewish, who has a close relationship to Jewish life, to the hopes and aspirations of the Jewish masses.'" While laying down such criteria for Jewish candidates, *The Day* nevertheless felt that there were "no Jewish political questions" in America and no "Jewish politics." Furthermore, a candidate nominated because he was Jewish would "not travel far with Jews" on Jewishness alone.

Commenting on the possibility of a Jew running for Governor of
New York in 1928, *The Day* wrote:

> Now, there is, for instance Col. Lehman in the Democratic party.
> He is now being mentioned as a possible candidate. If Col. Lehman
> would not have been a Jew, he would still have been a worthy can-
> didate for governor. . . . When, in addition, Col. Lehman is a Jew
> and a good Jew, a devoted and untiring worker for all important
> Jewish causes, the Jews would be particularly pleased if such an
> important person who is, in addition, a good Jew is nominated. We
> do not want Jewish politics in America. We do not want any Jewish
> candidate who would be nominated only because he is a Jew.[21]

Only those Jews intimately aware of the nature of Jewish politics
in eastern Europe understood *The Day*'s distinction between Jewish politics and the "compliment" of nominating a "good Jew"
for high office. Most second generation Jews considered it impossible to separate the recognition of a Jewish vote and Jewish
issues from that of Jewish individuals. The latter implied the
former and both constituted interrelated parts of Jewish ethnic
politics.

But while some Jews accepted as a compliment the nomination of a Jew for high office, others chafed at the limitations of the
balanced ticket. In 1926 Zionist leader Jacob deHaas denounced
the subtle prejudices in New York City ethnic politics which
forced Jews to lower their political aspirations. Admitting that
ethnicity was "an absolute part of American politics," deHaas
expressed outrage that "an opinion prevailed in political circles
that a Jew must not aspire to the office of U.S. Senator. I can understand that attitude in some other state," he continued, "but I
frankly could not understand it as guiding New York State politics." DeHaas acquiesced in the current political wisdom that no
Catholic could become President of the United States and no Jew
could become Mayor of New York (despite the city's large Jewish
population). But he concluded that "he who may only accept the
gifts that are offered to him and may not take what the law says
he is entitled to is a citizen of the second class." In 1928 Herbert
Lehman objected to pressures within the Democratic party to balance its ticket in response to the Republican nomination of Ottinger. Presenting the other side of deHaas's argument, Lehman
felt that the exigencies of the balanced ticket would force a Jew

inappropriately into a position of prominence. "Yes, I was mentioned for governor," he recalled, "but I never took it seriously. My name was considered only in default of getting somebody who was politically stronger than I. They did think about it," he continued, "because they knew that the Republican nominee was going to be Ottinger. Somebody thought that having me as his opponent—a man of the same religious faith—would be good." Lehman "felt it would have been very bad, and didn't hesitate so to express myself."[22]

The pressures of ethnic politics often left Jewish politicians in what they considered to be untenable positions. In the context of ethnic politics the widespread public anti-Semitism of the 1920s and 1930s tempered the ambition of some Jewish politicians. Nathan Straus Jr., twice elected to the New York State Senate from Manhattan on the Democratic ticket, felt constrained not to run for reelection in 1926 because another Jewish Democrat, Maurice Bloch, had been chosen Speaker of the Assembly. Straus's assessment of the limits of Democratic ethnic politics convinced him that he could not aspire to be leader of the Senate if a Jew already was presiding over the Assembly. Recalling his discussions regarding the mayoral nomination in 1933, Straus elaborated on his interpretation of ethnic politics: "I did go to the Commodore Hotel," he remarked, "and, at the meeting, was formally tendered the nomination for Mayor by the men representing the groups that constituted the so-called 'reform forces.' " Straus took the weekend to come to "one of the most difficult decisions of my life. The big obstacle," he remembered,

> was the fact that Herbert Lehman was Governor. It seemed to me extremely doubtful, looking at the matter objectively, that it would be advisable for there to be a Jewish Governor and a Jewish Mayor. Yet I did very much want the nomination, and my ambition had always been to be Mayor of New York.

Straus consulted a number of leading Jews. He asked newspaper publisher Paul Block his opinion and Block advised him to accept the nomination. Although Rabbi Stephen Wise was abroad, Straus cabled him. " 'Should a Jew be the next Mayor of New York?' He cabled back, 'No comma unless it is you.' I thought that this answer was a polite way of telling me that he did not approve in *any* case, and his answer was a big factor in my final decision," Straus admitted. He even went down to Washington to talk with Eugene Meyer, publisher of the Washington *Post*. Meyer was ambivalent. Finally Straus had a "long talk of a whole evening" with banker and philanthropist Felix Warburg.

> Mr. Warburg was most emphatic against my acceptance. He felt that it would not be at all wise for both the Governor of New York State and the Mayor of New York City to be Jews. . . . He thought it would be a bad thing all around, both as an American and as a Jew, to have the highest executive offices in both city and state occupied by Jews.[23]

Thus, although the possibility of Straus's nomination had been printed in several newspapers, which referred to Straus in flattering terms as "a prominent Jew of the Louis Marshall type," Straus declined the nomination. Like the process of ethnic political recognition itself, it is impossible to know how accurate Straus's evaluation of the situation was. Since he was offered the nomination, obviously not all politicians figured by his wary Jewish calculus.

Herbert Lehman's success in capturing and retaining the New York governorship for four successive terms during the Depression decade kept alive the issue of Jewish political visibility and its potential to stimulate anti-Semitism. Most Jews perceived Lehman's record as governor as a symbol of Jewish political success, but some concluded that Lehman's case illustrated the limitations of ethnic politics set by prejudice. In a letter to Lehman in 1939, Jewish journalist and editor of the New York *World*, Herbert Bayard Swope, indicated the dilemma Lehman raised for him "as an American and as a Jew."

> Al Smith was beaten for the Presidency by Prosperity and— Intolerance. You are being beaten—before you start—by Intolerance.
> Here is a man who has spent himself in the service of the people; a man who has made an extraordinary record as Governor, the first to hold his post *unbrokenly* for four terms; the *only one* (not excepting the President) who could have beaten the Republican candidate last year. He comes from the pivotal state. . . . With all these factors in his favor, there is not even a whisper of his name. And for only one reason—because of his faith.

However, Swope concluded, "in all fairness, I suppose I should admit that while your case does not prove *all* for our system, it has proved much that is good." Such comments from a journalist who never mentioned his Jewishness in public suggest the pain inherent in ethnic politics for some Jews.[24]

But Lehman's success also acclimated second generation Jews to the interethnic competition of ethnic politics. Jewish politicians like Steingut and Sobel saw the division in Brooklyn politics as a struggle between old timers and youth, between traditionalists and newcomers, although these splits often pitted Irish against Jew. In the 1920's they were hesitant to push for Jewish candidates on the Democratic party ticket, but in the next decade second generation Jewish politicians increasingly accepted the consequences of ethnic politics. Treated by others as a legitimate and potentially powerful voting bloc, New York Jewish politicians adapted themselves to the local traditions of ethnic politics. Success in entering politics at the neighborhood level encouraged Jews to press for their share of political rewards. Lehman recalled that when he sought the Democratic gubernatorial nomination in 1932, John McCooey, head of the powerful Brooklyn Democratic machine, opposed his efforts. "I think undoubtedly he would have remained against me," Lehman added, "had it not been for a statement by some of his leaders in Brooklyn, serving notice on him that regardless of any orders they might get from him, they were going to vote for me in the convention. When that revolt became strong enough, he took it into account."[25]

Compared with the situation in the early 1920s, this represented Jewish advancement within Democratic party ranks. But from the insider's vantage point, too, Jews still had a long journey before they reached the goal of political acceptance. Joel Slonim, Yiddish writer and poet and member of Tammany's Board of Strategy, claimed that although Jews made up 30 percent of Tammany's membership they accounted for only 10 percent of the leadership in the late 1930s. Other contemporary estimates agreed: Jews comprised 13 percent of the Democratic district leaders in Manhattan, 15 percent in the Bronx, and 23 percent in Brooklyn. The relatively large percentage in Brooklyn reflected the ambition and political acumen of second generation Jewish politicians. Given the Republican control of Brooklyn politics in

Herbert Lehman and Democratic party bosses in 1928. Front row,
left to right: Lehman, John J. Raskob, General William Marshall, Mayor
Frank Hague of Jersey City, New Jersey, John McCooey, and William F. Kenny.
Wide World photograph courtesy of the Herbert H. Lehman Archives.

the early 1920s, second generation Jews moved more quickly into
the Democratic party than they did in the Bronx, where Democratic politics were dominated by Tammany. Brooklyn Democrats
appreciated Jewish help in ousting the Republicans, and Jews
were able to use their growing strength in the county advan-
tageously. Sobel, for example, succeeded in convincing McCooey
to increase the number of representatives to the party council.
This move allowed Jews to enter the ranks of leaders without taking positions away from the Irish. When McCooey died in 1934,
Jewish district leaders helped to elect as his successor Frank V.
Kelly, a man more favorably inclined to F.D.R. and New Deal
politics and hence more congenial to Jewish Democrats.[26]

Recognition of the Jewish vote and its potency implied not
only a recognition of Jewish ethnicity and of Jewish leaders in
New York but of Jewish issues as well. The growing Jewish voter
support for the Democratic party and the increasing prominence
of Jewish Democratic party politicians in the 1920s and 1930s
paralleled the emergence of a liberal, urban-oriented ideology as
characteristic of New York Democratic politics. The party of the

1920s, which attracted second generation Jews, differed in important respects from the one immigrant Jews knew. Under the influence of Al Smith and Robert F. Wagner Sr., and with the benign approval of Tammany boss Charles Murphy, the Democratic party supported a number of key social welfare issues. Smith led a movement which "combined social reform with party regularity, new ideas with old styles." With Smith as governor, Tammany advocated such governmental reforms as the direct primary and women's suffrage, such labor reforms as social security and factory legislation, and such causes for the underprivileged as unemployment insurance and public housing. Tammany reformism was "a market-basket liberalism that concentrated on social welfare and economic reforms for the masses." Especially during the years of Smith's governorship (1922–1928), the state party became known for its attention to social and political reform and nonpartisan administration. "Smith represented something fresh in American life," Irving Howe observes. "He spoke in the accents of the urban masses; he cleared a path for recently arrived immigrant groups as they stumbled into mainstream politics; and at times he raised their inchoate needs and complaints to the level of serious issues." Second generation Jews who joined the Democratic party found this new liberal outlook congenial.[27]

Smith himself welcomed Jews into the party. He "eased the way for second generation Jewish intellectuals, the kind who a decade or two earlier might have become socialists, to enter old-line politics," Howe notes. Smith accorded praise and prominence to Jewish advisors like Belle Moscowitz and Joseph Proskauer. Not only did Smith's policies appeal to Jews but he specifically invited them into a new Catholic-Jewish brotherhood. At the annual meeting of the United Hebrew Charities in 1922 Smith spoke about "our people," Jews and Catholics, claiming that "throughout this land nothing speaks more eloquently, nothing stands out in greater justification of our people . . . than the care we personally take of our poor, our sick and afflicted." Not only were Jews and Catholics known "for our charity," but there were "no sensational divorces among our people. We belong to the family life of New York and of this State," Smith concluded. Many Jews eagerly embraced Smith's proffered harmony of Jew and Catholic in politics. Even Jewish Socialists had difficulty opposing Smith.

They attacked him "less for his record than for his associations."
When Smith ran for President in 1928, David Dubinsky, head of
the International Ladies Garment Workers Union and a devoted
Socialist, felt himself in a quandary because of Smith's critical help
during several bitter garment disputes in the 1920s. Dubinsky
refused to make speeches for Norman Thomas, the Socialist candidate, "because I really believed it would be better if Smith got
elected." Dubinsky recalled that the distressed reactions among
his Socialist friends "bothered me so much that I decided not to
register . . . because I still respected the Socialists and I was
afraid I might be tempted to vote for Smith." This was the only
time Dubinsky failed to vote when eligible. For less ideologically
inclined second generation Jews, the local clubhouse's camaraderie and opportunities for personal advancement cemented their
bond of allegiance to Smith's Democratic politics.[28]

If Smith welcomed Jews into the Democratic party, Lehman
made them feel at home. If Smith shook the faith of Jewish Socialists, Franklin Roosevelt shattered it. Under "Silent Dynamite"
Lehman, a transformed party emerged in the state and with it a
political consensus among New York Jews. A German-Jewish
banker, Lehman dissolved the allegiance of wealthy Jews to the
Republican party and he claimed the loyalty of Socialist Jewish
garment workers, who remembered his $50,000 loan to a
bankrupt ILGWU in 1926. Ten years later these Jewish Socialists
repaid their debt to Lehman and affirmed their support of Roosevelt's New Deal through the creation of the American Labor
Party. Established at a meeting of Jewish Socialists and leaders of
the predominantly Jewish garment unions, the ALP initially
sought "to insure a full labor vote for Roosevelt in 1936." Since
committed Jewish Socialists balked at the prospect of voting for
the capitalist parties (and especially for the party of Tammany),
the ALP gave them the opportunity to pull the lever for Roosevelt
and Lehman without compromising their ideological convictions.
Recognizing this, Democratic supporters of F.D.R. in the state
worked to get the ALP on the ballot. Edward Flynn's Bronx organization, with some misgivings, supported the ALP effort, while in
Brooklyn Sobel and Steingut and other Jewish Democrats printed
petitions for the ALP. Although the ALP polled 239,000 votes for
Roosevelt in the city, these turned out to be above the margin of

victory FDR needed; "curiously enough," Lazarus observed in retrospect, "the election would have gone the same way."[29]

But the ALP's success led to unintended results. Dubinsky and Alex Rose, a leader of the largely Jewish United Hatters, Cap and Millinery Workers International Union, decided to keep the ALP alive as a permanent third party in New York. With the support of such Socialists as Charney Vladeck, Rose assumed the job of Executive Secretary of the party. The ALP entered the 1937 mayoralty race, running a full slate of candidates for city offices, including the newly established City Council elected by proportional representation. Thus, as Lazarus noted, the ALP "served—without intending to do so—to break up some of the power of Tammany Hall." Indeed, Dubinsky recalled, the Democrats "wished we would drop dead. They insisted we were stealing their votes [but] . . . we were convinced we were appealing to the great mass of independent voters in New York as well as the old-line Socialists." Flynn and the Bronx Democratic machine recognized this, yet they refused to cooperate with the ALP, preferring to deal with the Republicans. But in Brooklyn, second generation Jewish Democrats often went along with the ALP. Steingut accepted ALP support in 1938.[30]

The ALP hastened the demise of the Socialist Party in New York. While estimates showed that the ALP polled only 20 percent of the Jews' vote in 1936, the following year approximately 40 percent of New York Jews voted for candidates on its ticket. In 1938 Lehman received crucial support from the ALP; over 30 percent of the New York Jews who voted for Lehman chose to pull the ALP lever rather than the Democratic one. The ALP marked the end of the immigrants' political radicalism. Through its choice of candidates, the ALP replaced the Socialists as the representative of the liberal political consensus of New York Jews.[31]

The ALP emphasized the importance of its political program or ideology in recruiting support. It encouraged its members to vote for candidates whom the party endorsed on the basis of their stand on specific issues. On the local level the ALP stood behind Mayor Fiorello LaGuardia because of his advocacy of low-rent municipal housing and slum clearance, bills to protect consumers, and adequate relief allowances for the unemployed. In state politics the ALP, a firm friend of Lehman, pushed for state funding of education, legal protection for unions, rent control legislation, and the strengthening of civil liberties. Nationally, the ALP considered itself, in party Secretary Alex Rose's words, "the permanent New Deal Party of our country." Rose argued that since the New Deal was "an accident of history," the ALP must "continue the traditions of the New Deal" and make "the philosophy of the New Deal a permanent school of thought." Thus the ALP repudiated both the Communist party and the Socialist party. As its paper explained in 1939, the ALP "was organized as a new political movement to promote progressive and labor interests within the framework of our present social system. . . . The American Labor Party is primarily concerned with problems of our own American life which we seek to solve in our own American fashion."[32]

The ALP did not shun local political practices. Though it began largely as a union enterprise, the ALP subsequently set up clubs. Through the clubs the ALP wedded its ideology to practical politics. In Brownsville, Bessie Wallman translated the ALP's concern for consumer protection into the practice of checking pushcart scales. Eager to obtain members for the young party, the local ALP club in the Grand Concourse ran a membership contest offering a vacation (two weeks at the Majestic Hotel or Ehrenreich's Manor) as prizes. Rose gave pointers on how to recruit party members: "Always bear in mind that each voter has a special problem, and that his or her interest can most easily be aroused by showing how the Labor Party can solve that problem." Rose's advice sounded as if it might have come from boss Murphy's Tammany Hall. "Get to know the people of your district and talk to them about the things that concern them," he counseled. But Rose added the ingredient neither Tammany nor the New Deal–oriented Brooklyn Jewish Democrats ever included: "our program." "Our program covers all of their needs; it is the only program that does," Rose asserted. "Your job is to convince them." Second generation Jewish Democrats like Sobel and Abrams never discussed the Democratic party program with voters. They appealed for support on personal grounds; issues were left to party leaders like Lehman to enunciate.[33]

The ALP's program, which it equated with the "philosophy" of the New Deal, represented the political ideology espoused by most second generation Jews by 1940. The process of transforming issues of social welfare and civil liberties, of internationalism and civil rights, into "Jewish" issues took two decades. A number of factors encouraged Jews to adopt these issues as their own. Jews' urban orientation facilitated the linking of social welfare concerns with ethnic recognition. Jewish grass-roots politics were urban politics, intimately tied to solving the varied problems afflicting city life. As apartment dwellers who traveled to work on the mass transit lines, Jews cared about the quality of the city's economic, social, and cultural services and saw politics as a means to ensure a decent life for themselves and their children. Jews also found opportunities for personal advancement through social welfare programs, especially those adopted during the Depression.

The political allegiances of their immigrant parents also inclined second generation Jews toward a distinctive Jewish liberalism. Lazarus observed that the "Jew of parents who came from the ghetto, has a curious tendency to seek out liberal political philosophy and to practice it." Lazarus recognized that such liberalism embodied contradictions. "You find a man who makes a great success in business and who should be voting a Republican ticket or a Tammany ticket because of his local business interests contributing sums of money to all sorts of liberal causes." But he concluded that such behavior was "an instinctive reaction to what the first generation hears in the household of the parent who comes from a ghetto." A second generation Jew and New Deal economist, Louis Walinsky, confirmed Lazarus' observation. The son of Ossip Walinsky, a Labor Zionist and an organizer of the Leather Goods Workers' Union, Louis Walinsky grew up in the Bronx where "the circle of parents' friends," a Jewish, intellectual, and radical group, shaped the environment.

> I remember one of my early memories is going to a Socialist Sunday school in the Bronx. My father was in politics—he ran for the state assembly—and of course the trade union group was a part of my youthful background. And my mother was a kind of suffragette and activist in the Women's Consumer League and in the Peace Society and a parader and all that.

For Walinsky, radicalism "was part of the atmosphere, it was the ambience, it was natural." Political scientist Arthur Liebman

Mothers and children at a May Day rally in the 1920s, where Jewish radicalism was "part of the atmosphere." *Courtesy of the YIVO Institute for Jewish Research.*

calls this type of Socialism "a community creed." To move to liberalism from a background in which respect for radical ideology was embedded and even institutionalized in the community required only a gradual transition. Second generation Jews, too, created a milieu in which their liberalism was as intrinsically Jewish as had been their parents' radicalism.[34]

The development of a constellation of issues considered "Jewish" and linked to liberalism as a political ideology also involved a selective process. Not all immigrant values were handed down intact to the second generation and not all issues were accepted into the pantheon of American Jewish liberalism. In fact, throughout the 1920s various Jewish groups competed to gain support for their programs, which included both symbolic and interest-group issues. In the 1920s Zionists focused largely on the former. They encouraged the city Board of Aldermen, the state legislature, and Congress to pass resolutions annually in support of the establishment of a Jewish homeland in Palestine. Zionists interpreted these resolutions as a measure of public concern for Jewish interests. In the context of New York politics, Zionists gradually won acceptance of such symbolic gestures as a yardstick of American acceptance of Jews. When rebuffed, Zionists and other Jews interpreted the action as a sign of anti-Semitism. In 1921 the Board of Aldermen failed to obtain unanimous consent to honor Albert Einstein and Zionist leader Chaim Weizmann, who were in the city on a Zionist fund-raising tour, by according them the "freedom of the city." Jews and Tammany politicians alike recognized the political affront. The Tammany leader on the Board prevailed on the Socialist Vladeck to answer the objections of the Republican whose prejudices were embarrassing Tammany. Vladeck agreed and through a convincing speech managed to get the Republican to retract his objection. Vladeck's speech revealed the extent to which Zionist aspirations were accepted by New York Jews as ethnic political currency. Challenged to explain his action by the anti-Zionist Bundist leader, Vladimir Medem, who was also visiting the city, Vladeck justified his support of the Zionist Weizmann as a defense of Jews as a group. "Vladeck raised the issue to a higher level by affirming that there exists an area of general Jewish interests from which socialists cannot exclude themselves," suggests radical activist Melech Epstein.[35]

Like the Zionists, Orthodox Jews tried to get their needs recognized as of general Jewish interest and incorporated into the Jews' emerging political program. In 1917 and 1922 New York State passed two kosher laws to assist Orthodox Jews by regulating the sale and preparation of kosher meat in New York. Orthodox Jews also pressed for bills to establish a five-day work week, to prevent the scheduling of civil service exams on Saturday, and to allow shopkeepers who closed on Saturday to remain open on Sunday. The most active lobbyist for these Jewish Sabbath measures, the Jewish Sabbath Alliance, promoted the bills in order not to penalize Jews who observed the Sabbath. However, the New York State kosher law remained the most successful effort on the part of Jewish politicians to bring the force of the secular state behind Jewish religious law. The other bills, affecting Gentiles as well as Jews, attracted neither sufficient Gentile support nor general Jewish interest and went down to defeat.[36]

Less traditional Jews defined anti-Semitism as a Jewish issue and concentrated on fighting it through legislation and proclamation. Although they viewed civil rights legislation as a Jewish issue, second generation Jewish politicians wrote their bills to apply to all citizens. In 1930 Republican Assemblyman Louis Lefkowitz introduced a bill making it a misdemeanor for an employer to discriminate against an employee on the basis of race, creed, or color. Franklin Roosevelt, then Governor of New York, rejected the bill as impractical and unenforceable. He urged education to fight anti-Semitic discrimination. In the late 1930s, however, Jewish efforts to erect legal barriers to discrimination met with more success. Jews gathered enough political support in 1938 to make it illegal for New York colleges to discriminate against individuals applying for admission. This civil rights legislation complemented efforts by Jewish politicians to develop a state university system. The difficulty Jewish politicians faced in obtaining legislative support for both religious and secular Jewish issues declined in the 1930s, as the Democratic party won more seats in the state legislature. As Speaker of the Assembly, Irwin Steingut helped to guide Jewish bills successfully through the legislature. Nevertheless, Steingut often sought non-Jewish sponsors of civil rights legislation in order to remove from the bills the stigma of being "Jewish."[37]

Jews in Congress faced similar difficulties in fighting anti-Semitism. Jewish Congressmen like Emanuel Celler pressed unsuccessfully for the liberalization of the immigration laws. He also urged Congressional investigations of such anti-Semitic organizations as the Ku Klux Klan and Henry Ford's *Dearborn Independent* in the 1920s and American fascist groups in the 1930s. Celler saw these issues as Jewish ones as well as of concern to all Americans. He recognized as well that his largely Jewish constituency supported American participation in efforts at international cooperation in the 1920s and governmental actions to break up large business trusts in the 1930s. Even the extreme left concurred occasionally and accepted a number of issues as Jewish. In 1924 a writer in the Communist Yiddish daily *Freiheit* observed that "in spite of the fact that the Jewish population in this country is divided into various classes and each class votes according to its own interests, it cannot be denied that there exists something that can be called a 'Jewish vote.'" The article continued, "in the present election it must be admitted that Mr. Coolidge, the representative of American reaction, the friend of the Ku Klux Klan, the man who signed the anti-immigration bill, does not deserve the vote of the Jews."[38]

The pursuit of these Jewish issues in the context of bipartisan ethnic politics produced limited gains until the advent of the New Deal. With the national success of Roosevelt and the Democratic party, second generation Jews sensed the legitimacy of their own political identity. Many New York Jews saw the election of 1936, when Roosevelt's opponents identified him with "Jewish interests," as a referendum on themselves. If some Republicans attacked the New Deal as the "Jew Deal," and the nation repudiated the Republicans, Jews, too, felt vindicated. Roosevelt's triumph in 1936 further cemented Jewish loyalty to the New Deal, and his blessing on the American Labor Party made even former Jewish Socialists feel welcome in the national Democracy. "Roosevelt, to many American Jews," writes journalist Stephen Isaacs, "was the next thing to Moses. To many who had left religion, he was the new Moses." The identification of Jewish issues or Jewish liberalism with New Deal liberalism by second generation Jews— despite the New Deal's mediocre record in such important areas of Jewish concern as immigration flexibility and civil rights—is central to an understanding of Jewish politics in the 1930s.[39]

Although most New York Jews moved toward support of the liberal wing of the Democratic party in the 1920s and 1930s, a handful of Jews remained prominent in the city's Republican and Socialist parties. Samuel Koenig served as Republican party leader in Manhattan for 22 years until his ouster in 1932. Similarly, in Brooklyn Meier Steinbrink actively directed Republican politics for many years. Morris Hillquit, the Socialist anti-war candidate for mayor in 1917, continued to be active in the city's Socialist party until the 1930s. Nevertheless, second generation Jews produced the amalgamation of votes, leadership, and ideology characterizing their successful emergence as a political ethnic group through the Democratic party. The Democratic clubhouse and the American Labor Party represented two roads New York Jews followed to enter the American political mainstream. The clubhouse emphasized camaraderie and the opportunity to get ahead, while the ALP stressed an ideological liberalism which it associated with the New Deal outlook; but both approaches pointed to the acculturation of the second generation and to its ethnic persistence.[40]

The Jewish liberalism which emerged as the political ideology of most second generation New York Jews derived from a variety of sources. At the neighborhood level liberalism began with Jewish support for Smith's social reformism, encouraged by second generation Jews' urban traditions, the heritage of their immigrant parents, and the welcome they received from the predominantly Irish politicians who preceded them in Democratic party politics. But second generation Jews also developed a complement of Jewish issues as part of their liberal ethnic politics. Concern for Jews abroad—often relatives who were suffering from anti-Semitism— added a form of internationalism and a commitment to Jewish peoplehood to Jewish political liberalism. The desire of second generation Jews to insulate themselves from discrimination in all areas—in housing, in private and government employment, in education, in recreation, and in business—led them to pursue civil rights as a Jewish political issue. In the 1920s and 1930s New York Jews also turned toward liberalism from a commitment to social justice. That they saw this commitment as consonant with Jewish tradition in part reflected their distance from Orthodox practice. Feeling comfortable in their neighborhoods, they drew selectively from Jewish tradition "to backstop their political liberalism." Other Jews drifted from Socialism toward liberalism. These Jews brought a religious commitment to politics. Indeed, some have argued that "the zeal of untraditional Jews for politics is their *de facto* religion." "Having lost the faith that there is a God, but not wanting to give up messianism," Rabbi Seymour Seigel suggests, "they go into politics." Imbued with a messianic outlook, these secular Jews identified political liberalism with America's civil religion, its ultimate source of values. From this perspective, liberalism as a Jewish ideology not only promised integration into American politics, but actually acquired the potential for salvation. Ironically, adherence to liberalism made Jews politically distinctive.[41]

The New York Jewish Democrat emerged in part from a traditional American ethnic politics of group loyalty, but his liberalism came to be ideological. Usually Jewish group interests supported Jewish Democratic ideology. Indeed, for many the two appeared to be coextensive. But to the extent that Jewish Democrats identified their New Deal beliefs with American civil religion itself, they loosened their ideology from its ethnic moorings. Ideological Jewish Democrats would rather vote for a Gentile liberal than a Jewish conservative. Vladeck articulated this Jewish view of ethnic politics in 1937 when he returned to the City Council on the ALP ticket. "For many years we have been telling our people that the real, the true bond of comradeship is not religion but kinship of aspirations and ideals," he argued. If Jews voted together, they did so as Americans of the liberal persuasion. Speaking "as a member of the Jewish faith," Vladeck explained that "intelligent Jews in this community resent the idea of just voting as Jews in any election and not as citizens. They resent the idea of voting, not on the basis of principle, not on the basis of the common good, but on the basis of religious or racial affiliations." Vladeck felt that, as citizens, Jews should share a "kinship" of liberalism rather than a "kinship" of ethnicity. Their "bond of comradeship" extended to all who agreed with their "aspirations and ideals." Understandably, Jews were collectively the most devout adherents of American liberalism as portrayed by Jews like Vladeck. In rejecting the old ethnicity of race and religion, they defined a new ethnicity of ideology—intensely Jewish and intensely American. For Vladeck and other ideological Jewish liberals, common beliefs shaped common voting patterns.[42] By 1940, the process of two decades of ethnic politics had brought New York Jews to a political consensus. Ideological ethnic politics replaced the class politics Jews previously practiced.

At home in the Democratic party, or at least the liberal urban wing of it, second generation Jews increasingly considered Jewish and Democratic concerns to be interwoven. The opportunity New York City Jews had enjoyed before the 1920s to search for advancement in a variety of political parties narrowed as second generation Jews faced the beginning of World War II. Democratic party allegiance, either on a local level through the clubhouse or an ideological level through support of New Deal social programs and internationalism, characterized second generation Jews. As Jews cemented these ties of loyalty to the Democratic party, assimilation into the American political system translated into support for liberal Democrats. Although second generation Jews did not embark consciously on a policy of ethnic politics in the 1920s, their widespread allegiance to the Democratic party by 1940 pointed to ethnic voting patterns.[43]

The historical setting of Democratic political power in New York City and the ethnic character of city politics drew second generation Jews into local, personal, ethnic Democratic party politics. As they gained confidence in their own ethnic viability in the political arena, New York Jews increasingly sought the spotlight as political candidates and appealed for support on ethnic lines. Although they remained concerned that anti-Semitism might be generated by visible Jewish political activity, second generation Jews pursued civic acceptance through the practices of ethnic politics. Nationally, the New Deal gave Jews further evidence of their political integration as it strengthened their ethnic ideological commitment. On the state level, Jewish ethnic politics combined personal style with Jewish issues, individual advancement with group recognition. For second generation Jews, Jewish political progress in America came to mean not only recognition of Jewish leaders but also espousal of Jewish issues. Through the Democratic party, second generation Jews in New York pursued the goal of political assimilation by striving for acceptance as an ethnic group. From the perspective of 1940, most Jewish Democrats could gauge the distance successfully traveled in the course of two decades, and take pride in Jewish achievement.

9

So then, we were admitted. But where? For what had we been prepared? Certainly not for the ritual despair of our forefathers . . . although we knew we could never resign from the old contract with the past, our long history bonded by memory and always annealed in the present. But what was our point of view? *What, in short, was the angle?*
A New York question, rhetorical, rebounding from its own answer! It was New York we were prepared for, and New York, half-Jewish, which took us in. New York! Ghetto of Eden! We go back always where we came from, in memory, to and from ourselves. The things that made us what we are made you.

Milton Klonsky, "The Trojans of Brighton Beach,"
Commentary (May 1947), p. 466.

At Home
in America

The vanguard second generation of the 1920s created the conditions for a renascent Jewish culture. As its ranks swelled in the 1930s and 1940s, the second generation consolidated its synthesis of American and Jewish values. Its institutional foundation grew from the symbiotic interaction of a Jewish middle-class ethnicity and forms of urban community. Within this framework the third generation would discover what it meant to be an American Jew. This new generation would carry the essential features of their parents' synthesis even into the affluent suburbs. The pluralist character of Jewish ethnicity in New York, with its strong secular flavor, would survive.

In the 1950s second generation Jews continued to nourish a world of unselfconscious Jewishness in their neighborhoods. They turned to their neighborhoods to translate what Jewishness meant into a livable reality and to their public institutions to give expression to the varied content of Jewish ethnicity. New York Jews experienced a sense of community in their neighborhoods. They felt at home where they lived. Through residential concentration, New York Jews often acquired a psychological attitude of a majority, in a country where they were a small minority. The clustering of thousands of Jews into city neighborhoods made Jewish living comfortable and natural.

Second generation Jews fit into the urban landscape of their lives, and most third generation Jews who followed them sought a similar sense of being at home. "Generally the Jew still lives in what are called Jewish neighborhoods—or now, Jewish suburbs," sociologist Herbert Gans observed in 1956. Furthermore, "his best friends are almost certain to be Jewish; and his wife likes to have the children play with other Jewish children wherever possible."[1] Although in the postwar period second generation Jews left the old neighborhoods of Flatbush for the fresh newness of Forest Hills, or moved up from the Grand Concourse to the hills of Riverdale, they quickly introduced into these areas the visible signs of Jewish ethnic group life. As Jews filled Riverdale's modern apartment buildings, they also tenanted its shops, opening bakeries and butchershops, clothing and book stores, delicatessens and delicacy shops. Yet not all Jews moved at the same speed. Moving to a new apartment or house required a rising income which the elderly did not often possess. Some Jews lingered in the old neighborhoods because they were ideologically committed to Orthodoxy or Yiddish radicalism and they wanted to remain close to their local institutions. The influx of refugees in the 1940s also strengthened these second generation neighborhoods and contributed to their longevity.

The postwar apartment shortage in New York City pushed Jews into the suburbs of Westchester, Long Island, and New Jersey as well as into new urban neighborhoods. But Jews chose suburbia and home ownership reluctantly. "Of course those Jews who moved into the mass-produced Levittown-type suburbs found that though they lived in separate houses their neighbors were still close by. On the other hand," Marshall Sklare notes perceptively, "there were no hallways or lobbies, as in apartment houses, for chance meetings, no elevators for quick exchanges of gossip and news, no corner luncheonettes for ready sociability, no street life to speak of. For many," he concludes, "the absence of these staples of the Jewish urban scene was a real deprivation." Yet even in the suburbs of Westchester or Long Island, where the signs of ethnicity were homogenized, Jews developed shorthand symbols of their presence. Real estate agents understood the codes. As Sklare points out, they came "to know what to stress in showing a suburban house to a prospective Jewish buyer—comfort, modernization, good schools, and easy access to shopping, transportation, and 'people.' Thus, even when Jews seemingly embrace suburbia, they still look for the urban virtues—convenience, cultural and social opportunities."[2]

The networks of builders and real estate operators, so important in directing Jewish residential dispersion in the 1920s, continued to operate effectively. By word of mouth as well as from advertising, Jews came to know that Trump built solid homes in Brooklyn or in Queens, and that Levitt offered substantial value on Long Island. Similarly "Abraham Kazan, having managed the Amalgamated Co-ops successfully through the depression, played the major role in launching post-war co-ops in the city. The success of these," Glazer and Moynihan point out, "led to other large co-operative developments, which have anchored large groups of middle income citizens to the inner city."[3]

Moving into new neighborhoods, second and third generation Jews participated in the city's expansion following the second World War. The New York metropolitan district grew to include the surrounding suburban areas, even parts of New Jersey. But the suburban sprawl only spotlighted the centrality of Manhattan. Residence in such formerly exclusive areas as Forest Hills or Riverdale did not erase the old dichotomy between New York and the ethnic neighborhood. The American, cosmopolitan city eluded second generation Jews and their children. The problem of residential exclusion also remained. Although second and third generation Jews took to the courts for redress more successfully than those who tried in the 1920s, gentlemen's agreements effectively kept Jews out of certain parts of the suburbs.

Yet if the postwar residential dispersion conformed to many of the precedents set by second generation Jews in the 1920s, it also diverged in some aspects. Unlike the urban growth of Queens, the suburban expansion followed highways rather than subway tracks. The automobile determined the structure of these new suburbs and in the process changed the basis of community. In 1959 sociologist Amitai Etzioni, with one eye on the modern suburbs, reviewed a reissue of Wirth's *The Ghetto*, arguing that "a group can maintain its cultural and social integration and identity" without having a neighborhood locus. Etzioni considered suburban American Jews to be a reference group based upon "a common identity, tradition, values, and consciousness" which is "maintained by communication and activated in limited social situations and core institutions." Etzioni provided an alternative explanation for the persistence of Jewish ethnicity. Looking at the Jewish suburban dispersion, Etzioni concluded that residential contiguity no longer functioned as a factor in maintaining Jewish-

ness. Yet while "private automobiles and telephones make it possible to have greater dispersion than previously," Nathan Kantrowitz shows that few New Yorkers took advantage of this
technology to forego residential concentration. Furthermore, residential segregation was characteristic of many ethnic groups in
the multiethnic metropolis. If the suburbs changed the structure
of Jewish residential concentration, they did not obliterate the
fact of segregation. "The history of the Jews in the United
States," C. Bezalel Sherman observed in the 1950s (with only a
touch of exaggeration) "may be written on the basis of the exchange of one area of compact Jewish settlement for another."
Residential concentration, the product of "internal desire and external avoidance," continued to provide the territorial foundation
for Jewish ethnic community.[4]

Within the new neighborhoods New York Jews again built institutions. Looking at Queens in 1955, Morris Freedman discovered that "for many Jewish families, settling here seems to have
involved a new adventure in Jewishness, expressing itself in formal affiliation, for the first time in their lives, with a Jewish community institution. The most obvious manifestation of this phenomenon," he continued, "is the burgeoning of 'community
centers' throughout the borough, especially in the more recently
developed areas." Postwar synagogue building eclipsed even the
1920s boom. Million dollar synagogue centers of modern architectural design attracted attention and comment. Freedman found
on Queens Boulevard

> two impressive centers in quick succession: in Rego Park, one of
> the first fashionable sections of the apartment belt, is a great white
> building looking somewhat like a bank, with a huge Star of David
> on one blank wall and flanked by stores; a little farther east is a
> substantial building, recently completed, reminiscent of a modern
> college auditorium—plain, high, out-thrust front with rows of steps
> leading up—which houses the Forest Hills Jewish Center.[5]

Jews appeared to be participating in the widely discussed national religious revival.

To some observers, the bright shiny synagogue centers suggested the final transformation of third generation Jews into an
American religious group. Will Herberg attributed the change to
the third generation, the one which wanted to remember all that

the second generation tried to forget. According to Herberg, Jewish ethnicity, the bane of second generation existence, went underground and reemerged with the third generation as Jewish religion, an American faith. As Marshall Sklare argued, the Jews became a middle-class ethnic church, "a fellowship whose members are differentiated from those belonging to other denominations by virtue of their special *descent* as well as by their doctrines or practices. In America the uniqueness of this type of church," Sklare wrote, "is its articulation of ethnicity and religiosity in a multi-ethnic society where ethnic groups are essentially minority groups, i.e., subordinate to a majority group presumed to be non-ethnic."[6] Especially in the suburbs, synagogues served as ethnic facilities, with religious services often taking a back seat to recreational and educational activities. Increasingly, as all religions became Americanized, they came to share common values.

These analyses of the postwar synagogue center suggest that it did not differ significantly from its earlier model. Third generation Jews—even more than their parents—established the synagogue center as the key local Jewish institution in the suburbs. The tangle of religion and ethnicity institutionalized in the synagogue center could not be unraveled. And, as attendance figures soon revealed, Jews' participation in worship services still did not come close to approximating the percentages reached by the religious revival in the Christian churches. If third generation Jews were now members of an American religious faith, they behaved in a most peculiar and unreligious manner. Gans called the Jewish revival "not a return to the observance of traditional Judaism, but a manifestation in the main of the new symbolic Judaism." An aspect of Jewish ethnicity, this new version of Jewish religion served "as a symbol for the expression of Jewishness."[7] Third generation Jews coupled symbolic Judaism with a staunch belief in an American civil religion. Indeed, their civil religious fundamentalism brought them into open conflict with their neighbors over the character of the local public schools.

Second and third generation suburban Jews fought the battle of separation of church and state with renewed vigor in the 1950s. Unlike the inconclusive skirmishes before the war, the struggles to ban prayers and to remove Christmas celebrations from the public schools often passed into the courts, occasionally reaching the Supreme Court. Jewish efforts to purge the public schools of Christian characteristics accompanied a fervent drive to promote faith in American civil religion. Second and third generation Jews often turned into a creed the constitutional clause separating church and state and the parallel article protecting religious freedom. They came to feel that, in Charles Liebman's words, "only separation of church and state assures the existence of religiously neutral areas of life where the Jew can function with his Jewish status as a matter of irrelevance." As the theories of progressive education had supported the efforts of second generation Jews to legitimate their ethnic separateness and their pluralist vision of American democracy, so the new concept of an American civil religion buttressed Jewish efforts to achieve respect and recognition from public school authorities. Similarly, Jews often accepted Christmas-Chanukah celebrations as a valid compromise, since this synthesis articulated America's supposed Judeo-Christian heritage.[8]

The attempt to gain acceptance from public school authorities paralleled a renewed struggle against discrimination in higher education. Armed with laws prohibiting discrimination in college admissions, New York Jews also pressed for an expanded state university system to accommodate those who flocked to college after the war. In this environment, the idea of a Jewish university reappeared. Under the energetic supervision of Dr. Samuel Belkin, Revel's successor, Yeshiva College further expanded into a university, adding new schools of graduate study as well as a college for women, Stern College. Yeshiva University also founded a medical school, named, ironically, not in honor of a famous Jewish doctor like Moses Maimonides, but for the world renowned physicist Albert Einstein. Unlike the College, the graduate schools were open to Jews and Gentiles alike. Thus Yeshiva University institutionalized a nonsectarian liberal educational ideal friendly to Jews but accessible to Gentiles, a goal which had been articulated by some early supporters of the College. Yeshiva University countered the effects of academic discrimination against Jews and underlined the valuable Jewish contribution to American higher education. It also symbolized the maturing of the second generation and reflected its love of American secular society. The building of this institution of higher learning represented the creative commitment of second generation American Jews.

Such creative expressions of Jewish ethnicity simultaneously strengthened communal philanthropy. The scope of philanthropy expanded in the postwar era as demands for funds escalated. In the wake of the Holocaust and the tension surrounding the creation of Israel, American Jews mobilized to provide financial assistance to their brethren. The tremendous need for money in turn boosted the prestige of philanthropy and restored its communal influence, even when the fund raising supported only local organizations, as was the case of New York Federation. During the 1950s New York Federation and the more recently established United Jewish Appeal refused to combine their fund-raising. In maintaining its independence, Federation held on to its pretensions to represent the New York Jewish community, but it also sought to broaden its constituency by establishing a separate neighborhood division for fund-raising. And, as the study of religion became a subject of scientific inquiry divorced from religious profession or practice, Federation inaugurated a department of religious affairs. Thus Federation leaders successfully maintained the primacy of philanthropy as the representative voice of the organized New York Jewish community.

Similarly undaunted by postwar developments, Jewish liberalism continued to reign as the ideology of American Jewish ethnicity. But the Cold War environment eroded the middle ground on which Jewish liberalism stood. The attack on Jewish Communists by organizations within the Jewish world as well as the anti-Communist hysteria provoked by Senator Joseph McCarthy disrupted Jewish radical activities. Although McCarthy and others succeeded in discrediting Communism (as Socialism had been routed in New York after World War I), they did not break most second generation Jews' ties to liberalism. Indeed, "McCarthy may have pushed Jews toward the Democratic party." Even ideological liberals like Alex Rose and David Dubinsky held on to their synthesis. In 1944 Rose and Dubinsky created the Liberal Party in New York when they lost control of the American Labor Party. They refused to join the Democrats or the Communists. Similarly, Jewish support for civil liberties, civil rights, the welfare state, and internationalism did not waver. In-

deed, many second generation Jews continued to see their liberal
ideology as an expression of their Jewishness. From their American experience, these Jews discovered an apparently integral relationship between Jewishness and liberalism, and on occasion even
used the latter to define the former. As the editor of *Commentary*
observed, they believed "that the essence of Judaism is the struggle for universal justice and human brotherhood" and asserted
"that anyone who fights for this ideal is to that degree more Jewish than a man who merely observes the rituals or identifies himself with the Jewish community." But the dwindling of a radical
alternative effectively realigned Jewish liberalism into an ideology
associated with the left rather than with a more conservative
American alternative to socialism. The new position of Jewish
liberalism on the left wing meant that Jews stood farther from the
American political consensus as the 1950s progressed. While
middle-class American Jewish liberalism developed as a synthesis
of Jewish ethnic concerns with the pragmatic tradition of American urban politics, the loyalty of second generation Jews to liberalism in the years after World War II anchored them to the
liberal wing of post–New Deal Democratic politics. In this situation, Jewish support of liberalism buttressed Jewish ethnicity in
an enduring fashion.[9]

The persistence of Jewish ethnicity after World War II
suggests, in Liebman's words, that "the essence of American Jewish identity, the core meaning of Judaism for many American
Jews, may very well be their social ties to one another." This pattern of Jewish associationalism "exists independently of other attributes of Jewish identity. It is a pattern found among all types
of Jews and in all types of Jewish communities, urban and suburban, wealthy and poor, first generation and third generation
American." Jewish associationalism, institutionally nurtured by
the middle-class urban neighborhoods of New York and supported by occupational concentration, gave birth to varied expressions of Jewish ethnicity. As a group, second generation Jews
acculturated thoroughly while preserving strong communal boundaries. "Some writers have regarded the flight from the Jewish
community as typical for a large part of second-generation
Jewry," Gans writes. "However, while many intellectuals may
have tried to escape, the great mass of Jews in this country never

even considered the possibility. They became middle class almost as a matter of course, assimilating culturally to the majority but continuing to live among Jews without questioning their own Jewishness or its ineluctability.''[10] While the synthesis involved the adaptation of American characteristics, the second generation assimilated these middle-class values into its ethnic identity. Indeed, so intensively did second generation Jews cultivate selected American values that their idiosyncratic American pantheon came to define their new Jewishness. The emergent Jewish culture was organizationally rooted in the fertile structures of New York life.

The appearance of an American Jewish ethnicity with the second generation highlights the important structural basis of Jewish life. Jewish values have never existed as the abstract expressions of a static religion. On the contrary, the dynamic of Jewish values appears in the structural context of community culture itself. Second generation Jews reconstructed that context through the urban neighborhood. They strengthened the neighborhood's associational patterns with a network of ethnic occupational ties. Such a base supported many ways to be Jewish and sustained diverse expressions of moral community. It nourished individual freedom in the context of rich institutional complexity. Middle-class Jewish ethnicity extended the ideal of a pluralist society as it rewove the web of urban community.

Appendix

All Jewish population figures in the United States are estimates; the government never has included religion as a question in its decennial censuses. Its enumeration of foreign-born and its census of mother tongues, including Yiddish, are excellent but do not allow one to obtain figures on second-generation Jews. The Censuses of Religious Bodies in 1926 and 1936 were supervised by H. S. Linfield for the Jews. His Jewish population figures are estimates, and his figures for congregations, synagogue buildings, and value of property, are based on secondary sources. A number of different methods have been used to obtain estimates of the Jewish population. Ira Rosenwaike, *Population History of New York City*, p. 111, considers most of the existing estimates to be "guesswork" except for those using Jewish mortality figures. Unfortunately, really reliable Jewish population statistics for Jews in New York City were never developed during the 1920s and 1930s and it would be exceedingly difficult, if not impossible, to reconstruct such figures.

The most popular method was used for at least forty years after it was pioneered by Alexander Dushkin in 1913 for his dissertation, published as *Jewish Education in New York City*. Called the "Yom Kippur" method, it involved estimating the number of Jewish pupils in the New York City public schools based on absences on Yom Kippur. In 1923 the Jewish Education Association began keeping records of Jewish pupils in the city public schools, and most subsequent Jewish population estimates use this data (for example, C. Morris Horowitz and Lawrence J. Kaplan *The Estimated Jewish Population of the New York Area 1900–1975*). For a detailed discussion of how the method is applied, including the statistical tools used, as well as some of its drawbacks, see Jewish Welfare Board, Part II: A Study of the Jewish Population of New York City, Survey of Recreational and Cultural Needs of the Jewish Population of New York City (New York: Jewish Welfare Board, 1946), TS, pp. 5–27, located in the New York Public Library. Obviously, there are many difficulties with the Yom Kippur method. For a general discussion of these problems see Sophia Robison, ed., *Jewish Population Studies*, p. 3, and Horowitz and Kaplan, p. 87. The main advantage of the Yom Kippur method was its low cost and relative speed. No Jewish agency in the 1920s and 1930s appeared willing to pay for more costly, although potentially more accurate, estimates of the Jewish population in New York City.

Other estimates of the New York City Jewish population include those done by sampling. Walter Laidlaw, ed., *Population of the City of New York 1890–1930*, who pioneered in developing a system of census tracts, estimated the religious population distribution of New York City from several sample surveys. Unfortunately both in 1900 and again in 1930 Laidlaw neglected to draw representative samples from Brooklyn, Queens, and Staten Island, and instead extended the data from Manhattan and the Bronx proportionately. Rosenwaike, p. 122, considers Laidlaw's figures "inaccurate" and Robison, p. 50, notes the "vast divergency" of Laidlaw's figures from Jewish Education Association estimates for the boroughs Laidlaw neglected to sample. A Cities Census Committee memorandum of March 24, 1928, in the American Jewish Historical Society, Council of Jewish Federations and Welfare Funds MSS, Box 163, observed that Laidlaw's figures for those boroughs, although conducted under Committee auspices, "need modification." (See the memorandum for details on Laidlaw's methodology.) In 1935 the Research Bureau of the Welfare Council of New York City conducted a survey, later published by Nettie P. McGill and Ellen N. Matthews, *The Youth of New York*, in which a sample of youth aged 16–24 was surveyed and religious distribution obtained. This sample is considered fairly reliable and the percentage of Jewish youth in New York City correlated with other estimates of the Jewish population. Robison discusses this survey, p. 6, as does Rosenwaike, pp. 123–24.

Given all of these problems with Jewish population estimates, it might be asked, why bother to use any at all? In this book the Yom Kippur figures have been followed (except for 1920 when Laidlaw's figures were used since there were no Yom Kippur figures) because they are the only estimates which attempt to measure Jewish population in neighborhoods of New York City. I have bothered with figures for several reasons. Despite the inaccuracies, the estimates provide the only way to make concrete a statement such as, "a large number of Jews lived on the Lower East Side." When a large number of Jews is seen as 250,000 Jews, it does not matter that there may have been in actuality 300,000 Jews or 200,000 Jews. The estimates give some perspective. In general, I have tried to emphasize movement when using population estimates— again to enhance the impressionistic historical data. When Jews describe the Harlem Jewish community as disappearing "overnight," the percent decline of the Jewish population adds another dimension to historical understanding. Needless to say, the figures should at all times be considered estimates and should be evaluated within the context of the other evidence presented.

For a detailed discussion of neighborhoods, their boundaries and populations, see my dissertation, "The Emergence of Ethnicity: New York's Jews 1920–1940," Columbia 1975.

Notes

Abbreviations

AJHQ	*American Jewish Historical Quarterly*
BJSR	Bureau of Jewish Social Research
CJFWF	Council of Jewish Federations and Welfare Funds MSS
FMW	Felix M. Warburg MSS
JCS	Jewish Communal Survey of Greater New York TSS
JDB	*Jewish Daily Bulletin*
JWB	Jewish Welfare Board
NYT	*New York Times*
OHM	Oral History Memoirs in Columbia University Oral History Library
WPA	Works Progress Administration: Historical Records Survey: Federal Writers Project TSS
YU	Yeshiva University Public Relations Department

1. New York Jews

1. Kehillah of New York City, "Preface," in *Jewish Communal Register*, p. 3; Ruppin, "Jewish Population of the World," p. 357; *The Encyclopedia Judaica*, 12: 1062.

2. Finkelstein quoted in Sklare, *The Jews*, p. v; Sklare, "The Sociological Study of New York Jewry and Its Relationship to the Study of American Jewry," unpublished paper; Bernheimer, *The Russian Jew in the United States*, pp. 117–23.

3. Howe, *World of Our Fathers*; Warshow, "Poet of the Jewish Middle Class," pp. 17–18.

4. For good definitions of assimilation and acculturation see Gordon, *Assimilation in American Life*, pp. 70–77. On intermarriage see Heiss, "Premarital Characteristics of the Religiously Intermarried," pp. 47–55, and Zukerman and Chenkin, "Problems Confronting the Researchers," pp. 158–67.

5. Howe, "Memoir of the Thirties," pp. 350, 352.

6. Kaplan, *Judaism As A Civilization*, pp. 76–77; Rosenwaike, *Population History of New York City*, pp. 79, 82–83, 109–10, 122–25.

7. Glazer and Moynihan, *Beyond the Melting Pot*, p. 18; Yancey, Erickson, and Juliani, "Emergent Ethnicity: A Review and Reformulation," pp. 391–400.

8. Howe, *World of Our Fathers*, pp. 122–23; Smith, "Religion and Ethnicity in America," p. 1155.

9. Rischin, *The Promised City*, pp. 237–57.

10. Rose, *"The Ghetto and Beyond,"* p. 5; Chudacoff, "A New Look at Ethnic Neighborhoods," p. 91; Kessner, *The Golden Door*, pp. 152–56; Gurock, *When Harlem Was Jewish*, pp. 40–41; Rischin, *The Promised City*, p. 93.

11. Kessner, *ibid.*, p. 169; Rischin, *ibid.*, pp. 51–75.

12. Howe, *World of Our Fathers*, pp. 250–51; Nahirny and Fishman, "American Immigrant Groups," pp. 316–17.

13. Howe, "Memoir of the Thirties," pp. 353–54; Gans, "American Jewry," pp. 422–23; Nahirny and Fishman, *ibid.*, pp. 320–21; Sklare, "The Sociological Study of New York Jewry and Its Relationship to the Study of American Jewry," unpublished paper.

14. *The Day* translated and quoted in JDB, October 22, 1924. French Jew quoted in Kriegel, "Generational Difference," p. 34. The quote goes on to elaborate generational succession: "The grandfather prays in Hebrew, the father reads the prayer in French, and the son does not pray at all. The grandfather observes all festivals, the father observes only Yom Kippur, the son does not observe any. The grandfather is still a Jew, the father has become an Israelite, and the son is simply a deist."

15. Kriegel, *ibid.*, pp. 31–35.

16. Ruth Glazer, "West Bronx," p. 584; Hooper-Holmes Bureau, Inc., *A Survey of the Buying Power and Buying Habits of the Readers of the Jewish Daily Forward*, p. 12.

17. Sherman, *The Jew Within American Society*, p. 226; Sklare, "The Sociological Study of New York Jewry and Its Relationship to the Study of American Jewry," unpublished paper.

18. Chudacoff, "New Look at Ethnic Neighborhoods," p. 89; Quandt, *From the Small Town to the Great Community*, pp. 3–10; Haller, "Recurring Themes," p. 280; Wirth, *The Ghetto*, pp. 254–61.

19. For a similar analysis of Chicago see Rosenthal, "Acculturation and Assimilation," p. 288.

20. Reich, "Economic Trends," pp. 161–69; Goren, *New York Jews and the Quest for Community*, pp. 186–213, 236–42; Nathan Glazer, *The Social Basis of American Communism*, pp. 136–48.

21. Rotenstreich's definition of a modern Jew is: "A Jew is a Jew when he is with other Jews," "Emancipation and Its Aftermath," pp. 56–57.

22. Rose, "The Ghetto and Beyond," p. 17; Charles Liebman, *The Ambivalent American Jew*, p. 66.

23. Fink and Richards, *Jewish Community Directory of Greater New York*, pp. 6–7; Postal and Koppman, *Jewish Landmarks in New York*, p. 7.

24. Berman, "That Is, Unless We Make It Ourselves," p. 4.

2. Jewish Geography

1. Rosenwaike, *Population History*, p. 84; Rischin, *Promised City*, p. 78; Cahan, *The Rise of David Levinsky*, pp. 89–91, describes this typical scene for David Levinsky.

2. Lee K. Frankel, "Introduction," in BJSR, *Jewish Population*, JCS, p. III; Laidlaw, *Population of the City of New York*, pp. 292–96; Horowitz and Kaplan, *Estimated Jewish Population*, pp. 98, 100, 102.

3. Howe, *World of Our Fathers*, pp. 130–31; Yoffeh, "Passing of the East Side," p. 274; Klaperman, *Story of Yeshiva*, p. 29; Jewish Communities, TS, WPA, Jews of New York, Box 3632; *Forward*, December 2, 1903, in Howe, *World of Our Fathers*, p. 133; Landesman, *Brownsville*, p. 95; BJSR, *Jewish Population*, JCS, pp. 4–10; Gurock, *When Harlem Was Jewish*, pp. 58–60.

4. Quoted in Still, *Mirror for Gotham*, p. 362; *Brooklyn Review* masthead; Rosenwaike, *Population History*, pp. 109–10, 131–32; Horowitz and Kaplan, *Estimated Jewish Population*, p. 21.

5. Goren, *New York Jews and the Quest for Community*, pp. 14–17; Sanders, *Downtown Jews*, p. 224; Rischin, *Promised City*, p. 98; *Forward*, July 4, 1926, as translated in *JDB*, July 7, 1926.

6. *JDB*, July 7, 1926; S. Mutterperl, in *Jewish Tribune*, March 9, 1928. In the 1920s the word "ghetto" almost always applied exclusively to Jewish neighborhoods. Concentrations of other ethnic groups acquired a different terminology (e.g. "little Italy" or "Chinatown"). Louis Wirth in *The Ghetto*, p. 6, notes that "the ghetto is, strictly speaking, a Jewish institution." But he continues,

> there are forms of ghettos that concern not merely Jews. There are little Sicilies, Little Polands, Chinatowns, and Black belts in our larger cities, and there are segregated areas, such as vice areas, that bear a close resemblance to the Jewish ghetto. . . . The ghetto may therefore be regarded as typical of a number of forms of community life that sociologists are attempting to explore.

Today the word ghetto carries exclusively Jewish overtones only for some Jews. Theodorson and Theodorson define a ghetto as "a segregated community, usually racially or culturally homogeneous, within a larger community. The isolation of the community may be enforced politically or economically or it may be voluntary." *Modern Dictionary of Sociology*, p. 174.

7. Report of the Seventy-ninth Street Settlement House, TS, FMW, Box 222, Henry Street Settlement, 1925.

8. R. Williams to M. Abelman, February 19, 1920, Interior Correspondence, CJFWF, Box 160, Brooklyn Federation of Jewish Charities; Horowitz and Kaplan, *Estimated Jewish Population*, pp. 98, 100, 102; BJSR, *Jewish Population*, JCS, pp. 2–7, Laidlaw, *Population of the City of New York*, pp. 292–96, 73–81.

9. Mutterperl, in *Jewish Tribune*, March 9, 1928; Bercovici, "The Greatest Jewish City in the World," *The Nation*, September 12, 1923, p. 261; *Population, Land Values and Government*, Rgional Survey of New York, 2: 60.

10. Spengler, *Land Values in New York*, pp. 89–91, 105–7; interview with Myron Eisenstein, 1973; Jewish Communities, TS, WPA, Jews of New York, Box 3632; Jewish Communal Center of Flatbush, *Twentieth Anniversary of Jewish Communal Center of Flatbush 1916–1936, Souvenir Journal*; quoted in *NYT*, May 6, 1973; Golden, *Greatest Jewish City in the World*, p. 105; *Bronx Art Deco Architecture: An Exposition*, Larcada Gallery, New York City, 1976.

11. Mutterperl, in *Jewish Tribune*, March 9, 1928; quoted in *NYT*, April 24, 1921; interview with Marcus Gilden, 1972; *NYT*, July 10, 1921, January 2, 1921; *Bronx Art Deco Architecture: An Exposition*, Larcada Gallery, New York City, 1976.

12. *NYT*, April 24, 1921; JWB, Study of Educational and Recreational Resources of Brooklyn (1925), TS, p. 20; interview with Myron Eisenstein, 1973; Jewish Communities, TS, WPA, Jews of New York, Box 3632; "Lenru" brochure, in possession of Myron Eisenstein.

13. Memorandum from Harry Schneiderman, quoted in memo to the staff of the Jewish Book from Charles C. Baldwin, August 21, 1941, WPA, Jews of New York, Box 3637; Halpern, "America Is Different," pp. 35–36.

14. *JDB*, July 7, 1926; Gold, *Jews Without Money*, pp. 158–59; Yoffeh, "Passing of the East Side," p. 274.

15. Horowitz and Kaplan, *Estimated Jewish Population*, p. 57, found this trend continuing into the 1950s. The index of dissimilarity which measures ethnic segregation when applied to Jews in New York City unfortunately relies only on the rough estimates of Jewish population available. The unit of measurement (the neighborhood) is rather large. Thus the index does not explain Jewish residential patterns within the neighborhood and the possibilities for increased Jewish-Gentile contact in a neighborhood only 50 percent Jewish in its population compared with one which is 80 percent Jewish. For an excellent discussion of the uses of an index of dissimilarity in measuring ethnic segregation and its implications for acculturation and assimilation see Lieberson, *Ethnic Patterns in American Cities*. For methodology see Dollar and Jensen, *Historian's Guide to Statistics*, pp. 125–26. For an analysis of residential segregation, using census tracts in New York which confirms these patterns for 1960, see Kantrowitz, *Ethnic and Racial Segregation*, pp. 11–32.

16. Horowitz and Kaplan, *Estimated Jewish Population*, pp. 98, 100, 102, 122; BJSR, *Jewish Population*, JCS, pp. 2, 4–7; Laidlaw, *Population of the City of New York*, pp. 292–96, 73–81, 275; Maller, "Study of Jewish Neighborhoods of New York City," pp. 275–76; Rosenwaike, *Population History of New York City*, p. 133. Robison, *Jewish Population Studies*, p. 5, presents divergent figures from the Jewish Education Association.

17. Laidlaw, *ibid.*, pp. 233–44; *Population, Land Values and Government*, Regional Survey of New York, 2: 29.

18. *Transit and Transportation*, Regional Survey of New York, 4: 40, 99.

19. *Transit and Transportation*, Regional Survey of New York, 4: 23, 32; Spengler, *Land Values in New York*, p. 86; *New York City Market Analysis* (1944); *New York City Guide*, p. 11.

20. Makielski, *Politics of Zoning*, pp. 7, 36, 111–12; interview with Myron Eisenstein, 1973; *NYT*, July 17, 1921.

21. Maller, "Study of Jewish Neighborhoods," p. 272; interview with Julius Borenstein, 1972; *NYT*, March 5, 1922, April 24, 1921; Wexelstein, *Building Up Greater Brooklyn*, p. vii; notice prior to dedication on January 11, 1925, of Jacob H. Schiff Center, FMW, Box 221, Jacob H. Schiff Center, 1924; Sullivan and Danforth, *Bronx Art Deco Architecture*, p. 13.

22. Bayor, *Neighbors in Conflict*, pp. 150–52; Sanders, *Downtown Jews*, pp. 2–6, 45.

23. *JDB*, February 3, 1927; Broun and Britt, *Christians Only*, p. 256; *NYT*, September 11, 1921; interview with Paula Goldwasser, 1972; Postal and Koppman, *Jewish Landmarks in New York*, p. 57; Weld, *Brooklyn Is America*, pp. 8–10; interview with Dr. Paul Ritterband, 1972.

24. *JDB*, February 3, 1927; Naomi Cohen, *Not Free to Desist*, pp. 384–87; Gurock, "The 1913 New York State Civil Rights Act," pp. 111–12.

25. Interview with Dr. Ira Eisenstein, 1973; interview with Charles Dash, 1972; interview with Dr. Paul Ritterband, 1972.

26. See Warner, *Streetcar Suburbs*, chs. 4, 6, 7, for an excellent presentation of the general development of suburbs, in this case in Boston. The Regional Survey of New York's volume on *Population, Land Values and Government*, suggests an ethnically distinct housing market in Queens, p. 64. See also *NYT*, October 2, 1921, for evidence of Italian builder network.

27. Howe, *World of Our Fathers*, p. 139; Cahan, *Rise of David Levinsky*, pp. 486, 464; Gold, *Jews Without Money*, p. 152; Epstein, *Pages from a Colorful Life*, p. 53; Landesman, *Brownsville*, p. 83, Gurock, *When Harlem Was Jewish*, pp. 45–49.

28. Fischel, *Forty Years*, pp. 31–32; Landesman, *Brownsville*, pp. 84–85; Epstein, *Jewish Labor*, 1: 372–74; Gurock, *When Harlem Was Jewish*, p. 33.

29. *NYT*, February 16, 1921, October 2, 1921, January 1, 1922, January 8, 1922, January 27, 1922; Epstein, *Jewish Labor*, 2: 328; Epstein, *Pages From A Colorful Life*, p. 53.

30. Interview with Myron Eisenstein, 1973; *NYT*, April 24, 1921; Fischel, *Forty Years*, p. 180.

31. Edith Isaacs, *Love Affair with a City*, pp. 49–50; State of New York, *Report of the State Board of Housing* (1932), pp. 15–17; Wexelstein, *Building Up Greater Brooklyn*, p. xvii.

32. Wexelstein, *ibid.*, pp. xvii–xx; Gold, *Jews Without Money*, p. 155.

33. *JDB*, March 14, 1929; American Jewish Committee, Minutes, 5 (April 14, 1929): 1458; Melvin Fagen, Jewish Workers In New York City, TS, pp. 2, 4, WPA, Jews of New York, Box 3629, Commerce; Broun and Britt, *Christians Only*, p. 260; quoted in *JDB*, January 9, 1927; Sullivan and Danforth, *Bronx Art Deco Architecture*, pp. 56–58.

34. Wexelstein, *Building Up Greater Brooklyn*, pp. 32–33, 46–48, 51–52, 55–56, 78–79, 99–100, 106–7; interview with Julius Borenstein, 1972; interview with Lou Berg, 1972; interview with David Tishman, 1973; interview with Myron Eisenstein, 1973.

35. Interview with David Tishman, 1973; interview with Julius Borenstein, 1972; Wexelstein, *Building Up Greater Brooklyn*, pp. 91–92, 99–100, 177–78, 197–98, 201; interview with Myron Eisenstein, 1973; interview with Marcus Gilden, 1972; interview with Lou Berg, 1972.

36. Interview with Julius Borenstein, 1972; interview with Marcus Gilden, 1972; interview with Lou Berg, 1972; interview with Jack Brakarsh, 1972; interview with David Tishman, 1973.

37. Melvin Fagen, Jewish Workers in New York City, TS, WPA, Jews of New York, Box 3629, Commerce; George Garvin, House Painting and Decorating, TS, WPA, Jews of New York, Box 3629, Commerce; "Jews in Trade Unions in New York City," *American Jewish Year Book*, 31 (1928–1929): 203–4; Epstein, *Jewish Labor*, 2: 326.

38. Harriet Kraus, "Evolution of the Alteration Painters Union," TS, p. 2, YIVO; Irving Ripps, Brownsville, TS, p. 3, WPA, Jews of New York, Box 3628; Kazin, *Walker in the City*, pp. 37–38.

39. Interview with Jack Brakarsh, 1972; interview with Lou Berg, 1972; interview with Julius Borenstein, 1972; Wexelstein, *Building Up Greater Brooklyn*, pp. 7–8, 55–56; Landesman, *Brownsville*, pp. 87–88.

40. Interview with Marcus Gilden, 1972; interview with Jack Brakarsh, 1972; interview with Lou Berg, 1972; interview with Julius Borenstein, 1972; interview with Myron Eisenstein, 1973; Landesman, *Brownsville*, p. 131; Trade Union and Labor Movement, TS, WPA, Jews of New York, Box 3633; Wexelstein, *ibid.*, p. 19.

41. Interview with Myron Eisenstein, 1973; interview with Marcus Gilden, 1972; interview with Jack Brakarsh, 1972; interview with Lou Berg, 1972; interview with Julius Borenstein, 1972.

42. Interview with Marcus Gilden, 1972; interview with Julius Borenstein, 1972; interview with David Tishman, 1973; interview with Lou Berg, 1972; Broun and Britt, *Christians Only*, p. 261; interview with Myron Eisenstein, 1973.

43. BJSR, *Jewish Population*, JCS, p. 7; Kazin, *Walker in the City*, pp. 9–10; Jewish Communities, TS, WPA, Jews of New York, Box 3632; *NYT*, June 12, 1921; interview with Julius Borenstein, 1972; JWB, Study of Educational and Recreational Resources of Brooklyn (1925), TS, p. 20; State of New York, *Report of the State Board of Housing* (1929), pp. 53–80.

44. Cahan, *Rise of David Levinsky*, p. 512; Schwartz quoted in Wexelstein, *Building Up Greater Brooklyn*, p. 196; Notice prior to dedication on January 11, 1925, in FMW, Box 221, 1924, Jacob H. Schiff Center.

45. Goldberger, in *NYT*, January 31, 1974; Just Plain Jews, TS, WPA, Jews of New York, Box 3632, Miscellaneous; Ruth Glazer, "West Bronx," p. 584; Sullivan and Danforth, *Bronx Art Deco Architecture*, pp. 9–13, quotes on pp. 11–12.

46. Bayor, *Neighbors in Conflict*, p. 20; interview with Irene Dash, 1978; Sklare, "Jews, Ethnics, and the American City," p. 72.

47. Locke, "Village Vision," pp. 84–137; interview with Myron Eisenstein, 1973; Blaine and Intrater, "Grandeur That Is Flatbush," p. 44.

48. Strauss, *Images of the American City*, p. 243; Kaplan, *Judaism As A Civilization*, p. 49.

49. Peck, in *NYT*, April 29, 1973, sec. 8 (real estate), p. 10; Locke, "Village Vision," pp. 84–137; Strauss, *ibid.*, p. 244; interview with Myron Eisenstein, 1973; *New York City Market Analysis* (1933).

50. State of New York, *Report of the State Board of Housing* (1929), p. 32; B. B. Weinrebe, Jewish Suburban Housing Movement, TS, pp. 6–7, WPA, Jews of New York, Box 3628; Trillin, "U.S. Journal: The Bronx," p. 49; *NYT*, May 3, 1977, p. 37; *New York City Guide*, p. 539.

51. Trillin, *ibid.*, p. 49.

52. Wexelstein, *Building Up Greater Brooklyn*, pp. 5–6; interview with Myron Eisenstein, 1973; *JDB*, April 28, 1929; Sullivan and Danforth, *Bronx Art Deco Architecture*, p. 7.

53. Blaine and Intrater, "Grandeur That Is Flatbush," p. 44; *New York City Guide*, p. 57; Goldberger, in *NYT*, January 31, 1974.

3. A World of Its Own

1. Gornick, "There Is No More Community," p. 4.

2. *Ibid.*; also Poster, "Twas a Dark Night in Brownsville," p. 461; Poplin, *Communities*, p. 7; Rosenthal, "Acculturation Without Assimilation," pp. 285–87; Sklare, *Conservative Judaism*, p. 47; Gans, "Origin and Growth of a Jewish Community," p. 247; Parenti, "Ethnic Politics," p. 721; Wirth, *The Ghetto*, pp. 241–62. All these offer theoretical discussions of the process of acculturation.

3. Wirth, "Bibliography," p. 190. It should be noted that Wirth felt that, "the neighborhood is typically the product of the village and small town. . . . While in the modern city we still find people living in close physical proximity to each other, there is neither close cooperation nor intimate contact, acquaintanceship and group consciousness accompanying this spatial nearness. The neighborhood has come to mean a small, homogeneous geographic section of the city, rather than a self-sufficing, co-operative, and self-conscious group of the population."

4. *The Fourth American City* (1927); Kazin, *Walker in the City*, p. 12; Gornick, "There Is No More Community," p. 4; Howe, "Memoir of the Thirties," p. 353.

5. Gornick, *ibid.*; Howe, *ibid.*; Park, "The Urban Community," pp. 60–61; Kazin, *ibid.*; Jewish Communities, TS, WPA, Jews of New York, Box 3632.

6. Glazer and Moynihan, *Beyond the Melting Pot*, p. 161, suggest the influence of institutions.

7. Mutterperl, *Jewish Tribune*, March 9, 1928.

8. *Forward*, July 4, 1926, as translated and quoted by *JDB*, July 7, 1926.

9. Landsmanshaftn, TS, WPA, Jews of New York, Box 3630, Organizations—Welfare; Landesman, *Brownsville*, p. 282; BJSR, *Report of the Executive Committee*, JCS, pp. 47–49, 37, 53–54; Jewish Communities, TS, WPA, Jews of New York, Box 3637.

10. Yoffeh, "Passing of the East Side," p. 266.

11. BJSR, Care of Jewish Aged of Manhattan and The Bronx, TS, p. 35; *New York City Market Analysis* (1933); *JDB*, September 2, 1930; Jonah Goldstein, The Place of the Alliance in the East Side, TS, located in the American Jewish Historical Society, Jonah Goldstein MSS, Box 3; WPA, Jews of New York, Box 3630, Organizations—Welfare.

12. *JDB*, December 9, 1926, December 21, 1927; H. K. Blatt, Jewish Communities, TS, p. 3, WPA, Jews of New York, Box 3632; *New York City Market Analysis* (1933); Aaron M. Frankel, "Back to Eighty-Sixth Street," pp. 169–70.

13. Howe, *World of Our Fathers*, pp. 132–33; Irving Ripps, Brownsville, TS, p. 1, WPA, Jews of New York, Box 3628; Landesman, A Neighborhood Survey, TS, p. 4a; Halpert, "Jews of Brownsville," p. 20; Landesman, *Brownsville*, p. 86; Kazin, *Walker in the City*, pp. 34–35; Poster, "Twas a Dark Night in Brownsville," pp. 459–60.

14. Halpert, *ibid.*, pp. 184–85; Landesman, *Brownsville*, pp. 170–89, 222–29, 234–36, 285–86; JWB, Study Of The Jewish Community Centers (1938), TS, p. 64; Tenenbaum, "Brownsville's Age of Learning," p. 177.

15. Quoted in Kranzler, *Williamsburg*, pp. 17–18; Rischin, *The Promised City*, p. 92; Daniel Fuchs, *Summer in Williamsburg*, p. 265.

16. Kranzler, *ibid.*, pp. 141–42, 45, 48–50; JWB, Report Of Preliminary Study (1923), TS, pp. 8–10; JWB, Jewish Community of Williamsburg (1936), p. 6.

17. JWB, Jewish Community of Williamsburg (1936), TS, p. 37; Kranzler, *ibid.*, pp. 167–69; 17–18; JWB, Study Of The Jewish Community Centers (1938), TS, pp. 158, 185.

18. *New York City Market Analysis* (1933); Gornick, "There Is No More Community," p. 4; JWB, Study of Bronx House (1939), TS, pp. 5, 10–11, 13, 18, 20, 121; Ferretti, *NYT*, October 21, 1977, pp. B1–B3; Ira Rosen, "The Glory That Was Charlotte Street," p. 74; JWB, Study Of The Educational And Recreational Resources Of The Bronx (1924), TS; Freedman, "Memoirs of a Pumpkin-Seed Peddler," p. 66.

19. JWB, Study Of Council House (1934), TS, pp. 24–26; Klaperman, *Story of Yeshiva*, p. 129; JWB, Study Of Bronx House (1939), TS, pp. 30–31, 34–35, 40, 89–95; *JDB*, October 6, 1930.

20. Jewish Communities, TS, WPA, Jews of New York, Box 3632; Howe, "Memoir of the Thirties," p. 353; Howe, *World of Our Fathers*, p. 614; Ruth Glazer, "West Bronx," p. 578.

21. *New York City Market Analysis* (1933); Jewish Communities, TS, WPA, Jews of New York, Box 3632; Jacobs, *Is Curly Jewish?*, p. 5; Howe, *ibid.*, p. 355; Just Plain Jews, TS, WPA, Jews of New York, Box 3632, Miscellaneous; Ruth Glazer, *ibid.*; *New York City Guide*, p. 517.

22. Jewish Communities, TS, WPA, Jews of New York, Box 3632; Jacobs, *ibid.*; Recreation Section: Synagogue Centers, JCS, TS, pp. A–B, 12–14, 22, CJFWF; Ruth Glazer, *ibid.*, p. 579.

23. BJSR, *Jewish Population*, JCS, p. 7; Jewish Communal Center of Flatbush, *Twentieth Anniversary of Jewish Communal Center of Flatbush 1916–1936, Souvenir Journal*, in WPA, Jews of New York, Box 3629, Religion; Wexelstein, *Building Up Greater Brooklyn*, p. xxvii; Blaine and Intrater, "*Grandeur That Is Flatbush*," p. 45; Jewish Sections of Brooklyn, TS, WPA, Jews of New York, Box 3633, Population; *JDB*, May 10, 1926, March 10, 1926; interview with Bella Golden, 1978.

24. Interior Correspondence, R. Williams to M. Abelman, February 19, 1920, CJFWF, Box 160, Brooklyn Federation of Charities; Borough Park, JCS, TS, CJFWF; *New York City Market Analysis* (1933); JWB, Study of the Educational and Recreational Resources of Brooklyn (1925), TS, p. 111.

25. Borough Park, JCS, TS, CJFWF; *JDB*, March 21, 1929, March 10, 1926, May 10, 1926.

26. *New York City Market Analysis* (1933); B. B. Weinrebe, Jewish Suburban Housing Movement, Part III—Cooperative Apartment Houses, trans. A. Richter, TS, p. 8, WPA, Jews of New York, Box 3628, Cooperative Activities; Trillin, "U.S. Journal: The Bronx," p. 50; J. M. Horden to E. Mozorowsky, April 10, 1935, CJFWF, Box 163.

27. B. Weinstein, Brighton Beach—A Jewish Suburb, trans. Betty Miller, TS, pp. 2–3, WPA, Jews of New York, Box 3628, Population: Brooklyn Localities; Coney Island, JCS, TS, CJFWF; New York Metropolitan Section—JWB, Recommendations for Extension Projects (1938), TS, p. 33; Klonsky, "Trojans of Brighton Beach," p. 462; *New York City Guide*, p. 471.

28. *New York City Market Analysis* (1933); Abelow, *History of Brooklyn Jewry*, pp. 15–22, 73–81; *JDB*, May 24, 1926, February 17, 1930; Minutes of the Meeting of the Distribution Committee, January 15, 1928, FMW, Box 245, 1925, New York Federation; H. K. Blatt, Jewish Communities, TS, pp. 2–3, WPA, Jews of New York, Box 3632.

29. *New York City Market Analysis* (1933), (1944).

30. Just Plain Jews, TS, WPA, Jews of New York, Box 3632, Miscellaneous; Ferretti, in *NYT*, October 21, 1977, p. B3; Howe, "Memoir of the Thirties," pp. 354–55.

31. Ira Rosen, "The Glory That Was Charlotte Street," p. 76; B. Weinstein, Brighton Beach—A Jewish Suburb, trans. Betty Miller, TS, pp. 2–3, WPA, Jews of New York, Box 3628, Population—Brooklyn Localities; Howe, *ibid.*; Golden, *Greatest Jewish City in the World*, p. 109.

32. Interview with Helen Miringoff, 1978; Kazin, *Walker in the City*, pp. 11–12; Klonsky, "Trojans of Brighton Beach," p. 463; Ferretti, in *NYT*, October 21, 1977, p. B3.

33. *Forward*, July 4, 1926, as translated and quoted by *JDB*, July 7, 1926.

34. Kazin, *Walker in the City*, pp. 11–12; Gornick, "There Is No More Community," p. 4; Howe, "Memoir of the Thirties," pp. 350–51.

35. Gornick, *ibid.*, Howe, *ibid.*, p. 351; Yoffeh, "Passing of the East Side," p. 275; *JDB*, April 1, 1930.

4. Ethnic Identity and the Neighborhood School

1. Tenenbaum, "Brownsville's Age of Learning," p. 174.

2. *The Evening Post*, August 9, 1918, quoted in Berkson, *Theories of Americanization*, p. 59; Dann, "Little Citizens," ch. 6.

3. Dann, *ibid.*, pp. 352–53; Berkson, *ibid.*, p. 72.

4. Michaelsen, *Piety in the Public School*, pp. 57, 11.

5. Tenenbaum, "Brownsville's Age of Learning," p. 174; Colin Greer, *Great School Legend*, pp. 116, 80.

6. Kligsberg, "Jewish Immigrants in Business," pp. 254–59; Gorelick, "Social Control," pp. 124–28.

7. Zangwill, *The Melting Pot*, p. 33; Mergen, "Another Great Prize," pp. 401–2; Gorelick, *ibid.*, p. 161; *JDB*, September 27, 1926.

8. Neumann, "Modern Jewish Experimental School," pp. 26–27; Poster, "Dark Night in Brownsville," p. 465.

9. Yoffeh, "Passing of the East Side," p. 271; Berrol, "Immigrants at School," p. 119.

10. Jewish Education Association, Jewish Child Population Study (1935), TS, in Board of Jewish Education files; Colin Greer, *Great School Legend*, p. 120; Dann, "Little Citizens," pp. 353–54.

11. Cole, *Unionization of Teachers*, p. 95; Gorelick, "Social Control," p. 222.

12. Berrol, "Immigrants at School," pp. 119–20; interview with Bella Golden, 1978.

Estimates of numbers of Jewish teachers in the public schools in 1927 and 1937 were based on names and derived from the New York City, Department of Education, *List of Members*. Bayor uses these lists and finds the same trends, see *Neighbors in Conflict*, pp. 26–27.

13. New York City Department of Education, *List of Members*; Zitron, *New York City Teachers Union*, pp. 128–30; Jewish Education Association, Jewish Child Population Study (1935), TS, in Board of Jewish Education files.

14. Interview with Irving Hudson, 1979; interview with Martin Dash, 1979.

15. Gorelick, "Social Control," p. 227; The Reminiscences of Theodore Fred Kuper, p. 122, in OHM; O'Shea, *Progress of the Public Schools*, pp. 5–7, 12.

16. Gorelick, "Social Control," p. 167; Landesman, *Brownsville*, pp. 162–63; *NYT*, October 2, 1921.

17. Gorelick, *ibid.*, pp. 181–82, 188, 98–99, 93.

18. Berrol, "Immigrants at School," pp. 63–64; Gorelick, *ibid.*, pp. 200–1; Zitron, *New York City Teachers Union*, p. 267; O'Shea, *Progress of the Public Schools*, pp. 17–20; Abelow, *History of Brooklyn Jewry*, p. 175; Howe, *World of Our Fathers*, p. 278; interview with Bella Golden, 1978.

19. O'Shea, *ibid.*, p. 21.

20. Interview with Bella Golden, 1978; Zitron, *New York City Teachers Union*, pp. 17–20, 30.

21. *JDB*, January 12, 1925; Abelow, *History of Brooklyn Jewry*, p. 178; *Brooklyn Review*, October 7, 1927; *Bronx Home News*, December 16, 1928.

22. Interview with Walter Metzger, 1975.

23. Gorelick, "Social Control," pp. 26, 101–3; Kessner, *Golden Door*, pp. 123–26.

24. Colin Greer, *Great School Legend*, p. 83; Maller quoted in Colin Greer, *ibid.*, p. 126; Maller, *School and Community*, pp. 247–49; Jewish Education Association, Jewish Child Population Study (1935), TS, in Board of Jewish Education files.

25. Interview with Judah Lapson, 1973; Howe, *World of Our Fathers*, p. 274.

26. Podhoretz, *Making It*, p. 14; interview with Zachary Baym, 1973.

27. Interview with Bella Golden, 1973; Rose, "The Ghetto and Beyond," p. 9.

28. Kazin, *Walker in the City*, pp. 21–22; interview with Raymond Feiden, 1973.

29. DeHass, *Louis D. Brandeis*, pp. 179, 203, 163, 185; Urofsky, *American Zionism*, p. 129; Trunk, "Cultural Dimension," pp. 364–65.

30. Gorelick, "Social Control," pp. 204–6; Kaplan, "Teacher's Institute," pp. 141–42; Friedlaender quoted in Cremin, *Transformation of the School*, p. 69.

31. Michaelsen, *Piety in the Public School*, pp. 145, 57, 136, 157–58; Dewey quoted in Itzkoff, *Cultural Pluralism*, p. 42.

32. Kaplan, *Judaism As A Civilization*, p. 490, 550 (fn. 9); Michaelsen, *ibid.*, p. 184.

33. Berkson, *Theories of Americanization*, p. 137; Nahirny and Fishman, "American Immigrant Groups," p. 319.

34. *JDB*, April 4, 1929; Winter, *Jewish Education*, p. 127; American Jewish Archives, Henry Hurwitz Menorah Association MSS, Box 77a, New York University.

35. *JDB*, May 4, 1930, May 7, 1929, January 11, 1929; Kaplan, *Judaism As A Civilization*, pp. 551–53; Chipkin as quoted in Winter, *ibid.*, pp. 125–27.

36. Chipkin, *ibid.*

37. O'Shea, *Progress of the Public Schools*, p. v; *JDB*, May 4, 1929, May 7, 1930; Lillian Zahn, Jews in Secular Education (1942), TS, in WPA, Jews of New York, Box 3632, Education; Lapson, "Hebrew in the Public Schools," no pg.

38. Interview with Irene Dash, 1978; Landesman, *Brownsville*, p. 163; Mason, *Great American Liberals*, *passim*; Lillian Zahn, Jews in Secular Education (1942), TS, in WPA, Jews of New York, Box 3632, Education; *NYT*, May 30, 1979; *JDB*, December 23, 1930.

39. *JDB*, April 1, 1930, June 9, 1930; interview with Rabbi George Ende, 1973; Epstein, *Jewish Labor*, 2: 272–77; Trunk, "Cultural Dimension," pp. 359, 362–72.

40. Gorelick, "Social Control," pp. 137, 139.

41. Pilch, "Early Forties to Mid-Sixties," p. 164; Halkin, "Hebrew in America," pp. 17–18; interview with Rabbi George Ende, 1973; interview with Judah Lapson, 1973; Jewish Education Association, Jewish Child Population Study (1935), TS, in Board of Jewish Education files.

42. *NYT*, March 16, 1922; *Brooklyn Review*, June 29, 1928; *JDB*, April 1, 1928, October 26, 1930.

43. *JDB*, January 27, 1926, January 28, 1926, June 15, 1931, June 16, 1931, January 15, 1932; *American Hebrew* quoted in *JDB*, January 28, 1926; Michaelsen, *Piety in the Public School*, pp. 30–33.

44. Goren, "Freedom and Its Limitations," p. 22; American Jewish Archives, Stephen Wise MSS, Box 1001; *JDB*, December 17, 1929, December 20, 1925; *Jewish Forum* quoted in *JDB*, December 7, 1930; Landesman, *Brownsville*, p. 161.

45. Jacobs, *Is Curly Jewish?*, pp. 8–9; Jewish Education Association, Jewish Child Population Study (1935), TS, in Board of Jewish Education files.

46. Sanders, *Reflections on a Teapot*, pp. 92–93.

47. Jacobs, *Is Curly Jewish?*, p. 91; Sanders, *Reflections on a Teapot*, pp. 132–33.

48. Interview with Walter Metzger, 1975.

49. Fishman, "Patterns of American Self-Identification," p. 229.

50. Board of Education statement quoted in Herlands, "Anti-Semitic Vandalism," p. 156; *NYT*, February 4, 1922; Bayor, *Neighbors in Conflict*, pp. 97–103.

51. Colin Greer, *Great School Legend*, p. 91.

5. From Chevra to Center

1. Sklare, *Conservative Judaism*, pp. 71–72.

2. Greeley, *The Denominational Society*, pp. 2–3, 108–9; Sklare, *ibid.*, pp. 35–38.

3. Doroshkin, *Yiddish in America*, p. 142; Cahan, *Rise of David Levinsky*, p. 109; Charles S. Liebman, "Orthodoxy in American Jewish Life," pp. 27–28; Nahirny and Fishman, "American Immigrant Groups," p. 316.

4. Feldstein, *Land That I Show You*, p. 258; Landesman, *Brownsville*, p. 208; Landesman, A Neighborhood Survey, p. 8; quote from Joseph Katz, Landsmanshaftn, TS, WPA, Jews of New York, Box 3637.

5. Landesman, A Neighborhood Survey, pp. 7–8.

6. JWB, Study Of The Educational And Recreational Resources Of Brooklyn (1925), TS, pp. 159–160; Landesman, *Brownsville*, pp. 209, 211; Kazin, *Walker in the City*, pp. 41–42; Landesman, A Neighborhood Survey, p. 9; *Temple Petach Tikvah News*, January 1938.

7. Halpert, "Jews of Brownsville," pp. 170–75, 191–92, 49; quote from E. Verschleisser, "Landmanshaft Constitutions," *Di Yidishe Landsmanshaftn fun New York*, p. 5, as translated by Doroshkin, *Yiddish in America*, p. 150; Landesman, *Brownsville*, p. 208.

8. Landesman, *Brownsville*, pp. 208–9; Halpert, *ibid.*, pp. 176–77.

9. Landesman, A Neighborhood Survey, p. 9; interview with Zachary Baym, 1973.

10. Landesman, *Brownsville*, pp. 208–10; Halpert, "Jews of Brownsville," p. 175; Landesman, A Neighborhood Survey, p. 8.

11. Landesman, *Brownsville*, pp. 213–17; JWB, A Study Of The Educational And Recreational Resources Of Brooklyn (1925), TS, p. 157; Landesman, A Neighborhood Survey, p. 11.

12. Interview with Lynn Goran, 1976.

13. Jewish Communal Center of Flatbush, "A Condensed History of the Jewish Communal Center of Flatbush," in *Twentieth Anniversary of the Jewish Communal Center of Flatbush 1916–1936*, WPA, Jews of New York, Box 3629, Religion; Levinthal quoted in Sklare, *Conservative Judaism*, p. 136.

14. "Minutes of Organization Meeting of the Brooklyn Jewish Center," *Jewish Center Bulletin: Dedication Number*, December 31, 1922; BJSR, Recreation Section, JCS, TS, pp. 3–6, CJFWF.

15. *Jewish Center Bulletin: Dedication Number*, December 31, 1922.

16. Sklare, *Conservative Judaism*, p. 135; BJSR, Survey of Jewish Recreational Facilities in Manhattan and the Bronx (1920), TS, pp. 80–82, in FMW, Box 198, 1920, Bureau of Jewish Social Research; Kraft, "Jewish Center Movement," pp. 121–22; Kaplan, *Judaism As A Civilization*, pp. 328, 428.

17. Kraft, *ibid.*, pp. 119–22, 135; Kaplan, *ibid.*, p. 425; Cross, *Church and the City*, p. xxxvi.

18. Charles S. Liebman, "Reconstructionism in American Jewish Life," pp. 4, 70; Goldberg, "25 Years of Brooklyn Jewish Center History," p. 7.

19. BJSR, Recreation Section, JCS, TS, pp. A–B, 12–14, 22, 3–4, CJFWF; Cross, *Church and the City*, pp. xxii–xxiv.

20. Ginzberg, *Agenda for American Jews*, p. 35.

21. BJSR, The Recent Development of Synagogue Centers, JCS, TS, p. 3, CJFWF.

22. BJSR, Recreation Section, JCS, TS, pp. A–B, 3–4, 6–8, CJFWF.

23. *JDB*, November 3, 1927; BJSR, *ibid.*, pp. 15, 18B–18D, CJFWF; Abelow, *History of Brooklyn Jewry*, pp. 90, 92; JWB, Study of the Jewish Community of Brooklyn (1935), TS, p. 34.

24. JWB, Study of the Jacob H. Schiff Center (1927), TS; BJSR, Recreation Section, JCS, TS, pp. 39–40, CJFWF; Jewish Communal Center of Flatbush, *Twentieth Anniversary of the Jewish Communal Center of Flatbush 1916–1936*, in WPA, Jews of New York, Box 3629, Religion.

25. *JDB*, November 3, 1927; *Brooklyn Jewish Center Review*, December 1934, pp. 1–2.

26. *JDB*, March 29, 1927; Heller, "Pattern for Synagogue Centers," pp. 82–83.

27. Interview with Bella Golden, 1978; BJSR, Recreation Section, JCS, TS, pp. 1–2, CJFWF.

28. Abelow, *History of Brooklyn Jewry*, pp. 64, 55–56, 29; *JDB*, December 24, 1929; Parzen, *Architects of Conservative Judaism*, pp. 107–10; Phillipson, *Reform Movement in Judaism*, pp. 377–79; Karp, *History of the United Synagogue of America*, p. 37; Sklare, *Conservative Judaism*, p. 75.

29. JWB, Study of the Jewish Community of Brooklyn (1935), TS, pp. 20–32; JWB, Study of the Uptown Talmud Torah (1937), TS, pp. 74–82; Sklare, *ibid.*, pp. 85–126.

30. Sklare, *ibid.*, pp. 102–9; *JDB*, July 9, 1930; Phillipson, *Reform Movement in Judaism*, pp. 377–79; Charles S. Liebman, "Orthodoxy in American Jewish Life," pp. 58–59.

31. BJSR, Recreation Section, JCS, TS, p. 78, CJFWF; JWB, Study of the Jewish Community of Brooklyn (1935), TS, pp. 20–32; JWB, Study of the Uptown Talmud Torah (1937), TS, pp. 74–82.

32. BJSR, *ibid.*

33. JWB, Study of the Jacob Schiff Center (1927), TS; Sklare, *Conservative Judaism*, pp. 93–97, Goldberg quote on p. 97; *JDB*, September 22, 1925.

34. *JDB*, December 24, 1929, June 9, 1929, August 20, 1931, August 10, 1931, September 14, 1928, June 8, 1931, August 17, 1930, September 22, 1925.

35. BJSR, Recreation Section, JCS, TS, pp. 78, 36D, CJFWF; Brooklyn Jewish Center, *Tenth Anniversary Dinner*, January 27, 1929; JWB, Study of the Jacob H. Schiff Center (1927), TS; Abelow, *History of Brooklyn Jewry*, pp. 81, 90.

36. BJSR, *ibid.*, pp. 43, G, CJFWF; JWB, *ibid.*; JWB, Study of the Jewish Community of Brooklyn (1935), TS, p. 22; Brooklyn Jewish Center, *Tenth Anniversary Dinner*, January 27, 1929.

37. JWB, Study of the Jewish Community of Brooklyn (1935), TS, p. 25; JWB, Study of the Jacob H. Schiff Center (1927), TS; BJSR, *ibid.*, pp. 47, 69, 6–7, CJFWF; Landesman, *Brownsville*, p. 216.

38. JWB, Study of the Jacob H. Schiff Center (1927), TS; JWB, Study of the Jewish Community of Brooklyn (1935), TS, pp. 26, 28; Goldberg, "25 Years," p. 17.

39. JWB, Study of the Uptown Talmud Torah (1937), TS, pp. 74–75, 77; BJSR, *ibid.*, pp. 62–66, CJFWF; Goldberg, *ibid.*

40. *JDB*, December 19, 1927, December 25, 1927, October 14, 1927; Zeitlin, *Disciples of the Wise*, pp. 50–51; BJSR, *ibid.*, p. 68, CJFWF; Goldberg, *ibid.*, pp. 37, 17; FMW, Box 244, 1925, Jacob H. Schiff Center.

41. BJSR, *ibid.*

42. BJSR, *ibid.*, pp. 45, 47, 62, 2–4, CJFWF; Doris Glassman, "The Jacob H. Schiff Center," TS, WPA, Jews of New York, Box 3630, Welfare—Jewish Settlement Houses; *JDB*, May 12, 1932; Levinthal quote in Sklare, *Conservative Judaism*, p. 136.

43. Kaplan, "The Way I Have Come," p. 311.

44. Heller, "Pattern for Synagogue Centers," pp. 82–83; Goldstein quote in Spitz, "Synagogue Center Marches On," p. 62.

45. JWB, Study of the Jacob H. Schiff Center (1927), TS.

6. A Collective Enterprise

1. Wiebe, *Search for Order*, chs. 3, 5–7.

2. Medalie, "New York Federation," pp. 117–34.

3. Goldin, *Why They Give*, pp. 82–83; Chipkin, "Judaism and Social Welfare," pp. 722–23, 730; Jick, *Americanization of the Synagogue*, pp. 6–10; Kutzik "Social Bases of Philanthropy," pp. 260, 275, 331, 591; Roseman, "American Jewish Community Institutions in their Historical Context," pp. 28–30.

4. Carnegie, *Gospel of Wealth*, pp. 12, 14–15, 18, quote on pp. 39–40; Fischel, *Forty Years*, p. xiv. Carnegie's original article in the *North American Review* was called "Wealth," but the ideas were labeled the "Gospel of Wealth" soon after and this rubric persisted. Bremner, *American Philanthropy*, pp. 105–7.

5. Mead, *The Lively Experiment*, pp. 142, 154; Morris and Freund, *Trends and Issues in Jewish Social Welfare*, p. 163.

6. Kutzik, "Social Bases," pp. 34–36; Medalie, "New York Federation," pp. 121, 133–34; Elazar, *Community and Polity*, pp. 160–61; conversations with Charles Liebman and Arthur Goren, 1977.

7. Goren, *New York Jews and the Quest for Community*, pp. 4–17, 57–74, quote on p. 74.

8. Curti, *American Philanthropy Abroad*, pp. 230–35, 243–44, 251–52, 258–60; Morris Engelman, *Four Years of Relief*, *passim*; Roseman, "American Jewish Community Institutions," p. 33; Magnes quoted in Goldin, *Why They Give*, p. 79.

9. Rosenfelt, *This Thing of Giving*, p. 325; *NYT*, October 18, 1918, December 22, 1915, December 22, 1916.

10. Billikopf, in Morris and Freund, *Trends and Issues*, p. 142; *The Golden Heritage*, pp. 51, 53.

11. Goldwasser, "Federation for Support of Jewish Philanthropies," pp. 142, 146; Abelow, *History of Brooklyn Jewry*, p. 263.

12. Kutzik, "Social Bases," pp. 831–34.

13. Quoted in *The Golden Heritage*, pp. 53–54.

14. Kutzik, "Social Bases," p. 834; *NYT*, September 12, 1921; *JDB*, August 1, 1926.

15. Quoted in "Shall We Have A Money Raising Dinner As Federation's Opening Event?"; also see "Suggestions for an Opening Event for the 1934 Campaign," both in FMW, Box 304, 1933, New York Federation.

16. Letter of Felix M. Warburg to Walter Beer, June 21, 1933, in FMW, Box 304, 1933, New York Federation; Kutzik, "Social Bases," pp. 605, 382; Goldwasser quoted in *The Golden Heritage*, p. 53.

17. G. Richard Davis to Benjamin Winter and Nathan Wilson, March 6, 1926, in FMW, Box 232, 1926, New York Federation.

18. Minutes of the Board of Trustees Meeting of New York Federation, December 14, 1925, in FMW, Box 228, 1925, New York Federation; Farra, *Financing of Social Work*, p. 17; New York Federation Blue Books for 1921, 1923, 1925, 1927; *The Golden Heritage*, p. 51.

19. Medalie, "New York Federation," p. 121; Federation for the Support of Jewish Philanthropic Societies of New York City, *Federation: Its Meaning and Purpose*, pp. 5–7; Lissner, Plan for Money Raising (1926), TS, pp. 12–13.

20. Joseph Willen, Conference Paper, TS, pp. 6–7, 11–12, in CJFWF, Box 166; *JDB*, December 5, 1926, December 13, 1927, September 13, 1928.

21. *JDB*, January 23, 1928; Fischel, *Forty Years*, p. 63.

22. *JDB*, August 30, 1931.

23. Romasco, *The Poverty of Abundance*, chs. 1, 4, 8; National Council of Jewish Federations and Welfare Funds and Bureau of Jewish Social Research, Jewish Family Society in Its Relation to the Public Agency, TS, pp. 1–5, 7–19, in New York Public Library; Morris and Freund, *Trends and Issues*, pp. 280–81; Sulzberger and Selekman, The Federation as the Vital Community Agency, TS, in FMW, Box 306, 1933, Social Agencies; *JDB*, November 14, 1927, September 26, 1929, May 24, 1926; A summary of a meeting on October 21, 1933, attended by David Heyman, Harry Lurie, Solomon Lowenstein, George Rabinoff, Joseph Willen, and Ira Younker to discuss the possibility of a national Federation, in FMW, Box 306, 1933, Social Agencies.

24. Farra, *Financing of Social Work*, p. 17; Report of Paul Adler and Benjamin Buttenweiser in FMW, Box 306, 1933, New York Federation; Minutes of the Special Meeting of the Board of Trustees, December 3, 1934, in FMW, Box 313, 1934, New York Federation.

25. Joseph Willen, Conference Paper, TS, pp. 6–7, 11–12, in CJFWF, Box 166; *JDB*, December 12, 1926.

26. Council of Fraternal and Benevolent Organizations, Closing the Ranks in Jewish Life, pp. 4, 6, quote on p. 7; Doroshkin, *Yiddish in America*, pp. 142–46; Jewish Benevolent Societies, TS, in CJFWF, Box 204; B. Rivkin, "Di sotziale role fun di landsmanshaftn," in Rontch, *Di yidishe landsmanshaftn*, pp. 68–108.

27. Bureau of Jewish Social Research, Digest of Proceedings, 1932, pp. 37–38.

28. *JDB*, November 18, 1924; Fink and Richards, *Jewish Community Directory*, p. 5.

29. Park, "The City," p. 123; Park, "The City as a Social Laboratory," pp. 7–8.

30. Quandt, *From Small Town to Great Community*, pp. 17, 25, 46–53, quote on pp. 17, 75; Park, "The City," p. 123.

31. Letter of January 12, 1926 quoted in BJSR, *Jewish Population*, JCS, p. iii; Dushkin, "Jewish Population of New York City," pp. 75–87; Jones, *American Immigration*, p. 276; Agenda for informal meeting with respect to proposed survey of Jewish philanthropic work of New York City, FMW, Box 226, 1925, BJSR. For a list of committee members see BJSR, *Report of the Executive Committee*, pp. 77–80.

32. *JDB*, December 29, 1925; letter of Samuel Goldsmith to A. R. Emanuel, April 18, 1930, in FMW, Box 269, 1930, BJSR.

33. Samuel Goldsmith to Lee K. Frankel in FMW, Box 201, 1921, BJSR.

34. Goren, *New York Jews and Quest for Community*, p. 236; Kehillah of New York City, *Jewish Communal Register of New York City*, p. 3.

35. BJSR, Progress of Study, JCS (September 1926), TS, in CJFWF; BJSR, *Report of the Executive Committee*, p. 77.

36. BJSR, Recreation Section: Study of Synagogue Centers in New York City, JCS, TS, pp. 8–9, 83, in CJFWF.

37. BJSR, *Report of the Executive Committee*, pp. 7, 57, 58–63; BJSR, Report Number 3, Health Section, ch. I, General Hospital Facilities, JCS (New York 1928), TS, pp. 8–9, in New York Public Library.

38. BJSR, *Report of the Executive Committee*, pp. 8, 19, 47, 55, 57, 59–63, quotes on pp. 8, 57; Karpf, "Decade of Jewish Philanthropy," p. 243.

39. *The Golden Heritage*, pp. 36, 42; Felix M. Warburg to William Engel, July 17, 1923, in FMW, Box 213, 1923, William Engel; Felix M. Warburg to Walter Rothschild, December 20, 1926, in FMW, Box 230, Brooklyn Federation; *JDB*, February 15, 1927, January 25, 1928.

40. *JDB*, March 8, 1928, January 25, 1928.

41. Quoted in the *JDB*, March 19, 1928, December 4, 1929, December 11, 1929, December 13, 1929; Lubove, *The Professional Altruist*, p. 158.

42. Solomon Lowenstein to Felix Warburg, October 13, 1930, also memo of September 17, 1930 and Jewish Hospital Proposal, in FMW, Box 263, 1930, New York Federation; *The Golden Heritage*, pp. 62–65; Minutes of the Board of Trustees of New York Federation, April 27, 1931, in FMW, Box 278, 1931, New York Federation.

43. Medalie, "New York Federation," pp. 119, 130.

7. Yeshiva College

1. Rothkoff, *Bernard Revel*, p. 74. Much of the story of Yeshiva College in the 1920s and 1930s can be found in this excellent biography. Rothkoff had access to the Yeshiva Archives and he reprinted many documents located there in several appendices. Unfortunately, the Archives remain closed to other scholars although the files of the Public Relations Department are open.

2. Klaperman, *The Story of Yeshiva University*, p. 149; Fischel, *Forty Years*, p. 164.

3. Interview with Dr. Hyman Grinstein, 1974; Fischel, *Forty Years*, p. 163.

4. Newman, *A Jewish University in America*, p. 9; Steinberg, *Academic Melting Pot*, pp. 12, 19–23; Wechsler, *The Qualified Student*, pp. 161–64.

5. Newman, *ibid.*, p. 11; Felix M. Warburg to Paul Sachs, October 8, 1922, FMW, Box 217, 1922; Lowell quoted in Wechsler, *ibid.*, p. 161.

6. Steinberg, *Academic Melting Pot*, p. 25; Newman, *ibid.*, p. 19; Dean quoted by Newman, *ibid.*, p. 11.

7. Newman, *ibid.*, pp. 10, 19, 41–44, Frank quote pp. 41, 44.

8. *Ibid.*, pp. 17–18, Frank quote pp. 42–44.

9. Rothkoff, *Bernard Revel*, pp. 74, 76–77; Levy, "Orthodox Jewry Rises to the Occasion," *NYT*, December 26, 1924.

10. Rothkoff, *ibid.*, pp. 76–77, 80–82.

11. Rothkoff, *ibid.*, p. 94; The Yeshiva Endowment Foundation, *Annual Report* (December 1936), pp. 6, 8.

12. Levy, *Historical Souvenir Journal*; "Prominent New York Real Estate Men To Supervise Construction of New Jewish Seminary and College," press release, December 17, 192?; "New York Jewish Women Undertake to Raise $100,000 For Yeshiva Dormitory," press release, in YU; *Brooklyn Review*, May 18, 1928; Yeshiva Synagogue Council, *Annual Convention* (New York, 1938); Fischel, *Forty Years*, pp. 347–48; "Yeshiva Thousand Dollar Dinner Begins New Era in Jewish Fund-Raising Efforts, Replacing Popular Appeal Which Has Lost Its Effectiveness, press release in YU.

13. Fischel, *Forty Years*, pp. 345–46; Rothkoff, *Bernard Revel*, p. 75; Klaperman, *Story of Yeshiva*, pp. 155, 129; Fischel, "New Yeshiva Buildings," n.p.; *JDB*, December 23, 1924.

14. Quoted in Rothkoff, *ibid.*, pp. 94–95.

15. *JDB*, December 23, 1924, October 19, 1928.

16. Rothkoff, *Bernard Revel*, p. 72; *JDB*, April 13, 1928; Revel, "Message and Meaning of Yeshiva," n.p.

17. Rothkoff, *ibid.*, p. 135; Wiernik, "Problem of Higher Jewish Education," n.p.

18. Klaperman, *Story of Yeshiva*, pp. 152, 162; *JDB*, October 16, 1928; Littauer and Enelow quoted in Ritterband and Wechsler, "The Role of the Jewish Academic," pp. 1–2; see also pp. 57–60.

19. Shands, "The Cheder on the Hill," pp. 262, 269, quote on pp. 266–67; Band, "Jewish Studies in American Liberal Arts," pp. 19–20; Lillian Zahn, Jews in Secular Education, TS, in WPA, Jews of New York, Box 3632, Education. Zahn notes that only 54 colleges and universities in the United States offered Hebrew language instruction as of 1942.

20. Rothkoff, *Bernard Revel*, pp. 79, 82, 135, 137; *JDB*, March 8, 1926; "Dr. Bernard Revel, President of Faculty, Defines in Interview, Yeshiva College Approach to Science and Religion Problem," press release, October 19, 1928, YU.

21. Rothkoff, *ibid.*, pp. 79–80, 119, 131–34, 137; Klaperman, *Story of Yeshiva*, includes an appendix of all honorary degree recipients. See also *Yeshiva College Catalog* for course offerings and credits.

22. Isaacs quoted in Rothkoff, *ibid.*, p. 137; also see pp. 135–36.

23. *JDB*, March 29, 1926, December 4, 1927, March 28, 1929, March 5, 1930, May 3, 1926; Harris Selig, "The Failure of the Hebrew Schools of America," press release, December 11, 1928, YU.

24. Revel quoted in Rothkoff, *Bernard Revel*, pp. 81–82; "Address by Samuel Levy at Million Dollar Music Festival At Madison Square Garden, May 23, 1926," press release, May 23, 1926, YU.

25. Louis Marshall to M. F. Seidman, January 8, 1924, in *Louis Marshall*, ed. Reznikoff, 2: 905; *American Hebrew*, January 31, 1924; *Brooklyn Review*, May 25, 1928.

26. "European and American Scholars Hail New York Yeshiva College Project," press release, 22 June 192?, YU.

27. *Brooklyn Review*, May 11, 1928; *B'nai B'rith Magazine* quoted in Klaperman, *Story of Yeshiva*, p. 153.

28. Klaperman, *ibid.*, pp. 150–51; *The Day* quoted in *JDB*, May 3, 1927; Trunk, "Cultural Dimension of American Jewish Labor Movement," pp. 365–66.

29. Rothkoff, *Bernard Revel*, pp. 138, 140–42, 147–48.

30. Klaperman, *Story of Yeshiva*, pp. 159–60; Parzen, *Architects of Conservative Judaism*, p. 105; Sklare, *Conservative Judaism*, pp. 193–94.

31. Revel, "Seminary and Yeshiva," in Rothkoff, *Bernard Revel*, pp. 268–75.

32. Sklare, *Conservative Judaism*, p. 166.

33. Felix M. Warburg to Isidore Singer, July 27, 1925, FMW, Box 224, 1925, Isidore Singer; Louis Marshall to Rabbi Solomon Gandz, December 3, 1928, in *Louis Marshall*, ed. Reznikoff, 2: 889; Sklare, *Conservative Judaism*, p. 193.

34. Revel, "Message and Meaning of Yeshiva," n.p.; Levy in *NYT*, November 23, 1936.

8. The Rise of the Jewish Democrat

1. Norman Salit, "Judaism and Americanism," radio address delivered over WEAF, October 31, 1928, in American Jewish Historical Society, Norman Salit MSS, Box 2.

2. On ethnic voting theory see Wolfinger, "Development and Persistence of Ethnic Voting," pp. 896–908. and Parenti, "Ethnic Politics," pp. 717–26.

3. Wolfinger, *ibid.*, p. 896; Samuel Lubell quoted in Glazer and Moynihan, *Beyond the Melting Pot*, p. 168. For a good summary of immigrant politics see Howe, *World of Our Fathers*, pp. 360–94, and Rischin, *The Promised City*, pp. 147–51.

4. Halpern, "Roots of American Jewish Liberalism," pp. 208–9; Postal and Koppman, *Jewish Landmarks*, pp. 73–81; Howe, *World of Our Fathers*, pp. 361–62, 366–68; Rischin, *The Promised City*, pp. 147–51; Gorenstein, "Portrait of Ethnic Politics," pp. 204–8, 218–21.

5. Herling, "Vladeck," p. 87; Howe, *World of Our Fathers*, p. 318.

6. *NYT*, August 12, 1921, August 31, 1921, November 10, 1921; Shannon, *Socialist Party of America*, pp. 149–55, 168–81. For voting documentation see *The City Record, Official Canvass*. The precentages are derived from the total votes cast for the top three candidates (except in mayoralty races) and thus are somewhat inflated.

7. Schorenstein story from Costikyan, *Behind Closed Doors*, p. 325; interview with Beadie Markowitz, 1975; interview with Stanley Steingut, 1975.

8. Costikyan, *ibid.*, pp. 325–26.

9. *The City Record, Official Canvass*; interview with Beadie Markowitz, 1975.

10. Moscow, *Politics in the Empire State*, p. 130; interview with Nathan Sobel, 1975; interview with Stanley Steingut, 1975; *The City Record, Official Canvass*.

11. Peel, *Political Clubs of New York City*, p. 251; also pp. 61–69 on the structure of local politics in New York City in the 1920s; Costikyan, *Behind Closed Doors*, p. 96.

12. Interviews with Stanley Steingut, Nathan Sobel, George Abrams, 1975.

13. Interviews with Nathan Sobel, Stanley Steingut, George Abrams, 1975; Costikyan, *Behind Closed Doors*, p. 96.

14. *JDB*, February 2, 1931, January 11, 1930, March 6, 1931, March 15, 1931, January 10, 1928, January 18, 1928, August 8, 1928, May 10, 1927, December 4, 1925, February 14, 1926; The Reminiscences of Walter Mack Jr., p. 9, OHM; *Brooklyn Review*, September 26, 1927; Peel, *Political Clubs*, p. 179; interviews with Stanley Steingut, Robert Steingut, George Abrams, Ray Feiden, Nathan Sobel, 1975.

15. *JDB*, April 28, 1930, May 1, 1930; Peel, *Political Clubs*, pp. 286–87; interviews with Nathan Sobel, George Abrams, 1975. In the late 1940s Biederman staged an unsuccessful primary fight against Steingut in the 18th A.D.

16. Lowi, *At the Pleasure of the Mayor*, pp. 7, 34; The Reminiscences of Reuben Lazarus, p. 446, OHM.

17. Reuben Lazarus, *ibid.*; Lowi, *ibid.*, p. 7; Herling, "Vladeck," p. 87; Golden and

Pozzi, Jews of New York in Politics and Civics (1941), TS, in WPA, Jews of New York, Box 3628.

18. Stephen Isaacs, *Jews and American Politics*, pp. 217–24.

19. Marshall statement in *JDB*, October 10, 1928; letter to unnamed individuals in FMW, Box 239, 1927, American Jewish Committee.

20. Minutes of the Executive Committee of the American Jewish Committee, 7, (November 10, 1940): 205–206. Located in the American Jewish Committee Library.

21. Translated in the *JDB*, September 14, 1928.

22. *JDB*, September 28, 1926; Reminiscences of Herbert H. Lehman, p. 242, OHM.

23. Reminiscences of Nathan Straus Jr., pp. 69, 75–77, OHM.

24. Herbert Bayard Swope to Herbert H. Lehman, July 14, 1939, in Herbert H. Lehman Archives, Herbert Bayard Swope, File 805. Emphasis in the original. Stephen Isaacs, *Jews and American Politics*, mentions Swope and his Jewishness on pp. 44, 58.

25. Reminiscences of Herbert H. Lehman, p. 225, OHM; interviews with Nathan Sobel and Stanley Steingut, 1975.

26. Morton Deutsch, Government and Politics, TS, in WPA, Jews of New York, Box 3628; Golden and Pozzi, Jews of New York in Politics and Civics (1941), TS, in WPA, Jews of New York, Box 3628; interview with Nathan Sobel, 1975; Garrett, *LaGuardia Years*, pp. 52–53, 305.

27. Howe, *World of Our Fathers*, p. 385; Weiss, *Charles Francis Murphy*, p. 90; Garrett, *LaGuardia Years*, pp. 59–60; Dawidowicz and Goldstein, *Politics in a Pluralist Democracy*, pp. 84–87.

28. Howe, *World of Our Fathers*, pp. 386–87; Josephson and Josephson, *Al Smith*, pp. 192–98, 257–59, 285–86; Smith speech in *NYT*, January 11, 1922; Dubinsky and Raskin, *David Dubinsky* p. 264.

29. The Reminiscences of Reuben Lazarus, p. 411, OHM; Golden and Pozzi, Jews of New York in Politics and Civics (1941), TS, in WPA, Jews of New York, Box 3628; Garrett, *LaGuardia Years*, p. 259; interviews with Nathan Sobel, Stanley Steingut, 1975; Howe, *World of Our Fathers*, p. 391.

30. The Reminiscences of Reuben Lazarus, p. 411, OHM; Dubinsky and Raskin, *David Dubinsky*, pp. 268–71; Garrett, *LaGuardia Years*, p. 263; interview with Stanley Steingut, 1975.

31. Bayor, *Neighbors in Conflict*, pp. 41, 47.

32. Fielding, "A Brief Review of the ALP in 1938–1939–1940 at City Hall and the "Twelve Point" Municipal Program for 1941" (1941), TS, pp. 1–5, in New York Public Library; American Labor Party, *Legislative Facts*, no. 11; *News of the Week*, June 26, 1939, May 15, 1939.

33. *News of the Week*, September 17, 1938, November 5, 1938, August 13, 1938; interviews with George Abrams, Nathan Sobel, 1975.

34. The Reminiscences of Reuben Lazarus, p. 447, OHM; Walinsky quoted in Stephen Isaacs, *Jews and American Politics*, p. 90; Arthur Liebman, "Ties That Bind," p. 293.

35. *NYT*, April 6, 1921, April 7, 1921; Epstein, *Profiles of Eleven*, pp. 346–47.

36. *JDB*, June 4, 1930, March 1, 1931, November 25, 1931, October 10, 1924; *Daily News Bulletin*, January 21, 1923.

37. *JDB*, June 25, 1930; *Daily News Bulletin*, June 28, 1938; interview with Stanley Steingut, 1975; Wechsler, *Qualified Student*, pp. 193–99.

38. Translated in the *JDB*, November 4, 1924; Celler, *You Never Leave Brooklyn*, pp. 79–94, 114–17, 222–29, 233–35.

39. Feingold, *The Politics of Rescue*, pp. 8–9, 298–304; Stephen Isaacs, *Jews and American Politics*, p. 156.

40. Lawrence Fuchs, *The Political Behavior of American Jews*, p. 67; *JDB*, September 30, 1927; Shannon, *Socialist Party of America*, p. 104; Postal and Koppman, *Jewish Landmarks*, pp. 73–81.

41. Himmelfarb and Seigel quoted in Stephen Isaacs, *Jews and American Politics*, pp. 7, 19–20; Lawrence Fuchs, "Introduction," p. 185.

42. Quoted in Herling, "Vladeck," p. 93.

43. On voting trends see Lawrence Fuchs, "American Jews and the Presidential Vote," p. 401.

9. At Home in America

1. Gans, "American Jewry," p. 425.

2. Sklare, "Jews, Ethnics, and the American City," p. 73.

3. Glazer and Moynihan, *Beyond the Melting Pot*, p. 152.

4. Etzioni, "The Ghetto," p. 258; Kantrowitz, *Ethnic and Racial Segregation*, pp. 6–7; Sherman, *Jew Within American Society*, pp. 150, 152.

5. Freedman, "New Jewish Community in Formation," p. 36.

6. Sklare, *Conservative Judaism*, p. 35; Herberg, *Protestant, Catholic, Jew*, pp. 184–98, 231–46.

7. Gans, "American Jewry," p. 427.

8. Charles Liebman, "American Jewry," p. 134; Pfeffer, *Church, State, and Freedom*, pp. 397–412.

9. Dawidowicz and Goldstein, *Politics in a Pluralist Democracy*, pp. 76–80, 86–90, quote on p. 89; "Jewishness and the Younger Intellectuals: A Symposium," *Commentary* (April 1961), p. 310.

10. Charles Liebman, "American Jewry," pp. 140–41; Gans, "American Jewry," p. 426.

Bibliography

Primary Sources

Archival Material
American Jewish Archives. Association for Jewish Children. Jewish Child Care
    Association. Papers and bylaws.
—— Jesse Bullowa MSS.
—— Rabbi J. X. Cohen MSS.
—— Jacob Cohen MSS.
—— Congregation Adas Jeshirim. Minutes. 1920–1927.
—— Congregation Temple Beth Emeth of Flatbush. Minutes. 1920–1934.
—— Benedict Glazer MSS.
—— Graduate School for Jewish Social Service MSS.
—— Rudolph Grossman. Sermons.
—— Hebrew Tabernacle Congregation. Minutes. 1920–1940.
—— Henry Horowitz Menorah Association MSS.
—— Stanley M. Isaacs MSS.
—— The Judeans. Minutes. 1930–1940.
—— Horace Kallen MSS.
—— National Foundation of Temple Sisterhood. Round Table Speeches. 1922.
—— Gustavus Rogers MSS.
—— Union of American Hebrew Congregations MSS. 1920–1940.
—— Felix M. Warburg MSS. 1920–1936.
—— Stephen Wise MSS.
American Jewish Committee. Minutes of the Executive Committee. 1920–1940.
    American Jewish Committee Library.
American Jewish Historical Society. Cyrus Adler MSS.
—— B'nai B'rith Manhattan-Washington Lodge MSS.
—— Congregation Shearith Israel MSS.
—— Council of Jewish Federations and Welfare Funds MSS. Includes Jewish
    Communal Survey of Greater New York TSS.
—— Philip Cowan MSS.
—— Israel Goldberg MSS.
—— Jonah Goldstein MSS.

—— Graduate School for Jewish Social Work MSS.

—— Hebrew Orphan Asylum MSS.

—— Jewish War Veterans MSS.

—— Max J. Kohler MSS.

—— Samuel Kohs MSS.

—— Norman Salit MSS.

Columbia University. Herbert H. Lehman Archives.

Federation of Jewish Philanthropies of New York. Minutes of Meeting of the Board of Trustees. 1922–1936.

Federation of Jewish Philanthropies of New York. Minutes of the Meeting of the Distribution Committee. 1928.

New York City Municipal Archives. Works Progress Administration. Historical Records Survey. Federal Writers Project. Factbook.

—— Works Progress Administration. Historical Records Survey. Inventory of Records of Churches. Jewish Synagogues.

—— Works Progress Administration. Historical Records Survey. Federal Writers Project. Jews of New York.

—— Works Progress Administration. Historical Records Survey. Federal Writers Project. Racial Groups in New York.

Yeshiva University Public Relations Department. Press Releases. 1924–1940.

Young Men's Hebrew Association. Minutes of the Board of Directors of the Young Men's Hebrew Association. 1921–1924.

Newspapers and Bulletins

American Hebrew. 1924.

American Jewish Committee. *Information Bulletins.* 1927–1938.

American Jewish Year Book. 1920–1970.

Bronx Home News. 1928.

Brooklyn Jewish Center Bulletin. 1922–1927.

Brooklyn Jewish Center Review. 1927–1934.

Brooklyn Review. 1926–1928.

Daily News Bulletin. 1923–1924; 1937–1938.

Federation Family. 1927–1928.

Jewish Daily Bulletin. 1923–1940.

Jewish Tribune. 1928.

Lifelines. 1926. Published by the United Jewish Campaign of New York. Located in American Jewish Archives.

New York Jewish Citizen. 1929.

New York Times. 1920–1924, 1927–1929, 1932–1933, 1935–1936.

News of the Week. 1936–1940.

Temple Petach Tikvah News. 1938–1939.

Interviews

George Abrams, 1975.

Zachary Baym, 1973.

Lou Berg, 1972.

Julius Borenstein, 1972.
Jack Brakarsh, 1972.
Charles Dash, 1972.
Irene Dash, 1978.
Martin Dash, 1979.
Ira Eisenstein, 1973.
Myron Eisenstein, 1973.
George Ende, 1973.
Raymond Feiden, 1973.
Marcus Gilden, 1972.
Bella Golden, 1973, 1978.
Paula Goldwasser, 1972.
Lynn Goran, 1976.
Hyman Grinstein, 1974.
Irving Hudson, 1979.
Judah Lapson, 1973.
Beadie Markowitz, 1975.
Walter Metzger, 1975.
Helen Miringoff, 1978.
Paul Ritterband, 1972.
Nathan Sobel, 1975.
Robert Steingut, 1975.
Stanley Steingut, 1975.
David Tishman, 1972.

Oral Memoirs
Columbia University Oral History Project.
"Reminiscences." Edward Greenbaum.
—— Stanley Isaacs.
—— Solomon Klein.
—— Samuel Koenig.
—— Theodore Fred Kuper.
—— Reuben Lazarus.
—— Herbert H. Lehman.
—— Walter Mack, Jr.
—— Nathan Straus, Jr.
—— Leonard Wallstein.

Secondary Sources

Unpublished Typescripts and Dissertations
Anania, Joseph. Report on the interdependence of Italians and Jews living in New York City and the effects of Recent Italian governmental Decrees on relations between Italians and Jews living in New York City. New York, 1938. TS. American Jewish Committee Library.

Berrol, Selma. "Immigrants at School: New York City, 1898–1914." Diss. CUNY 1967.

Bronx Council of Social Agencies. A Study of the Lower Bronx. New York: Bronx Council of Social Agencies, 1939. TS. Located in Jewish Welfare Board Library.

Bureau of Applied Social Research, Columbia University. Voting Behavior of American Ethnic Groups, 1936–1944. New York: Bureau of Applied Social Research, 1948. TS. Located in American Jewish Committee Library.

Bureau of Jewish Social Research. Care of Jewish Aged of Manhattan and the Bronx. New York: Bureau of Jewish Social Research, 1933. TS. Located in the New York Public Library.

—— Digest of Proceedings: Continuing Committee of Jewish Federation Executives. New York: Bureau of Jewish Social Research, 1932. TS. Located in New York Public Library.

—— Employment Facilities for Jews of New York City. Summary. Jewish Communal Survey of Greater New York. New York: Bureau of Jewish Social Research, n.d. Located in New York Public Library.

—— Family Welfare Section: Summary Statement. Report no. 2. Jewish Communal Survey of Greater New York: Bureau of Jewish Social Research, 1929. TS. Located in New York Public Library.

—— Health Section: Summary Statement. Report no. 4. Jewish Communal Survey of Greater New York. New York: Bureau of Jewish Social Research, 1929. TS. Located in New York Public Library.

—— Income and Expenditures of Jewish Federations and Welfare Funds for 1931 and Comparison with 1930 and 1929. New York: Bureau of Jewish Social Research, 1933. TS. Located in New York Public Library.

—— Personnel-Pension Study of the Personnel Employed in Organizations Affiliated with the Federation for the Support of Jewish Philanthropic Societies of New York City. New York: Bureau of Jewish Social Research, 1927. TS. Located in Ameican Jewish Archives.

—— Professional Tendencies Among Jewish Students in Colleges, Universities and Professional Schools. New York: Bureau of Jewish Social Research, 192? TS. Located in American Jewish Archives.

—— The Status of Jewish Child Care in New York City—1930. New York: Bureau of Jewish Social Research, 1931. TS. Located in New York Public Library.

—— A Study of the Jewish Blind in New York City (Exclusive of Brooklyn). Jewish Communal Survey of Greater New York. New York: Bureau of Jewish Social Research, 1930. TS. Located in New York Public Library.

—— Survey of Jewish Recreational Facilities in Manhattan and the Bronx. New York: Bureau of Jewish Social Research, 1920. TS. Located in American Jewish Archives.

—— Volume of Service and Financial Operations of Jewish Placing-Out Agencies in 1930. New York: Bureau of Jewish Social Research, 1931. TS. Located in New York Public Library.

Cohn, Martin and Arnold Gurin. A Study of National Civic-Protective Agencies.

New York: Council of Jewish Federations and Welfare Funds, 1945. TS. Located in American Jewish Committee Library.

Dann, Martin E. " 'Little Citizens': Working Class and Immigrant Childhood In New York City, 1890–1915." Diss. CUNY 1978.

Davie, Maurice E. Report on the 1938–39 Polls on Anti-Semitism. New York: Department of Public Reaction, American Jewish Committee, 1940. TS. Located in American Jewish Committee Library.

Fielding, Benjamin. A Brief Review of the ALP in 1938–39–40 at City Hall and the "Twelve Point" Municipal Program for 1941. 1941. TS. Located in the New York Public Library.

Ganin, Zvi. The Jewish Response to Anti-Semitism in the Context of Intergroup Relations in Boston and New York City 1938–1948. n.p. 1971. TS. Located in American Jewish Committee Library.

Goldstein, Judith. "The Politics of Ethnic Pressure: The American Jewish Committee as Lobbyist, 1906–1917." Diss. Columbia 1972.

Gorelick, Sherry. "Social Control, Social Mobility and the Eastern European Jews: An Analysis of Public Education in New York City, 1880–1924." Diss. Columbia 1975.

Halpert, Max. "Jews of Brownsville 1880–1925." Diss. Yeshiva 1958.

Herlands, William B. Investigation of Anti-American and Anti-Semitic Vandalism: Report. New York: Department of Investigation, 1944. TS. Located in American Jewish Committee Library.

Hoenig, Sidney B. Toward an Understanding of the Jews. Brooklyn, 1935. TS. Located in American Jewish Committee Library.

Institute of Social Research, Columbia University. An American Disciple of Adolf Hitler: A Study of the Nazi Propaganda Methods Used by Joseph E. McWilliams of the American Destiny Party in the 1940 Election Campaign. New York: Institute of Social Research, 194?. TS. Located in American Jewish Committee Library.

Jewish Education Association. Jewish Child Population Study. New York: Jewish Education Association, 1935. TS. Located in Board of Jewish Education files.

Jewish Welfare Board. Findings and Recommendations in Regard to Williamsburg YM & YWHA. New York: Jewish Welfare Board, 1941. TS. Located in Jewish Welfare Board Library.

—— Jewish Community of Williamsburg. New York: Jewish Welfare Board, 1936. TS. Located in Jewish Welfare Board Library.

—— Memorandum Re: Jewish Population and Membership Information for YM and YWHA of the Bronx. New York: Jewish Welfare Board, 1934. TS. Located in Jewish Welfare Board Library.

—— Part II: A Study of the Jewish Population of New York City. New York: Jewish Welfare Board, 1946. TS. Located in the New York Public Library.

—— Preliminary Summary of the Study of the Recreational and Educational Resources of the Brooklyn Jewish Community. New York: Jewish Welfare Board, 1925. TS. Located in Jewish Welfare Board Library.

—— Proposed Program and Budget for Bronx House—New York City. New

York: Jewish Welfare Board, 1932. TS. Located in Jewish Welfare Board Library.

—— Proposal for the Establishment by the Uptown Talmud Torah, 132 East 111th Street, of a Branch at the Jacob H. Schiff Center, 2510 Valentine Avenue Bronx, N.Y. New York: Jewish Welfare Board, 1938. TS. Located in Jewish Welfare Board Library.

—— Recommendation Made to the Jacob H. Schiff Center Bronx, N.Y. New York: Jewish Welfare Board, 1933. TS. Located in Jewish Welfare Board Library.

—— Report of Preliminary Study on the Practicability of the Williamsburg YM And YWHA Considering Plans for Erecting A New Building. New York: Jewish Welfare Board, 1923. TS. Located in Jewish Welfare Board Library.

—— Study and Appraisal of Program of Jewish Activities of the Jewish Community House of Bensonhurst, Brooklyn, N.Y. New York: Jewish Welfare Board, 1937. TS. Located in Jewish Welfare Board Library.

—— Study of Bronx House, New York City. New York: Jewish Welfare Board, 1939. TS. Located in Jewish Welfare Board Library.

—— Study of Council House and Its Immediate Area in the Borough of the Bronx. New York: Jewish Welfare Board, 1939. TS. Located in Jewish Welfare Board Library.

—— Study of Council House and Its Immediate Area in the Borough of the Bronx. New York: Jewish Welfare Board, 1934. TS. Located in Jewish Welfare Board Library.

—— Study of Dormitory Facilities in Brooklyn with Special Reference to Jewish Residents. New York: Jewish Welfare Board, 1933. TS. Located in Jewish Welfare Board Library.

—— Study of Educational and Recreational Resources and Needs of the Borough of Brooklyn, New York City. New York: Jewish Welfare Board, 1925. TS. Located in Jewish Welfare Board Library.

—— Study of the Educational and Recreational Resources and Needs of the Jewish Community of the Borough of the Bronx, New York City. New York: Jewish Welfare Board, 1924. TS. Located in Jewish Welfare Board Library.

—— Study of the Institutional Synagogue in relation to Harlem, New York City. New York: Jewish Welfare Board, 1938. TS. Located in American Jewish Historical Society.

—— Study of the Jacob H. Schiff Center and Its Needs. New York: Jewish Welfare Board, 1927. TS. Located in Jewish Welfare Board Library.

—— Study of the Jewish Community of Bath Beach, Brooklyn with Reference to Social and Recreational Facilities and Needs. New York: Jewish Welfare Board, 1922. TS. Located in Jewish Welfare Board Library.

—— Study of the Jewish Community of Brooklyn for the YMHA of Brooklyn. New York: Jewish Welfare Board, 1935. TS. Located in Jewish Welfare Board Library.

—— Study of the Jewish Community Centers Affiliated with Brooklyn Federation of Jewish Charities. New York: Jewish Welfare Board, 1938. TS. Located in Jewish Welfare Board Library.

—— Study of the Uptown Talmud Torah and Jacob H. Schiff Center. New York: Jewish Welfare Board, 1937. TS. Located in Jewish Welfare Board Library.

Kutzik, Alfred. "Social Bases of American Jewish Philanthropy." Diss. Brandeis 1967.

Landesman, Alter. A Neighborhood Survey of Brownsville. (A Report Prepared for the Members of the Society). n.p. n.d. TS. Located in the New York Public Library.

Lissner, Herman. Plan for Money Raising for Federation for the Support of Jewish Philanthropic Societies for New York City. New York, 1926. TS. Located in American Jewish Archives.

Locke, David. "The Village Vision." Diss. Brown 1971.

Lurie, Harry. Jewish Defense Activity in the United States; an inventory of four civic-protective agencies. New York: General Council for Jewish Rights of the American Jewish Committee, American Jewish Congress, B'nai B'rith, and Jewish Labor Committee, 1938. TS. Located in American Jewish Committee Library.

National Council of Jewish Federations and Welfare Funds and Bureau of Jewish Social Research. Federation Financing of Jewish Social Work in 1934: The Income and Expenditures of Sixty-Eight Federations and Welfare Funds and Their Local Beneficiary Agencies. New York: National Council of Jewish Federations and Welfare Funds and Bureau of Jewish Social Research, 1935. TS. Located in New York Public Library.

—— Jewish Family Society in its Relation to the Public Agency: A Study of Current Relationships in Forty-Three Cities. New York: National Council of Jewish Federations and Welfare Funds and Bureau of Jewish Social Research, 1935. TS. Located in New York Public Library.

New York Metropolitan Section—Jewish Welfare Board, Inc. Recommendations for Extension Projects to be conducted by New York Metropolitan Section—Jewish Welfare Board, Inc. in East Bronx, East Flatbush (Brooklyn), and Coney Island. New York: New York Metropolitan Section—Jewish Welfare Board, Inc., 1938. TS. Located in Jewish Welfare Board Library.

Ritterband, Paul. "The Changing Composition of a Conflict Group." unpub. article.

Ritterband, Paul and Harold Wechsler. "The Role of the Jewish Academic in Jewish Affairs." Paper presented at University of Cincinnati, October 31, 1978.

Saveth, Edward N. Theories of cultural adjustment of Jews in America; prepared in connection with the Conference on Jewish adjustment in America. New York: Library of Jewish Information, American Jewish Committee, 1945. TS. Located in American Jewish Committee Library.

Silverberg, I. Activity Survey of Bronx YM and YWHA—1930. New York: Jewish Welfare Board, 1933. TS. Located in Jewish Welfare Board Library.

Sklare, Marshall. "The Sociological Study of New York Jewry and Its Relationship to the Study of American Jewry." Paper presented at Conference on Culture and Community Among New York Jews, January 29, 1979, at New York City.

Stewart, William James. "A Political History of the American Labor Party 1936–1944." MA thesis, American University 1959.

Sulzberger, Frank L. and Ben M. Selekman. The Federation as the Vital Community Agency: A Report of the Committee on Finances and Governmental Welfare Policies of the National Council of Jewish Federations and Welfare Funds. January 1934. TS. Located in American Jewish Archives.

Taft, Sigmund C. A Study and Evaluation of the Jewish Community Councils of Bensonhurst, Borough Park, Flatbush and Williamsburg, Neighborhoods in the Borough of Brooklyn in New York City. New York: New York School of Social Work, Columbia University, 1943. TS. Located in Jewish Welfare Board Library.

Published Reports, Books, and Articles

Abelow, Samuel. History of Brooklyn Jewry. New York: Scheba Publishing Company, 1937.

American Jewish Committee. The Anti-Jewish Propaganda Front: A Bulletin of Information of Anti-Jewish Agitation and Counter Activities. 1937–1938.

—— Memorandum on the Street Disturbances in New York City. New York: American Jewish Committee, 1939.

American Labor Party. Handbook. September 1937.

—— Legislative Facts, no. 11. New York: Research Department, American Labor Party, 1939.

Band, Arnold J. "Jewish Studies in American Liberal Arts Colleges and Universities." American Jewish Year Book, 67 (1966): 3–30.

Baron, Salo W. The Jewish Community: Its History And Structure To The American Revolution. 3 vols. Philadelphia: Jewish Publication Society of America, 1942.

Bayor, Ronald H. Neighbors in Conflict: The Irish, Germans, Jews, and Italians of New York City. Baltimore: The Johns Hopkins University Press, 1978.

Ben-Horin, Meir. "From the Turn of the Century to the Late Thirties." A History of Jewish Education in America. Ed. Judah Pilch. New York: National Curriculum Research Institute of the American Association for Jewish Education, 1969, pp. 54–113.

Bercovici, Konrad. "The Greatest Jewish City in the World." The Nation, September 12, 1923, pp. 259–261.

Berkson, Isaac B. Theories of Americanization: A Critical Study: With Special Reference to the Jewish Group. New York: Teachers College, Columbia University, 1920.

Berman, Marshall. "That Is, Unless We Make It Ourselves." InterChange, April 1977, pp. 4–8.

Bernheimer, Charles S., ed. The Russian Jew in the United States. Philadelphia, 1905.

Blaine, Marge and Roberta Intrater. "The Grandeur That Is Flatbush." New York, August 14, 1978.

Bremner, Robert H. *American Philanthropy*. The Chicago History of American Civilization. Chicago: University of Chicago Press, 1960.

Bressler, Marvin. "Selected Family Patterns in W. I. Thomas' Unfinished Study of the *Bintel Brief*." *American Sociological Review*, 17 (1952): 563–72.

Brooklyn Jewish Center. *The Jewish Center Bulletin: Dedication Number*, December 31, 1922.

——— *Tenth Anniversary Dinner*, January 27, 1929.

Broun, Heywood and George Britt. *Christians Only: A Study in Prejudice*. New York: The Vanguard Press, 1931.

Bureau of Jewish Social Research. *Activities of the Bureau of Jewish Social Research for the Year 1933*. New York: Bureau of Jewish Social Research, 1934.

——— *Child Care Study*. New York: Bureau of Jewish Social Research, 1922.

——— *Studies in the New York Jewish Population*. Jewish Communal Survey of Greater New York. New York: Bureau of Jewish Social Research, 1928.

——— *Report of the Executive Committee*. Jewish Communal Survey of Greater New York. New York: Bureau of Jewish Social Research, 1929.

——— *A Report for the Year 1930*. New York: Bureau of Jewish Social Research, 1931.

Burgess, Ernest W. "The Growth of the City: An Introduction to a Research Project." *The City*. Robert E. Park and Ernest W. Burgess. 1925; rpt. Chicago: University of Chicago Press, 1967, pp. 47–62.

Cahan, Abraham. *The Rise of David Levinsky*. 1917; rpt. New York: Harper, 1960.

Carnegie, Andrew. *The Gospel of Wealth*. New York: Century, 1900.

Celler, Emanuel. *You Never Leave Brooklyn: The Autobiography of Emanuel Celler*. New York: John Day Company, 1953.

Chipkin, Israel. "Judaism and Social Welfare." *The Jews: Their History, Culture, and Religion*. ed. Louis Finkelstein. Philadelphia: Jewish Publication Society of America, 1949. 1: 713–744.

Chudacoff, Howard P. "A New Look at Ethnic Neighborhoods: Residential Dispersion and the Concept of Visibility in a Medium-Sized City." *The Journal of American History*, 60, no. 1 (June 1973): 76–93.

Citizens Union of New York. *Voters' Directory*. 1925–1940.

The City Record, Official Canvass of the Votes cast in the counties of New York, Bronx, Kings, Queens and Richmond, 1921–1939.

Cohen, Bernard. *Sociological Changes in American Jewish Life Reflected in Selected Jewish Literature*. Rutherford, New Jersey: Fairleigh Dickinson University Press, 1972.

Cohen, Naomi. *Not Free To Desist: The American Jewish Committee 1906–1966*. Philadelphia: The Jewish Publication Society of America, 1972.

Cohn, Werner. "The Politics of American Jews." *The Jews: Social Patterns of an American Group*. Ed. Marshall Sklare. New York: Free Press, 1958, pp. 614–26.

Cole, Stephen. *The Unionization of Teachers: A Case Study of the UFT*. New York: Praeger, 1969.

Committee on the Study of Racial and Religious Problems in Employment. *Resume of the Preliminary Survey of the Problem of Discrimination Against Jews in Employment in New York City.* New York: Committee on the Study of Racial and Religious Problems in Employment, 1931.

Costikyan, Edward. *Behind Closed Doors: Politics in the Public Interest.* New York: Harcourt, 1966.

Council of Fraternal and Benevolent Organizations. *Closing the Ranks in Jewish Life: A New Instrument for Community Understanding.* New York: Council of Fraternal and Benevolent Organizations, 1936.

Cremin, Lawrence A. *The Transformation of the School: Progressivism in American Education, 1876–1957.* New York: Vintage Books, 1961.

Cross, Robert, ed. *The Church and the City 1865–1910.* New York: Bobbs-Merrill, 1967.

Curti, Merle. *American Philanthropy Abroad: A History.* New Brunswick, N.J.: Rutgers University Press, 1963.

Cutlip, Scott M. *Fund Raising in the United States: Its Role in America's Philanthropy.* New Brunswick, N.J.: Rutgers University Press, 1965.

Dawidowicz, Lucy S. and Leon J. Goldstein. *Politics In A Pluralist Democracy: Studies of Voting in the 1960 Election.* New York: Institute of Human Relations Press, 1963.

The Day. 20 Years of Service. New York: *The Day,* 1934.

De Haas, Jacob. *Louis D. Brandeis: A Biographical Sketch.* New York: Bloch, 1929.

Dinin, Samuel. "Twenty Five Years of Teacher Training." *Jewish Education,* 7 (1935): 25–34.

Dollar, Charles M. and Richard J. Jensen. *Historian's Guide to Statistics: Quantitative Analysis and Historical Research.* New York: Holt, Rinehart and Winston, 1971.

Doroshkin, Milton. *Yiddish in America: Social and Cultural Foundations.* Rutherford, N.J.: Fairleigh Dickinson University Press, 1969.

Dubinsky, David and A. H. Raskin. *David Dubinsky: A Life with Labor.* New York: Simon and Schuster, 1977.

Dushkin, Alexander. "Congregation and Community in Jewish Education." *Jewish Education,* 1 (1929): 73–82.

—— *Jewish Education in New York City.* New York: Bureau of Jewish Education, 1918.

—— "The Jewish Population of New York." *Jewish Communal Register of New York City 1917–1918.* New York: Lipshitz Press, 1918, 75–89.

East Midwood Jewish Center. *East Midwood Jewish Center Dedication Journal.* New York, 1929.

Eisenberg, Israel L. "The Principal's Job—An Activity Analysis." *Jewish Education,* 3 (1931): 164–72.

Eisenberg, Louis and Elliot Rosenberg. *A Stripe of Tammany's Tiger.* New York: Robert Speller, 1966.

Elazar, Daniel J. *Community and Polity: The Organizational Dynamics of American Jewry.* Philadelphia: Jewish Publication Society, 1976.

Encyclopedia Judaica. 16 vols. Jerusalem, Israel: Keter Publishing House, 1971.

Engelman, Morris. *Four Years of Relief and War Work by the Jews of America 1914–1918.* New York: n.p., 1918.

Epstein, Melech. *Jewish Labor in U.S.A.* 2 vols. 1950, 1953; rpt. New York: KTAV Publishing House, Inc., 1969.

—— *Pages from a Colorful Life.* Miami Beach: I. Block Publishing Company, 1971.

—— *Profiles of Eleven.* Detroit: Wayne State University Press, 1965.

Etzioni, Amitai. "The Ghetto—A Re-Evaluation." *Social Forces,* 37 (1959): 258–61.

Farra, Kathryn. *Financing of Social Work in the City of New York, Studies of Federated Financing: Federation for the Support of Jewish Philanthropic Societies.* New York: Research Bureau, Welfare Council of New York City, 1931.

Federal Writers Project. *New York Panorama.* New York: Random House, 1938.

Federation for the Support of Jewish Philanthropic Societies of New York City. *Blue Book.* New York, 1921, 1923, 1925, 1927, 1929.

—— *Facts to help you solicit Federation gifts.* n.p. n.d.

—— *Federation: Its Meaning and Purpose.* New York, 1927.

Feingold, Henry. *The Politics of Rescue: The Roosevelt Administration and the Holocaust, 1938–1945.* New Brunswick, N.J.: Rutgers University Press, 1970.

Feldstein, Stanley. *The Land That I Show You: Three Centuries of Jewish Life in America.* Garden City, N.Y.: Anchor Press/Doubleday, 1978.

Ferretti, Fred. "After 70 Years, South Bronx Street Is at a Dead End." *New York Times,* October 21, 1977, pp. B1–B3.

Fink, Reuben and Bernard Richards, eds. *Jewish Community Directory of Greater New York: A Guide to Central Organizations and Institutions—Relief, Welfare, Religious, Cultural, Educational and Other Leading Agencies.* New York: The Jewish Information Bureau, 1947.

Firey, Walter. "Sentiment and Symbolism as Ecological Variables." *American Sociological Review,* 19 (1945): 140–48.

Fischel, Harry. "The New Yeshiva Buildings." *Historical Souvenir Journal.* New York: Yeshiva College Building Fund, 1926, n. pg.

—— *Forty Years of Struggle for a Principle.* Ed. Herbert S. Goldstein. New York: Bloch Publishing Company, 1928.

Fishman, Joshua A. "Patterns of American Self-Identification Among Children of a Minority Group." *YIVO Annual,* 10 (1955): 212–66.

Flynn, Edward. *You're the Boss: The Practice of American Politics.* 1947; rpt. New York: Collier Books, 1962.

The Fourth American City—The Jewish Community of New York, A Book of Facts About the Jewish Field, New York, Chicago, and National. New York: The Jewish Daily Forward, 1927.

Frankel, Aaron M. "Back to Eighty-Sixth Street." *Commentary,* August 1946, pp. 169–74.

Frankel, Lee K. "Introduction." Bureau of Jewish Social Research. *First Section: Studies in the New York Jewish Population.* Jewish Communal Survey of Greater New York. New York: Bureau of Jewish Social Research, 1928, pp. III–V.

Freedman, Morris. "Memoirs of a Pumpkin-Seed Peddler." *Commentary*, July 1947, pp. 64–69.

—— "New Jewish Community in Formation." *Commentary*, January 1955, pp. 36–47.

Fuchs, Daniel. *Summer in Williamsburg.* 1934; rpt. New York: Avon Books, 1972.

Fuchs, Lawrence. "American Jews and the Presidential Vote." *American Political Science Review*, 49 (1955): 385–401.

—— "Introduction." *American Jewish Historical Quarterly*, 66 (December 1976): 181–89.

—— *The Political Behavior of American Jews.* Glencoe, Illinois: The Free Press, 1956.

Gans, Herbert. "American Jewry: Present and Future." *Commentary*, May 1956, pp. 422–30.

—— "The Future of American Jewry: Part II." *Commentary*, June 1956, pp. 555–63.

—— "The Origin and Growth of a Jewish Community in the Suburbs: A Study of the Jews of Park Forest." *The Jews: Social Patterns Of An American Group.* Ed. Marshall Sklare. New York: Free Press, 1958, pp. 205–48.

—— *The Levittowners: Ways of Life and Politics in a New Suburban Community.* 1967; rpt. New York: Vintage Books, 1969.

—— "The Suburban Community and Its Way of Life." *Neighborhood, City, and Metropolis: An Integrated Reader in Urban Sociology.* Eds. Robert Gutman and David Popenoe. New York: Random House, 1970, pp. 297–309.

—— *The Urban Villagers: Group and Class in the Life of Italian Americans.* 1962; rpt. New York: The Free Press, 1965.

—— "Urbanism and Suburbanism as Ways of Life: A Re-evaluation of Definitions." *Neighborhood, City, and Metropolis: An Integrated Reader in Urban Sociology.* Eds. Robert Gutman and David Popenoe. New York: Random House, 1970, pp. 70–85.

Gamoran, Emanuel. *Changing Conceptions in Jewish Education.* New York: The Macmillan Company, 1924.

Garrett, Charles. *The LaGuardia Years: Machine and Reform Politics in New York City.* New Brunswick, N.J.: Rutgers University Press, 1961.

Gartner, Lloyd P., ed. *Jewish Education in the United States: A Documentary History.* New York: Teachers College Press, 1969.

Ginzberg, Eli. *Agenda for American Jews.* New York: Privately Printed, 1949.

Glazer, Nathan. *American Judaism.* The Chicago History of American Civilization. Chicago: University of Chicago Press, 1957.

—— *The Social Basis of American Communism.* New York: Harcourt, Brace & World, Inc., 1961.

Glazer, Nathan, and Daniel Patrick Moynihan. *Beyond the Melting Pot: The*

Negroes, Puerto Ricans, Jews, Italians, And Irish of New York City. Cambridge: The M.I.T. Press, 1963.

Glazer, Ruth. "West Bronx: Food, Shelter, Clothing." *Commentary,* June 1949, pp. 578–85.

Gold, Michael. *Jews Without Money.* 1930; rpt. New York: Avon Books, 1965.

Goldberg, Joseph. "Twenty Five Years of Brooklyn Jewish Center History." *Jubilee Book of the Brooklyn Jewish Center, Published in commemoration of the twenty-fifth anniversary of its founding.* New York, 1946, pp. 7–38.

Goldberger, Paul. "Style Moderne—Kitsch or Serious—Is in Vogue, ART DECO." *New York Times,* January 31, 1974.

Golden, Harry. *The Greatest Jewish City in the World.* Garden City, New York: Doubleday, 1972.

The Golden Heritage: A History of the Federation of Jewish Philanthropies of New York from 1917 to 1967. New York: Federation of Jewish Philanthropies of New York, 1969.

Goldin, Milton. *Why They Give: American Jews and Their Philanthropies.* New York: Macmillan, 1976.

Goldwasser, I. Edwin. "The Work of Young Men's Hebrew and Kindred Associations in New York City." *Jewish Communal Register of New York City 1917–1918.* New York: Lipshitz Press, 1918, pp. 476–81.

—— "Federation for the Support of Jewish Philanthropies of New York City." *American Jewish Year Book* 20 (1918–1919): 113–46.

Gordon, Milton M. *Assimilation in American Life: The Role of Race, Religion and National Origins.* New York: Oxford University Press, 1964.

Gorn, Arthur A. *New York Jews and the Quest for Community: The Kehillah Experiment, 1908–1922.* New York: Columbia University Press, 1970.

—— "Freedom and Its Limitations: The Jewish Immigrant Experience." Gratz lecture, 1979.

Gorenstein, Arthur. "A Portrait of Ethnic Politics: The Socialists and the 1908 and 1910 Congressional Elections on the East Side." *Publications of the American Jewish Historical Society,* 50 (March 1961): 202–38.

Gornick, Vivian. "There Is No More Community." *InterChange,* April 1977, pp. 4–5.

Greeley, Andrew M. *The Denominational Society: A Sociological Approach to Religion in America.* Glenview, Ill.: Scott, Foresman and Company, 1972.

—— *That Most Distressful Nation: The Taming of the American Irish.* Chicago: Quadrangle Books, 1972.

Greer, Colin. *The Great School Legend: A Revisionist Interpretation of American Public Education.* New York: Basic Books, 1972.

Greer, Scott. "The Social Structure and Political Process of Suburbia." *American Sociological Review,* 25 (1960): 514–26.

—— "Urbanism Reconsidered: A Comparative Study of Local Areas in a Metropolis." *American Sociological Review,* 21 (1956): 19–25.

Grinstein, Hyman B. *The Rise of the Jewish Community of New York 1654–1860.* Philadelphia: The Jewish Publication Society of America, 1945.

Gurock, Jeffrey S. *When Harlem Was Jewish, 1870–1930.* New York: Columbia University Press, 1979.

—— "The 1913 New York State Civil Rights Act." *AJS Review,* 1 (1976): 93–120.

Halkin, Abraham. "Hebrew in America." *Hebrew Comes to Life: The Role of the Hebrew Language and Culture in the Life of the Jewish People.* New York: Histadruth Ivrith of America, n.d., pp. 13–20.

Haller, Mark H. "Recurring Themes." *The Peoples of Philadelphia: A History of Ethnic Groups and Lower Class Life, 1790–1940.* Eds. Allen F. Davis and Mark H. Haller. Philadelphia: Temple University Press, 1973.

Halperin, Samuel. *The Political World of American Zionism.* Detroit: Wayne State University Press, 1961.

Halpern, Ben. "America Is Different." *The Jews: Social Patterns Of An American Group.* Ed. Marshall Sklare. New York: The Free Press, 1954, pp. 23–29.

—— "The Roots of American Jewish Liberalism." *American Jewish Historical Quarterly,* 66 (December 1976): 190–214.

Handlin, Oscar. *The Uprooted: The Epic Story of the Great Migration That Made the American People.* Boston: Little, Brown, 1952.

Hansen, Marcus Lee. *The Problem of the Third Generation Immigrant.* Rock Island, Ill.: Augustana Historical Society, 1938.

Hartmann, Edward George. *The Movement to Americanize the Immigrant.* New York: Columbia University Press, 1948.

Heiss, Jerold S. "Premarital Characteristics of the Religiously Intermarried in an Urban Area." *American Sociological Review,* 25 (February 1960): 47–55.

Heller, Abraham. "The Pattern for Synagogue Centers." *Jubilee Book of the Brooklyn Jewish Center, Published in commemoration of the twenty-fifth anniversary of its founding.* New York, 1946, pp. 81–83.

Herberg, Will. *Protestant, Catholic, Jew: An Essay in American Religious Sociology.* Garden City, New York: Doubleday, 1960.

Herling, John. "Baruch Charney Vladeck." *American Jewish Year Book,* 41 (1939): 79–93.

Higham, John. *Strangers in the Land: Patterns of American Nativism 1860–1925.* 1963; rpt. New York: Atheneum, 1970.

Hooper-Holmes Bureau, Inc. *A Survey of the Buying Power and Buying Habits of the Readers of the Jewish Daily Forward.* New York: The Jewish Daily Forward, 1942.

Horowitz, C. Morris and Lawrence J. Kaplan. *The Estimated Jewish Population of the New York Area 1900–1975.* New York: Federation of Jewish Philanthropies of New York, 1959.

Howe, Irving. "A Memoir of the Thirties." *Steady Work.* New York: Harcourt, 1966, pp. 349–64.

Howe, Irving with Kenneth Libo. *World of Our Fathers.* New York: Harcourt, 1976.

Isaacs, Edith S. *Love Affair with a City: The Story of Stanley M. Isaacs.* New York: Random House, 1967.

Isaacs, Stephen D. *Jews and American Politics.* Garden City, New York: Doubleday, 1974.

Itzkoff, Seymour W. *Cultural Pluralism and American Education.* Scranton, Pa.: International Textbook Company, 1969.

Jacobs, Paul. *Is Curly Jewish? A Political Self-Portrait Illuminating Three Turbulent Decades of Social Revolt 1935–1965.* 1965; rpt. New York: Vintage Books, 1973.

Janowsky, Oscar. *The JWB Survey.* New York: Dial Press, 1948.

Jewish Communal Center of Flatbush. *Twentieth Anniversary of Jewish Communal Center of Flatbush 1916–1936, Souvenir Journal.* n.p. n.d.

Jewish Statistical Bureau. *Digest of Events of Jewish Interest.* 1932–1934.

Jick, Leon A. *The Americanization of the Synagogue, 1820–1870.* Hanover, N.H.: Brandeis University Press, 1976.

Jonassen, Christen T. "Cultural Variables in the Ecology of an Ethnic Group." *American Sociological Review,* 14 (February 1949): 32–42.

Jones, Maldwyn Allen. *American Immigration.* Chicago: University of Chicago Press, 1960.

Josephson, Matthew. *Life among the Surrealists: A Memoir by Matthew Josephson.* New York: Holt, Rinehart and Winston, 1962.

Josephson, Matthew and Hannah. *Al Smith: Hero of the Cities, A Political Portrait Drawing on the Papers of Frances Perkins.* Boston: Houghton Mifflin, 1969.

Kallen, Horace Meyer. *Culture and Democracy in the United States: Studies in the Group Psychology of the American Peoples.* New York: Boni and Liveright, 1924.

Kantrowitz, Nathan. *Ethnic and Racial Segregation in the New York Metropolis: Residential Patterns Among White Ethnic Groups, Blacks, and Puerto Ricans.* New York: Praeger, 1973.

Kaplan, Mordecai M. "Affiliation With The Synagogue." *Jewish Communal Register of New York City 1917–1918.* New York: Lipshitz Press, 1918, pp. 117–22.

—— *Judaism As A Civilization: Toward a Reconstruction of American-Jewish Life.* 1934; rpt. New York: Schocken Books, 1967.

—— "The Teachers Institute and Its Affiliated Departments." *The Jewish Theological Seminary: Semi-Centennial Volume.* Ed. Cyrus Adler. New York: The Jewish Theological Seminary of America, 1939, pp. 121–43.

—— "The Way I Have Come." *Mordecai M. Kaplan: An Evaluation.* Eds. Ira Eisenstein and Eugene Kohn. New York: Jewish Reconstructionist Foundation, 1952, pp. 283–321.

Karp, Abraham. *A History of The United Synagogue of America 1913–1963.* New York: United Synagogue, 1964.

Karpf, Maurice. "A Decade of Jewish Philanthropy." *B'nai B'rith Magazine,* February 1932, pp. 145–48.

Kazin, Alfred. *A Walker in the City.* New York: Harcourt, 1951.

Kehillah of New York City. *Jewish Communal Register of New York City 1917–1918.* New York: Lipshitz Press, 1918.

Kennedy, Ruby Jo Reeves. "Single or Triple Melting Pot? Intermarriage Trends in New Haven 1870–1940.'' *American Journal of Sociology*, 49 (1944): 331–39.

Kessner, Thomas. *The Golden Door: Italian and Jewish Immigrant Mobility in New York City 1880–1915*. New York: Oxford University Press, 1977.

Klaperman, Gilbert. *The Story of Yeshiva University*. London: Macmillan, 1969.

Kligsberg, Moses. "Jewish Immigrants in Business: A Sociological Study.'' *The Jewish Experience In America*. Ed. Abraham J. Karp. New York: KTAV Publishing House, 1969.

Klonsky, Milton. "The Trojans of Brighton Beach.'' *Commentary*, May 1947, pp. 462–66.

Knoke, David and Richard Felson. "Ethnic Stratification and Political Cleavage in the United States, 1952–1968.'' *American Journal of Sociology*, 80 (1974): 630–42.

Kraft, Louis. "The Jewish Center Movement.'' *Mordecai M. Kaplan: An Evaluation*. Eds. Ira Eisenstein and Eugene Kohn. New York: Jewish Reconstructionist Foundation, 1952, pp. 119–36.

Kranzler, George. *Williamsburg: A Jewish Community in Transition*. New York: Philipp Feldheim, Inc., 1961.

Kriegel, Annie. "Generational Difference: The History of an Idea.'' *Daedalus*, Fall 1978, pp. 23–38.

Laidlaw, Walter, ed. *Population of the City of New York 1890–1930*. New York: Cities Census Committee, 1932.

Landesman, Alter. *Brownsville: The Birth, Development and Passing of a Jewish Community*. New York: Bloch, 1969.

Lapson, Judah. "Hebrew in the Public Schools.'' *Jewish Frontier*. rpt. New York: Jewish Education Committee, 1953.

Lehrer, Leibush. "The Jewish Secular School.'' *Jewish Education*, 8 (1936): 33–43.

Lestchinsky, Jacob. "The Economic and Social Development of the Jewish People.'' *The Jewish People, Past and Present*. New York: Central Yiddish Culture Organization, 1946. 1: 391–406.

Lester, Robert MacDonald. *Forty Years of Carnegie Giving*. New York: Scribner's, 1941.

Levy, Samuel. "Orthodox Jewry Rises to the Occasion.'' *Historical Souvenir Journal*. New York: Yeshiva College Building Fund, 1926. n. pg.

Lieberson, Stanley. *Ethnic Patterns in American Cities*. New York: Free Press, 1963.

Liebman, Arthur. "The Ties That Bind: The Jewish Support for the Left in the United States.'' *American Jewish Historical Quarterly*, 66 (December 1976): 285–321.

Liebman, Charles S. *The Ambivalent American Jew: Politics, Religion, and Family in American Jewish Life*. Philadelphia: Jewish Publication Society of America, 1973.

—— "Orthodoxy in American Jewish Life.'' *American Jewish Year Book*. Philadelphia: Jewish Publication Society, 1965. 66: 21–98.

—— "Reconstructionism in American Jewish Life.'' *American Jewish Year Book*. Philadelphia: Jewish Publication Society, 1970. 71: 3–100.

—— "American Jewry: Identity and Affiliation." *The Future of the Jewish Community in America.* Ed. David Sidorsky. New York: Basic Books, 1973, pp. 127–52.

Liptzin, Solomon. *Generation of Decision.* New York: Bloch, 1958.

Lowi, Theodore J. *At the Pleasure of the Mayor: Patronage and Power in New York City 1898–1958.* New York: Free Press, 1964.

Lubell, Samuel. *The Future of American Politics,* 3d ed., revised. New York: Harper, 1965.

Lubove, Roy. *The Professional Altruist: The Emergence of Social Work As A Career, 1880–1930.* Cambridge: Harvard University Press, 1965.

Magnes, Judah L. "Introductory Remarks on Religious Affairs." *Jewish Communal Register of New York City 1917–1918.* New York: Lipshitz Press, 1918, pp. 111–16.

Major Economic Factors In Metropolitan Growth and Arrangement: A Study of Trends and Tendencies in The Economic Activities Within the Region of New York and Its Environs. Regional Survey of New York and Its Environs. New York: Regional Plan of New York and Its Environs, 1927.

Makielski, Stanislaw J. Jr. *The Politics of Zoning: The New York Experience.* New York: Columbia University Press, 1966.

Maller, Julius B. "A Study of Jewish Neighborhoods of New York City." *Jewish Social Service Quarterly,* 10 (1934): 271–76.

—— *School and Community: A Study of the Demographic and Economic Background of Education in the State of New York.* The Regents' Inquiry. New York: McGraw-Hill, 1938.

Margoshes, Samuel. "The Verband Movement in New York City." *Jewish Communal Register of New York City 1917–1918.* New York: Lipshitz Press, 1918, pp. 1328–36.

Mark, Yudel. "Changes in the Yiddish School." *Jewish Education in the United States: A Documentary History.* Ed. Lloyd Gartner. New York: Teachers College Press, 1969, pp. 188–94.

Mason, Gabriel Richard, ed. *Great American Liberals.* 1956; rpt. Freeport, N.Y.: Books for Libraries Press, 1971.

Marshall, Louis. *Louis Marshall, Champion of Liberty: Selected Papers and Addresses.* Ed. Charles Reznikoff. 2 vols. Philadelphia: Jewish Publication Society of America, 1957.

McGill, Nettie P. and Ellen R. Matthews. *The Youth of New York.* New York: Macmillan, 1940.

Mead, Sidney E. *The Lively Experiment: The Shaping of Christianity in America.* New York: Harper, 1963.

Medalie, George Z. "New York Federation—After Twenty-Five Years." *American Jewish Year Book,* 45 (1943–44): 117–34.

Mergen, Bernard. " 'Another Great Prize': The Jewish Labor Movement in the Context of American Labor History." *YIVO Annual,* 16 (1976): 394–423.

Metzker, Isaac., ed. *A Bintel Brief: Sixty Years of Letters from the Lower East Side to the Jewish Daily Forward.* Garden City, New York: Doubleday & Company, Inc., 1971.

Michaelsen, Robert. *Piety in the Public School.* London: Macmillan, 1970.

Morris, Robert and Michael Freund, eds. *Trends and Issues in Jewish Social Welfare in the United States, 1899–1952*. Philadelphia: Jewish Publication Society of America, 1966.

Moscow, Warren. *Politics in the Empire State*. New York: Knopf, 1948.

Nahirny, Vladimir C. and Joshua A. Fishman. "American Immigrant Groups: Ethnic Identification and the Problem of Generations." *Sociological Review*, 13 (1965): 311–26.

National Appeals Information Service. *Bureau of Jewish Social Research*. New York: Bureau of Jewish Social Research, 1929.

—— *Menorah Movement*. New York: Bureau of Jewish Social Research, 1929.

—— *National Council of Jewish Women*. New York: Bureau of Jewish Social Research, 1929.

—— *The National Desertion Bureau, New York, N.Y.* New York: Bureau of Jewish Social Research, 1930.

Neumann, Fannie. "A Modern Jewish Experimental School—In Quest of a Synthesis." *Jewish Education*, 4, no. 1 (1932): 26–36.

Newman, Louis I. *A Jewish University in America?*. New York, n.p., 1923.

New York City. Department of Education. *List of Members of Board of Education, Local School Boards, Officials, Employees and Supervising and Teaching Staffs*, July 1, 1927, to December 31, 1927. rpt. City Record Supplement, January 31, 1928.

—— *List of Members Of Board of Education, Local School Boards, Officials, Employees and Supervising and Teaching Staffs*, May 1, 1937 to March 31, 1938. rpt. City Record Supplement, April 30, 1938.

New York City Guide. Federal Writers Project. New York: Random House, 1939.

New York City Market Analysis. New York: *The New York Herald-Tribune*, The *News* and The *New York Times*, 1933.

—— New York: *The New York Herald Tribune*, The *News* and The *New York Times*, 1944.

Novak, Michael. *The Rise of the Unmeltable Ethnics: Politics and Culture in the Seventies*. New York: Macmillan, 1971.

Oneal, James. *An American Labor Party: An Interpretation*. New York: Rand School Press, 1936.

O'Shea, William J. *Progress of the Public Schools, May 1, 1924–July 31, 1929*. New York: Board of Education, The City of New York, 1929.

Parenti, Michael. "Ethnic Politics and the Persistence of Ethnic Identification." *American Political Science Review*, 61 (1967): 717–26.

Park, Robert E. "Assimilation, Social." *Encyclopedia of the Social Sciences*. Eds. Edwin R. A. Seligman and Alvin Johnson. New York: Macmillan, 1930. 2: 281–83.

—— "The City As A Social Laboratory." *On Social Control and Collective Behavior*. Ed. Ralph H. Turner. Chicago: University of Chicago Press, 1967, pp. 3–18.

—— "The City: Suggestions for the Investigation of Human Behavior in the Urban Environment." *Classic Essays on the Culture of Cities*. Ed. Richard Sennett. New York: Appleton-Century-Crofts, 1969, pp. 91–130.

—— "Community Organization and the Romantic Temper." *The City*. Eds. Robert E. Park and Ernest W. Burgess. 1925; rpt. Chicago: University of Chicago Press, 1967, pp. 113–22.

—— "Human Migration and the Marginal Man." *Classic Essays on the Culture of Cities*. Ed. Richard Sennett. New York: Appleton-Century-Crofts, 1969, pp. 131–42.

—— "Racist Assimilation in Secondary Groups." *On Social Control and Collective Behavior*. Ed. Ralph H. Turner. Chicago: University of Chicago Press, 1967, pp. 114–32.

—— "The Urban Community as a Spatial Pattern and a Moral Order." *Ibid.*, pp. 55–68.

Park, Robert E. and Ernest W. Burgess. *Introduction to the Science of Sociology*. Ed. Morris Janowitz. 1921; rpt. Chicago: University of Chicago Press, 1969.

Parzen, Herbert. *Architects of Conservative Judaism*. New York: Jonathan David, 1964.

Peck, Richard. "Flatbush Shaped by History's Hand." *New York Times*, April 29, 1973, sec. 8 (real estate), p. 10.

Peel, Roy V. *The Political Clubs of New York City*. Port Washington, New York: Ira J. Friedman, 1935.

Perlmutter, Nathan. *A Bias of Reflections: Confessions of an Incipient Old Jew*. New Rochelle, New York: Arlington House, 1972.

Pfeffer, Leo. *Church, State and Freedom*. Boston: Beacon Press, 1953.

Phillipson, David. *The Reform Movement in Judaism*. New York: Macmillan, 1931.

Pilch, Judah. "From the Early Forties to the Mid-Sixties." *A History of Jewish Education in America*. Ed. Judah Pilch. New York: National Curriculum Research Institute of the American Association for Jewish Education, 1969, pp. 121–76.

Piliver-Podolier Society, Inc. *15th Anniversary Banquet and Ball 1915–1930*. New York: n.p., 1930.

Podhoretz, Norman. *Making It*. New York: Random House, 1967.

Poplin, Dennis E. *Communities: A Survey of Theories and Methods of Research*. New York: Macmillan, 1972.

Population, Land Values And Government: Studies of the Growth and Distribution of Population and Land Values; and of Problems of Government. Regional Survey of New York And Its Environs, vol. 2. New York: Regional Plan of New York and Its Environs, 1929.

Postal, Bernard and Lionel Koppman. *Jewish Landmarks in New York: An Informal History and Guide*. New York: Hill and Wang, 1964.

Poster, William. "Twas a Dark Night in Brownsville." *Commentary*, May 1950, pp. 458–66.

Quandt, Jean B. *From the Small Town to the Great Community: The Social Thought of Progressive Intellectuals*. New Brunswick, N.J.: Rutgers University Press, 1970.

Reich, Nathan. "Economic Trends." *The American Jew: A Composite Portrait*. Ed. Oscar Janowsky. New York: Harper, 1942, pp. 161–69.

Revel, Bernard. "The Message and the Meaning of the Yeshiva." *Historical Souvenir Journal*. New York: Yeshiva College Building Fund, 1926, n. pg.

Rich, J. C. *60 Years of the Jewish Daily Forward*. New York: Forward Association, 1957.

Rischin, Moses. *The Promised City: New York's Jews 1870–1914*. 1962; rpt. New York: Corinth Books, 1964.

Robison, Sophia, ed. *Jewish Population Studies*. Jewish Social Studies Publications, no. 3. New York: Conference on Jewish Relations, 1943.

Romasco, Albert U. *The Poverty of Abundance: Hoover, the Nation, the Depression*. New York: Oxford University Press, 1965.

Rontch, Isaac E. ed. *Di yidishe landsmanshaftn fun new york*. New York: Y. L. Peretz Shreiber Farein, 1938.

Rose, Peter I. "The Ghetto and Beyond." *The Ghetto and Beyond: Essays on Jewish Life in America*. Ed. Rose. New York: Random House, 1969, pp. 3–18.

Roseman, Kenneth D. "American Jewish Community Institutions In Their Historical Context." *The Jewish Journal of Sociology*, 16 (June 1974): 25–38.

Rosen, Ben. "Survey of Jewish Education in New York City." *Jewish Education*, 1 (1929): 82–96.

Rosen, Ira. "The Glory That Was Charlotte Street." *The New York Times Magazine*. October 7, 1979.

Rosenfelt, Henry. *This Thing of Giving*. New York: Plymouth Press, 1924.

Rosenthal, Erich. "Acculturation Without Assimilation: The Jewish Community of Chicago, Illinois." *American Journal of Sociology*, 66 (1960): 275–88.

Rosenwaike, Ira. *Population History of New York City*. Syracuse, New York: Syracuse University Press, 1972.

Ross, H. Lawrence. "Uptown and Downtown: A Study of Middle-Class Residential Areas." *American Sociological Review*, 30 (1965): 255–59.

Rotenstreich, Nathan. "Emancipation and Its Aftermath." *The Future of the Jewish Community in America*. Ed. David Sidorsky. New York: Basic Books, 1973, pp. 46–61.

Rothkoff, Aaron. *Bernard Revel: Builder of American Jewish Orthodoxy*. Philadelphia: Jewish Publication Society of America, 1972.

Rothschild, Richard. *Summary of Polls on Anti-Semitism, 1938–1942*. New York: American Jewish Committee, Public Information and Education Department, 1943.

Ruppin, Arthur. "The Jewish Population of the World." *The Jewish People, Past and Present*. New York: Central Yiddish Culture Organization, 1948. 1: 349–59.

Sackler, Harry. "The Kehillah of New York." *Jewish Communal Register of New York City 1917–1918*. New York: Lipshitz Press, 1918, pp. 5–68.

Saenger, Gerhart and Harry M. Shulman. *A Study of Intercultural Behavior and Attitudes Among Residents of the Upper West Side*. New York: Mayor's Committee on Unity, 1947.

Sandberg, Neil C. *Ethnic Identity and Assimilation: The Polish-American Community: Case Study of Metropolitan Los Angeles*. Praeger Special Studies in

United States Economic, Social, and Political Issues. New York: Praeger, 1974.

Sanders, Ronald. *The Downtown Jews: Portraits of an Immigrant Generation.* New York: Harper, 1969.

—— *Reflections on a Teapot.* New York: Harper, 1972.

Sayre, Wallace and Herbert Kaufman. *Governing New York City: Politics in the Metropolis.* New York: Russell Sage Foundation, 1960.

Schlesinger, Benjamin, ed. *The Jewish Family: A Survey and Annotated Bibliography.* Toronto: University of Toronto Press, 1971.

Schuman, Wendy. "Change Bends 'Spine' in Brooklyn." *New York Times*, January 20, 1974, sec. 8 (real estate), p. 8.

Shands, A. L. "The Cheder on the Hill: Some Notes on C.C.N.Y." *The Menorah Journal*, March 1929, pp. 264–69.

Shannon, David A. *The Socialist Party of America: A History.* 1955; rpt. Chicago: Quadrangle Books, 1967.

Sherman, C. Bezalel. *The Jew Within American Society: A Study in Ethnic Individuality.* Detroit: Wayne State University Press, 1965.

Sklare, Marshall. "Introduction." *The Jews: Social Patterns of an American Group.* Ed. Sklare. New York: Free Press, 1958, pp. 3, 43–44, 169–72, 323–24, 435–36, 505–8.

—— "Jews, Ethnics, and the American City." *Commentary*, April 1972, pp. 70–77.

—— *Conservative Judaism: An American Religious Movement.* Glencoe, Illinois: Free Press, 1955.

Smith, Timothy. "Religion and Ethnicity in America." *American Historical Review*, 83, no. 5 (December 1978): 1155–85.

Spengler, Edwin H. *Land Values in New York in Relation to Transit Facilities.* New York: Columbia University Press, 1930.

Spicer, Edward H. "Acculturation." *International Encyclopedia of the Social Sciences.* Ed. David L. Sills. New York: Macmillan, 1968, 1: 21–25.

Spitz, Leon. "The Synagogue Center Marches On, The History of the Synagogue Center Movement in the United States." *Jubilee Book of the Brooklyn Jewish Center*, Published in commemoration of the twenty-fifth anniversary of its founding. New York, 1946, pp. 53–66.

State of New York. *Report of the State Board of Housing.* 1928–1939.

Stedman, Murray Jr. and Susan Stedman. *Discontent at the Polls: A Study of Farmer and Labor Parties 1827–1948.* New York: Columbia University Press, 1950.

Steinberg, Stephen. *The Academic Melting Pot: Catholics and Jews in American Higher Education.* A Report Prepared for the Carnegie Commission on Higher Education. New York: McGraw-Hill, 1974.

Still, Bayrd. *Mirror For Gotham.* New York: New York University Press, 1956.

Strauss, Anselm L. *Images of the American City.* 1961; rpt. New Brunswick, N.J.: Transaction Books, 1976.

Sullivan, Donald G. and Brian J. Danforth. *Bronx Art Deco Architecture: An Exposition.* New York: Hunter College, City University of New York, 1976.

Taeuber, Karl E. and Alma F. Taeuber. *Negroes in Cities: Residential Segregation and Neighborhood Change.* 1965; rpt. New York: Atheneum, 1969.

Teller, Judd L. *Strangers and Natives: The Evolution of the American Jew from
1921 to the Present.* New York: Delacorte Press, 1968.

Temple Israel of New York City. *75th Anniversary.* n.p., n.d.

Tenenbaum, Samuel. "Brownsville's Age of Learning." *Commentary,* August
1949, pp. 173–78.

Teper, Lazare. *Report on the Discrimination Against Jews in the Field of Employment.* New York: Jewish Labor Committee, 1936.

Thernstrom, Stephen. "Immigrants and WASPS: Ethnic Differences in Occupational Mobility in Boston, 1890–1940." *Nineteenth-Century Cities: Essays in
the New Urban History.* Eds. Stephen Thernstrom and Richard Sennett.
New Haven: Yale University Press, 1969, pp. 125–64.

Theodorson, George A. and Achilles G. Theodorson. *Modern Dictionary of Sociology.* New York: Thomas Y. Crowell, 1969.

*Transit and Transportation: And a study of Port and Industrial Areas and
Their Relation to Transportation.* Regional Survey of New York and Its
Environs, vol. 4. New York: Regional Plan of New York and Its Environs,
1928.

Trillin, Calvin. "U.S. Journal: The Bronx." *The New Yorker,* August 1, 1977,
pp. 49–54.

Trunk, Isaiah. "The Cultural Dimension of the American Jewish Labor Movement." *YIVO Annual,* 16 (1976): 342–93.

United States Department of Commerce. Bureau of the Census. *Religious Bodies: 1936, Selected Statistics for the United States By Denominations and
Geographic Divisions.* Washington, D.C.: Government Printing Office,
1946.

Urofsky, Melvin I. *American Zionism from Herzl to the Holocaust.* Garden City,
N.Y.: Doubleday, Anchor, 1975.

Warner, Sam Bass Jr. *The Private City: Philadelphia in Three Periods of its
Growth.* 1968; rpt. Philadelphia: University of Pennsylvania Press, 1971.

—— *Streetcar Suburbs: The Process of Growth in Boston 1870–1900.* 1962; rpt.
New York: Atheneum, 1969.

Warner, W. Lloyd and Leo Srole. *The Social Systems of American Ethnic
Groups.* New Haven: Yale University Press, 1945. Yankee City Series, volume 3.

Warshow, Robert S. "Poet of the Jewish Middle Class." *Commentary,* May
1946, pp. 17–22.

Weber, Max. "The Nature of the City." *Classic Essays on the Culture of Cities.*
Ed. Richard Sennett. New York: Appleton-Century-Crofts, 1969, pp.
23–46.

Wechsler, Harold S. *The Qualified Student: A History of Selective College Admission in America.* New York: Wiley, 1977.

Weinryb, Bernard. "Jewish Immigration and Accommodation to America." *The
Jews: Social Patterns of An American Group.* Ed. Marshall Sklare. New
York: Free Press, 1958. pp. 4–22.

Weiss, Nancy Joan. *Charles Francis Murphy, 1858–1924: Respectability and*

Responsibility in Tammany Politics. Northhampton, Mass.: Smith College, 1968.

Weld, Ralph Foster. *Brooklyn Is America.* 1950; rpt. New York: AMS Press, 1967.

Welfare Council of New York City. *A Survey of Work for Boys in Brooklyn.* New York: Welfare Council of New York City, 1931.

Wexelstein, Leon. *Building Up Greater Brooklyn with Sketches of Men Instrumental in Brooklyn's Amazing Development.* New York: Brooklyn Biographical Society, 1925.

Weyl, Nathaniel. *The Jew In American Politics.* New Rochelle, New York: Arlington House, 1968.

Wiebe, Robert. *The Search For Order, 1877–1920.* New York: Hill and Wang, 1967.

Wiernik, Peter. "The Problem of Higher Jewish Education in America." *Historical Souvenir Journal.* New York: Yeshiva College Building Fund, 1926, n.pg.

Winter, Nathan. *Jewish Education in a Pluralist Society: Samson Benderly and Jewish Education in the United States.* New York: New York University Press, 1966.

Wirth, Louis. "A Bibliography of the Urban Community." *The City.* Eds. Robert E. Park and Ernest W. Burgess. 1925; rpt. Chicago: University of Chicago Press, 1967, pp. 161–230.

—— *The Ghetto.* 1928; rpt. Chicago: University of Chicago Press, 1956.

—— "Urbanism As A Way of Life." *Classic Essays on the Culture of Cities.* Ed. Richard Sennett. New York: Appleton-Century-Crofts, 1969, pp. 143–64.

Wolfinger, Raymond. "The Development and Persistence of Ethnic Voting." *American Political Science Review,* 59 (1965): 896–908.

Yancey, William, Eugene P. Erickson, and Richard N. Juliani. "Emergent Ethnicity: A Review and Reformulation." *American Sociological Review,* 41, no. 3 (June 1976): 391–400.

Yeshiva College. *Yeshiva College Catalog.* 1928–1940.

The Yeshiva Endowment Foundation. *Annual Report: Insuring the Life of Judaism,* December 1936.

Yoffeh, Zalmen. "The Passing of the East Side." *The Menorah Journal,* December 1929, pp. 264–75.

Zangwill, Israel. *The Melting Pot.* New York: Macmillan, 1909.

Zeitlin, Joseph. *Disciples of the Wise: The Religious and Social Opinions of American Rabbis.* Teachers College, Columbia University Contributions for Education, no. 908. 1945; rpt. Freeport, N.Y.: Books for Libraries Press, 1970.

Zitron, Celia Lewis. *The New York City Teachers Union 1916–1964: A Story of Educational and Social Commitment.* New York: Humanities Press, 1968.

Zuckerman, Jacob T. and Alvin Chenkin. "Problems Confronting the Researcher on Intermarriage in a Metropolitan Area." *Intermarriage and Jewish Life: a Symposium.* Ed. Werner J. Cahnman. New York: Herzl Press, 1963, pp. 158–67.

Index